THE COSMIC SELF

THE COSMIC SELF

A Penetrating Look at Today's New Age Movements

TED PETERS

HarperSanFrancisco

A Division of HarperCollins*Publishers*

Library of Congress Cataloging-in-Publication Data

Peters, Ted.
    The cosmic self : a penetrating look at today's New Age movements /
    Ted Peters.—1st ed.
        p.   cm.
    Includes bibliographical references and indexes.
    ISBN 0–06–066506–8 (alk. paper)
    1. New Age movement.   2. Christian life—1960- I. Title.
BP605.N48P47   1991
261.2'993—dc20
                                         89-45947
                                          CIP

92 93 94 95 96 HCMG 12 11 10 9 8 7 6 5 4

Manufactured in the United Kingdom by HarperCollins Publishers Ltd.

Contents

Preface

The new age is here. It is everywhere. But one needs to be ready to recognize it. Look for the pictures of bright sky on magazine covers, where a few clouds drift on the margins so that you look past them toward infinity. Read the tabloids sold in supermarkets for articles on reincarnation, crystals, and channeling. Check the shelves of your local health food store and talk to a nurse about holistic health practices. Listen for new age jargon that has become integral to our contemporary vocabulary, such as "negative energy" or "connectedness." Note how TV commercials exploit the slogans when the U.S. Army tells potential recruits to "Be All That You Can Be" or when MasterCard mimics Werner Erhard's est with "Master the Possibilities."

The new age is in the news. The whole world read in August 1987 about the Harmonic Convergence, when hundreds gathered at Mount Tamalpais in Marin County, California. In the spring of 1988 President Ronald Reagan tried to fend off embarrassment when it was revealed that his wife, Nancy, regularly consulted an astrologer and advised her husband to make political decisions only at auspicious moments. On April 23, 1990, the world held its breath, waiting to see if Elizabeth Clare Prophet's prophecy about the nuclear holocaust and the subsequent advent of the new age would come to fulfillment. It didn't.

Actress Shirley MacLaine published a headline-grabbing book in 1983, *Out on a Limb,* and made a TV miniseries recounting her quest for a "higher self." She reported adventures with extraterrestrials, out-of-body experiences, reincarnation, and channeling. This has brought the actress considerable attention, some less than kind. *San Francisco Chronicle* television critic John Carman described her five-hour miniseries as "deliriously wacko." One cartoon showed two lizards sitting on a rock with one saying, "There it is again . . . a feeling that in a past life I was someone named Shirley MacLaine." Oprah Winfrey, on the other hand, told her TV viewers that she reads metaphysical books, and said to Shirley MacLaine on the air, "Since I read *Out on a Limb,* I've been a changed, spiritually evolving person."

Elizabeth Taylor and George Hamilton tell reporters they practice Transcendental Meditation, and rock singer Tina Turner has announced that she chants at a Buddhist shrine. Hollywood stars know they will be quoted if they say something outrageous, and the extravagances of the new age provide an inventory of respectable but outrageous things to say.

Although Berkeley, where I work, already bears the ambiance of new age consciousness, every spring I like to cross the bay in the direction of San Francisco to attend the annual Whole Life Expo and see the new age in its concentrated form. Here the prophets and practitioners mix with the adepts and aficionados in a marathon of deep breathing and deep sharing. Former television preacher Terry Cole-Whittaker preaches that "Your Cup Runneth Over and Over and Over." Sylvia Brown, founder of the Nirvana Foundation, speaks on "Centering of Self." Timothy Leary, the LSD guru of the 1960s, offers "hands-on methods for expanding consciousness." In addition to lectures and workshops, booksellers sell books, health food dealers sell yummies, and artists present their crafts. Services and wares include acupuncture, psychic readings, tarot, hypnotherapy, prayer power, spiritual healing, crystal color wands, electronic juicers, herbal medicines, vitamins, and new age travel packages. Everywhere new age music gently tugs at the ears while tract distributors hand you ream upon ream of inspiring literature and advertisements.

Is the new age movement demonic or divine? If one reads some of the conservative Christian literature on the topic, the answer is clear: it is demonic! If one quizzes a meditating mystic, the opposite answer is equally clear: it is divine! Or perhaps things are not so clear; the answer might be more subtle. A genuine new age advocate would probably suggest that it is misleading to ask whether the movement is demonic or divine because the question is itself an example of the dichotomous thinking of Western Aristotelian logic, which assumes a sharp distinction between true and false, right and wrong. The new age would like to take us beyond these apparent dichotomies into a wholism that harmonizes all. The new age seeks to heal what was previously the pain of separation.

This is a book about the new age by someone who is both sympathetic and critical. I am sympathetic because of the wholesome values the movement teaches: world peace, inner peace, healing of division, attention to personal experience, optimism about the future, and cosmic consciousness. I am critical because in its haste to find personal bliss by identifying the self with the cosmos, the new age has inadvertently fallen into a gnostic form of the spiritual quest. By "gnostic," I mean it pursues human and cosmic salvation by pursuing esoteric knowledge, by pursuing higher consciousness. Such gnosticism is doomed to failure because it is unrealistic. It naively assumes that if we can think better, then reality will somehow be better. New age gnosticism fails to accept the full reality and pervasiveness of sin and brokenness; and it likewise denies the reality of God's grace in the work of salvation.

What I think we need to do is examine the new age carefully and, to borrow a phrase from the New Testament, try to "test the spirits" (1 John 4:1; Cor. 12:10). We need to ask: what in new age health practices and meditative techniques is helpful? What in new age teachings aids us in the pursuit of truth? What is serious and what is silly? What is harmless and what is harmful? What appears to be the case, and what is the reality behind the appearance? In trying to test the spirits, I wish to do something quite different from what either conservative critics or mainline Christian theologians have been doing until now.

The conservative critics miss the subtleties and beauties of new age spirituality while embarrassing the Christian tradition in their failure to see anything other than the literal truth of otherwise profound religious statements. To test the spirits, in contrast, means we will take the time to see what is going on.

Mainline church leaders have largely ignored the equivalent of a religious H-bomb in sustained explosion for nearly three decades now. Bishops and theologians in this period have certainly become conscious of the Church's responsibility in the nonreligious sectors of society. They have begun to exercise this responsibility by trying to influence secular politics in behalf of justice for the poor and in favor of a nuclear peace. These are important things to do, no doubt. Nevertheless, while church leaders have been occupying themselves with the world of secular politics, millions of people have begun to turn once again to religion. They are embarking on a spiritual quest: they want to find the source and meaning of their existence; to regain a sense of transcendent divinity; and to find a way to integrate human beings with one another, with nature, and with the whole of reality. Because the churches in North America seem to be becoming less and less religious, seekers of truth have begun to look for religion elsewhere. They have found it. What they have found, among other things, goes by the name "new age." What other theologians ignore, I wish to explore.

Our method in this book is somewhat journalistic. It belongs to what Alfred North Whitehead called philosophical assemblage: the gathering together of relevant resources and data and readying them for organization, analysis, synthesis, and constructive thought. Many different things travel with the label "new age." They need to be located and sorted out. What they have in common needs to be identified. Our task is to identify the teachings of the new age and ready them for examination from a theological perspective.

The perspective I will take here is that of a Christian theologian. Theology is a form of pursuing knowledge. Some call it the science of God. It attempts to understand the deepest workings of the inner soul as well as the infinite expanses of an unfathomable universe. It seeks to understand all things with reference to their creator, God. It tries to discern the significance of God's love and graciousness as exhibited in the death and resurrection of Jesus Christ. It looks for signs of spiritual guidance in the ordinary and extraordinary dimensions of daily life. It proposes that we live with the mystery of reality while at the same time it tries to understand it.

Theologians have a curious relationship to mystery. On the one hand, they stand or even kneel before the mystery of existence in sheer awe and wonder. In their view, the ultimate mystery that lies beneath all things has a quality of holiness about it, and this holiness should not be violated; it is sacred. So the first mandate of theologians is to protect the mystery—that is, to remind us that *mystery really is mysterious;* and, of course, we should never presume to know more about it than we actually do.

On the other hand, theology is a science that pursues understanding and knowledge. It does so on the basis of revelation. Christian theologians believe the ultimate mystery behind all things is not passive and inert. Rather, it is active. It has not remained silent. It has spoken. Out of the depths of mysterious silence a word has been emitted, a word by which all of the created universe has come into existence. In addition, the word took on flesh and blood and became a living person. So, the second mandate of theologians is to ponder the significance of this revelatory event in light of everything else we experience and understand.

Theologians know something, but not everything. This is a nondogmatic approach to Christian dogma. I like to picture the theological enterprise as an island of understanding in a giant sea of surrounding mystery. This is where we find ourselves. We have solid ground on which to stand, to be sure. But we cannot assume that the borders of this *terra firma* extend far enough to include everything within them. There is much that lies beyond our mental beaches, even beyond our horizon. Yet something impels us to lift up our eyes and strain them to look at the horizon. When we do so, miraculously the horizon seems to move and our world of understanding seems to grow.

The depth of the sea reminds us of the depths to be plumbed within our own souls. We need not just look out to find mystery. It lies within as well. The more we descend into the caverns of our own existence, the greater the mystery becomes. The more we understand, the more we realize the extent of what lies beyond understanding. This is the curious paradox: the greater the understanding, the greater the mystery.

This internal search can be frightening, of course, especially if we descend deeper and deeper and begin to think there may be no bottom. We tremble at viewing the abyss of emptiness, thinking that at the bottom there is only death and nothing beyond. To avoid this fear we may cut short our journey of inner exploration and return to the surface. By returning to the surface I mean yielding to the temptation of accepting a prepackaged dogmatic explanation for what we find within ourselves. We return to the surface prematurely when we attempt to explain our experience before we have the experience. Religious dogma frequently cuts us short in this way. So also does new age dogma. In fact, any philosophical world view can be guilty of cutting us short, if we permit it. What Christian theologians seek to do is permit, if not encourage, the dive into the deepest reaches of our inner souls. Under the guidance of God's Spirit, we can accept the reality that the abyss connotes meaninglessness, that it speaks of emptiness, loneliness, and death. Yet also under the guidance of God's Spirit, there is a return to life again—not a superficial return, by any means, but rather a resurrection. By God's grace we are given a re-rootedness in the ultimate reality that is life-giving. The result is participation in the death and resurrection of the divine life itself.

Acknowledgments

I would like to say thank you to Professor Ann C. Lammers for her critical review of the first version of this manuscript and for her valuable editorial suggestions. I want to thank Lisa Stenmark, my teaching assistant, for indexing. I wish to thank as well Heidi Michelson, my student secretary for two years, for whose help on this and other manuscripts I am most grateful. Finally, I wish to express personal gratitude to Roland Seboldt, my editor, for his counsel and encouragement over the last decade.

I dedicate this book to Paul and Julie Bongfeldt, our family friends. Such friendship would make life worth living in the new age, or in any age for that matter.

Ted Peters
Berkeley

THE COSMIC SELF

Chapter One

The New Age Is Here . . .
and Everywhere

The crowd was beginning to move out of the restaurant banquet room. I had finished my lecture. The program was over. People were shaking my hand, some thanking me for the presentation. Many were relating their own experiences. Out of the corner of my eye I noticed a woman and man waiting. I sensed that she especially wanted to talk, but her strategy was to wait until others were out of earshot.

My lecture had been on new age religion. A group of pastors had invited me to be the speaker for their midwinter theological conference to address the new age phenomenon. The new age had entered their community and their churches, and they knew it. Could a theologian be of help?

Finally an opening appeared, and the woman introduced herself. The man, whom I took to be her husband, looked about the room. I could not tell if he wanted this conversation to take place or not. She did. I could see it in her wistful eyes.

"I'm so glad you did not make this a laughing matter," she remarked once the small talk was under way. "Many pastors just laugh this off. I'm afraid to talk to them."

"What is your tie to the new age?" I queried.

"Channeling," she said. Then she hastened to add, "But I've given it up. I don't do it anymore." But her face spoke of great sadness. If she had given it up, I asked myself, then why the present melancholy? Eventually we got to the point.

"My daughter is still into channeling. She's into it in a big way. In fact, she has moved out and we don't communicate anymore."

I asked her to continue. She and her daughter had sought to invoke the spirits of the dead together until the mother started to back off. "I was the one who gave her the first book," she said. "I introduced her to it. Now look what I've done!"

I sensed feelings of guilt here. Yet I was becoming aware of the conversational buzz around us. "Look, if you want to talk about this some more . . ." I offered an opening. Yes, of course, she would try to attend my lectures the next day and then we would look for an opportunity to talk. I never saw her again. Perhaps the other lecture topics didn't interest her, or perhaps something else intervened to prevent follow-up. Yet there was serious hurt here. And because she was afraid of being laughed at, she was likely inhibited from raising her concern with the one person upon whom she should be able to rely for help—her pastor.

Pastors and Personal Piety

The pastors and priests leading our parishes are for the most part poorly equipped to minister in the new age atmosphere. A number of contradictory reasons for this exist. Although our clergy are allegedly religious leaders, they do not necessarily have a high opinion of religion. Although they preach and teach about things spiritual, they may be quite unsure what "spiritual" means. Although they lead prayer during worship service every Sunday, they may find little personal fulfillment in private prayer during the week. Although the religious symbols of the Christian religion speak of heaven and earth and things cosmic, many of our pastors have already consigned such things to outdated mythology and superstition. They believe religion is existential and ethical, not metaphysical or cosmological.

Why? Most of today's clergy were trained at a time when we in the Church believed the world around us had forsaken things religious. We thought the world view of natural science would soon eradicate religion from the Western world. We were taught in seminary that our preaching and teaching had to become "relevant" to the modern world, and by this we meant the *secular* world. We imbibed the view that religion is superstition. If the Christianity we were going to teach was to be relevant, then it needed to shed its offensive religious trappings. For many of the more radical students in the 1960s, Dietrich Bonhoeffer's words "religionless Christianity" became a slogan.

Students and theologians were writing another chapter in the history of liberalism. In the wake of the philosophy of Immanuel Kant, liberal Protestant theology for the last century and a half had been somewhat embarrassed that the Christian faith spoke so unabashedly about transcendent powers such as God's grace, angels, and resurrection of the dead. Such things do not fit the world of nature as our scientists describe it. Spiritual truths are not empirical, not testable. Ancient religious claims about heavenly realities now appeared to be outdated superstitions, if not outright frauds. This meant our intellectual leaders had to look for an honest way for Christian theologians to make a living. So they transmuted many so-called otherworldly concerns into this-worldly concerns. They reoriented Christian faith away from picturing our world as an arena where God does battle with demonic forces and directed our attention instead toward our ethical responsibility, toward transforming the social and political world. Ethics is credible within the limits of reason alone, so an ethical Christianity would not violate the secularity of the modern world view. This long process of adjusting to the modern world—a secular world that was trying to shed its religious clothes—was the context in which many clergy since World War II received their theological education.

One seminary student in the 1960s with whom I studied had a 4D draft status. Because he was preparing for the ministry, he was exempt from military service. He was also an ethical protestor against the U.S. war in Vietnam. "I just don't identify with the tradition of prayer," he told me. "I don't really talk to God. I think it's sort of psychological. What I do in prayer is talk to myself through the use of God-language." Perhaps here we could say Ludwig Feuerbach and Karl Marx had won. These nineteenth-century philosophers had seemingly convinced us that our understanding of God was a human projection and that enlightened modern people ought really to be naturalists and humanists. The psychological or existential value of our religion was what mattered, not its truth regarding the nature of reality.

But things have changed overnight. No sooner had we adjusted to the nonreligious world view than the modern world flipped. Now religion is back. It has not fully returned to the churches, however. Oh, yes, there was a decade of charismatic fervor in the late 1960s and early 1970s, but most churches were successful at confining it to the periphery so as to prevent it from having an impact on doing business as usual. Squeezed out of the established churches, the Christian charismatics found one another across denominational lines through their own small groups and large assemblies. They achieved a practical ecumenism that denominational leaders, for all their committee meetings, failed to accomplish. My point here is that the revival of religious consciousness has had some impact on the churches. Nevertheless, the largest explosion of religious consciousness lies outside the Christian camp entirely, entering only occasionally to borrow Christian symbols for other uses. The new age has exploded like a religious H-bomb, and the fallout is everywhere.

The New Age: What Is It?

What is the new age, anyway? Is it a religious cult? No, although much of what the cults teach can be seen in new age doctrines. Is it a business? No, although thousands of entrepreneurs make money selling new age products. Is it a political movement? No, although it has an international political platform dedicated to world peace and ecological balance. Is it a social movement? No, although this comes closer to identifying it. It is too loose a conglomeration of separate groups to be considered a movement in any unified social sense.[1] Perhaps it is best thought of as a phenomenon of cultural consciousness. It consists of a set of cosmological ideas and spiritual practices that nobody owns but that are widely shared by diverse groups and individuals. New age ideas travel fast because they are borne by the electronic and print media.

New age teachings reflect a love-hate relationship with the modern Western world. On the one hand, they admire and imbibe the intellectual power of modern science. On the other hand, they seek to retrieve premodern religious beliefs and practices—especially from India and sometimes China—and incorporate them into Western technological society. In a 1981 presidential letter to the International Transpersonal Association, Stanislav Grof writes: "It seems to be the perfect time and place to celebrate the increasing convergence of Western physics and Eastern metaphysics, of modern consciousness research and Eastern spiritual systems." At bottom, the new age is a phenomenon of cultural synthesis that is attempting to recover a religious grounding for understanding ourselves and the cosmos that is our home.

New age practitioners have discovered the secret of religious success in America. The secret is this: you can ask Americans to convert to a new set of beliefs, but do not ask them to give up their previous affiliations. As proof of this principle I offer the case of dispensationalism. John Nelson Darby (1800–1882), who developed the idea of the seven dispensations to describe the history of the world, visited America numerous times and tried to convince American Christians to abandon their respective denominations and meet together simply in the name of the Lord. He failed. Darby went home to his native England frustrated, mumbling that the churches were "more worldly in America than anywhere." Darby's ideas were published shortly thereafter by C. I. Scofield in the famous *Scofield Reference Bible,* which is now widely read and accepted by Evangelicals. Thus, Darbyism didn't end there; today it is alive and well. Americans can affirm almost any new idea—no matter how preposterous—as long as they are not required to abandon earlier commitments.

Acting upon this principle, new age prophets are making converts; and their teachings are being adopted without apparent cognitive dissonance by Protestants, Roman Catholics, Jews, atheists, as well as the growing number of Buddhists and Hindus in North America. Built into the new age teachings is the principle of inclusivity. They do not seek disagreement or conflict, but rather harmony. By rejecting the apparent conflicts that divided the competing dogmatisms of the past, new age teachings give the impression of raising up our present commitments into a higher set of unifying beliefs. New age philosophers add to what exists. They do not replace; or, at least, so it seems. The result is that new age theories

and techniques integrate themselves rapidly into our existing churches, businesses, and educational institutions.

The Serious New Age

What is at the heart of the matter? Is the new age only a collection
of hype and eccentricity? Is it only one more reason to hate California? Jonathan Adolph, senior editor of *New Age Journal,* argues that
beneath the hype is a serious mood to the new age that promises
good things for planet Earth. There is reason for the whole world
to be optimistic, he says, and new age consciousness capitalizes on
this optimism. He cites the widespread study of human consciousness and growing interest in mysticism. He cites the increasing credibility of holistic medicine, biofeedback, and relaxation training. He
cites a rise in what he calls "ethical purchasing," buying stock or
products based on social criteria such as divestment from South
Africa. He cites growth in the Green movement with its advocacy of
ecological awareness and nonviolent political action. He cites the
increased use of natural methods of fertilization and pest control
that may reduce toxic poisoning of the environment. These are the
items Adolph puts at the center of the new age. On the fringe he
locates crystals, which supposedly help the body realign its energy
field, and channeling, a form of necromancy whereby ancient entities allegedly speak through earthly mediums. Adolph is critical of
the media's superficial treatment of new age activities; he does not
want these fringe practices to distract us from the important agenda
at the center of new age thinking.[2]

David Spangler, former codirector of Findhorn Foundation in
Scotland and now in a state of "creative hibernation" in Issaquah,
Washington, similarly tries to identify the serious center of the new
age and put some distance between it and the paranormal. Spangler
emphasizes that "new age" is a symbol for a dimension of enrich-
ment within ordinary life.

> The New Age is essentially a symbol representing the human heart
> and intellect in partnership with God building a better world that
> can celebrate values of community, wholeness and sacredness. It is a
> symbol for the emergence of social behavior based on a worldview

that stimulates creativity, discipline, abundance and wholeness; it is a symbol for a more mature and unobstructed expression of the sacredness and love at the heart of life. It has very little to do with the emergence of psychic phenomena.[3]

Spangler dubs the new age a "metaphor" for living daily in the ordinary world with a creative and transformative spirit. It coordinates the human self with the planetary self. It is spiritual in that it seeks a constant openness to the presence of God, to love and possibility. It is political in that it promulgates a global ethic founded on a sense of embracing community.

> The New Age deals with issues of planetarization and the emergence of an awareness that we are all one people living on one world that shares a common destiny. The New Age represents social, political, economic, psychological, and spiritual efforts to recognize and include all that our modern society has tended to exclude: the poor, the dispossessed, the feminine, the ecological, and inwardly, all the painful repressed and unintegrated material that Carl Jung called the shadow.[4]

Marilyn Ferguson, the author of *The Aquarian Conspiracy*, the virtual bible of the new age, describes the movement as a kind of invisible college engaged in personal and global transformation. Her word *conspiracy* means literally to share the spirit, and the shared spirit is one of optimistic innovation.

> For the first time in history, humankind has come upon the control panel of change—an understanding of how transformation occurs. We are living in *the change of change,* the time in which we can intentionally align ourselves with nature for rapid remaking of ourselves and our collapsing institutions.
>
> The paradigm of the Aquarian Conspiracy sees humankind embedded in nature. It promotes the autonomous individual in a decentralized society. It sees us as stewards of all our resources, inner and outer. It says that we are *not* victims, not pawns, not limited by conditions or conditioning. Heirs to evolutionary riches, we are capable of imagination, invention, and experiences we have only glimpsed.[5]

Editor of the *Brain/Mind Bulletin* and popular lecturer on the new age circuit, Ferguson eschews silliness and seeks to ground her optimism in the work of respectable scientists and scholars.

Despite the protestations of these new age figures, however, it is not easy to separate the wheat from the chaff. What Adolph and Spangler identify as the serious new age is seldom separable from the hype, the paranormal, or the kooky. The lifeblood of the new age is the media. Except in the cults, no magisterium is appointed to guarantee orthodoxy. Ideas and techniques just float and mix and combine. The house of the new age can be entered through any of a large number of different doors. Therefore, it will be necessary for us to look at the broad spectrum of phenomena usually labeled "new age" and then try to sift through these phenomena to discern the essential teachings.

Terry and the Center of the Universe

"Terry's put on a few pounds," I thought to myself as we exchanged a bit of small talk on my way into her workshop session at the 1988 Whole Life Expo in San Francisco. Reverend Terry Cole-Whittaker had always appeared slim and trim and healthy on her Sunday morning TV show. Her flashy blond hair and blazing countenance were dazzling. She was a volcano erupting with enviable vitality. In a voice akin to that of a revivalist preacher, she told her audiences to look for God within, not without. This divinity within us that she was calling forth would empower our personalities. Her preaching fired us up so that we believed we could fulfill our own wishes by taking the initiative. It was an exciting and profitable message. Terry looked beautiful when she delivered it, and she still does.

Then she quit. She announced on the air that she was so besieged by the burdens of managing a multimillion-dollar televangelism business that she needed some relief. She was tired of the acrimony and infighting among her employees. So she gave up her TV show, telling her supporters that she had married a man who would move her to Hawaii and support her. It was "bye, bye" to mainland hubbub and "hello" to Pacific tranquillity.

But now she is back, not as a TV preacher but heading up a new age organization called Adventures in Enlightenment. She leads retreats at her home in Maui and on her farm in Washington state. She sells books and tapes and trips abroad. "I used to be called 'Reverend Terry,'" she says with a Phyllis Diller laugh at herself; "Now I'm irreverend Terry."

Her message is clear and forceful: I should love myself. I should acknowledge that deep inside I am beautiful and capable. I am "insignificant," meaning that my *significance* lies *in* me. I am "incurable" meaning that I am *curable* from with*in*. The problem is that we feel unworthy because our society teaches us to look outside for our answers. The schools teach us to ask the experts. Theologians teach us to ask them what we should believe. So we look to our teachers to pat us on the head and tell us we are worthy. We assume that we need to look outside ourselves to get validated. But all this is misdirected, she says. Instead we should turn inward. Our validation comes from within. We create it ourselves. The first step is to give ourselves permission to say, "I am worthy."

"Forgiveness is an insult," Terry adds. It contradicts our own self-created worthiness. Why should we let anybody else forgive us? If we yield to allowing others to forgive us, then this is a sign that we have judged ourselves and found ourselves wanting. Instead, we should avoid judging ourselves, she advises. Then the need for forgiveness will never arise. When we confront a situation that reveals an inadequacy on our part, we should consider this revelation a learning experience. Consign the inadequacy to the past. Do not apologize for it. Say, "Now I know better." Then embrace a new and better future.

Similarly, Terry cannot accept Jesus' statement that "the Son makes you free" (John 8:36). We do not need Jesus to set us free, says Terry. We set ourselves free.

How do we do this? We do it by "accessing the flow." We assume that the world is filled with an abundant supply of everything we need and want. The supply is unlimited. If we think there is a limit, then the problem is in what we think, not in reality. For example, the supply of love is inexhaustible. If we feel we do not have enough love in our life, then this is due to our having shut love off. All we need do in this instance is open ourselves to receive it. Then it will flow in from the universal energy supply that governs our cosmos.

This universal energy supply is what Terry calls God. Actually, she has many names for it. She says that in earlier years she called it Christ. Now the names are optional. Her current favorite is "the goddess," because she is currently on a personal exploration of the power of the feminine in her life and being. The most accurate title, she admits, is "the center of the universe."

Regardless of the name, what she emphasizes is that the goddess always gives, and gives abundantly. Like a mother watching over her children, the goddess at the center of the universe never says no. Rather, she only says yes! yes! yes! Blessings are unlimited.

What we have here is a doctrine of the cosmic self. Now one might ask: just what is the relationship between the self that creates its own worthiness and the center of the universe that bequeaths to us these blessings? Terry answers: they are one and the same. There is no external God. There is no God who is watching over our moral activities, just waiting until judgment day to place a crown on our head and tell us we have done well. Rather, we place the crown on our own head. Once we have given ourself the permission to declare ourself worthy, we have also given ourself access to the unlimited flow of universal energy. We have opened ourself to our higher self, and our higher self is the center of the universe.

When the subject of Terry's extra weight came up in her presentation that day in San Francisco, she patted her tummy and announced with another Phyllis Diller–style laugh that she believed in salvation through indulgence. Food tastes good. We should enjoy it just as we should enjoy the sexual intimacy of husband and wife. What we are after is fulfillment, not denial. That is what the center of the universe wants for us.

Terry's workshop includes deep breathing exercises, as does almost every activity in new age spirituality. With eyes closed in meditative stillness, we inhale slowly while Terry talks to us softly. We are asked to envision three things: (1) What do I want? (2) What would it be like to get it? and (3) What would gratitude for getting what I want feel like? With the air we breathe in power, blessing, and gratitude.

The workshop concludes with a tripartite chant. Following Terry we recite:

I love myself.
I am enough.
I am worthy.

This, she says, is "the fast path to bliss."

I cannot help but think of someone who shares the same basic commitment to the cosmic self but whose life-style could not be more opposite: Mother Krishnavai. A few years ago I traveled with a German colleague to southern India to engage in Hindu-Christian dialogue. We visited the widely renowned Hindu saint at Anandi Ashram. Then in her eighties and on a sickbed, she graciously granted us an audience and discussed philosophical matters. Determined to attain *mukti* or enlightenment during this lifetime, Mother Krishnavai gave herself over to strict asceticism, yoga, and meditation for forty years. After four decades of the strictest self-denial, she announced that she no longer felt any sexual desire. Shortly thereafter she attained cosmic consciousness, the sense that she is at one with the whole of reality. This has now given her *ananda*—that is, bliss.

What a contrast with Terry Cole-Whittaker's salvation through indulgence and the fast path to bliss! Where does this idea of the fast path to bliss come from? What Terry is doing is streamlining something otherwise rough and subtle. She is packaging and distributing what were previously the raw materials mined at a place called Esalen in California.

California's Esalen

What a place, California! Like a sustained chain reaction, California is a state of mind constantly exploding with new ideas. As the American frontier moved west, it hit its limit at the shores of the Pacific. The adventurous spirit that took the pioneers across the plains, mountains, and deserts did not dissolve in the waters of the great ocean, however. Rather, the adventure turned inward. Geographical expansion became consciousness expansion. Explorers of the landscape became explorers of the human mind. And just as the forty-niners had come west to seek their fortunes in gold, today's

Californians are seeking a richness of the inner life. As if they have been drinking the waters of the Pacific—an ocean named in honor of peacefulness—new age seekers are thirsting for a deep peace they believe can only be found within the human soul.

One weekend each spring I along with my wife, Jenny, and some close friends, Rabbi Hayim and Nancy Perelmuter, drive down the California coast to Big Sur and spend a few days at Las Rocas, a house near Torre Canyon. At dusk we watch the sunset from the point, a comfortable spot atop a cliff that drops five hundred feet down to the pounding waves and sea lions below. Above we can see the steep green hills rising another two thousand feet, marking the eastern horizon. Whether looking west or looking up into the clear celestial expanse, one cannot help but think about things infinite. "How tiny I feel," said Nancy during our 1988 pilgrimage while staring off at Venus rising in the evening sky, "especially when I think about the immensity of our universe. But it's peaceful to think about it. It feels good."

In such a location one can understand the birth of the Esalen Institute in the 1960s and the legacy it has left to the new age movement. In 1961 two Stanford University graduates, Michael Murphy and Richard Price, took over proprietorship of the Murphy family property at Big Sur and began what is now a continuing search for psychological wholeness. Murphy had entered into the practice of meditation earlier during a stint at Sri Aurobindo's ashram in Pondicherry, India. To America he imported Aurobindo's practice of mystical meditation, his notion of evolutionary development, and his philosophy of synthesizing the physical with the spiritual. At Esalen he and Price sponsored a series of think tank–style seminars with the aim of transforming what had just come to be known as the *human potential movement* into the *consciousness revolution*.

In the summer of 1962 connection was made with Abraham Maslow. Maslow, along with Carl Rogers, was the intellectual architect of the human potential movement. Rogers had given us the term *self-realization*, and Maslow *self-actualization*. These psychologists were focusing attention on what makes for psychological health, not on what is dysfunctional. A healthy person is a self-actualizing person, Maslow had said in his widely read book *Motivation and Personality*. Self-actualizing people have certain identifiable characteristics. For example, they are spontaneous and natural; they are at home with wonder and awe. They enjoy life. They are autonomous, occasionally unconventional, even detached. They are quite aware of their own impulses, desires, opinions, and subjective reaction patterns. Healthy people focus on problems outside of themselves; they do not see themselves as problems. They are capable of deeper and more profound interpersonal relations than are ordinary people. They are creative, unhostile, and have a sense of humor. In contrast to neurotics, most importantly, self-actualizing people accept themselves; they exhibit "a relative lack of overriding guilt, of crippling shame, and of extreme or severe anxiety."[6]

Of striking significance was Maslow's observation that a large number of healthy self-actualizing people have had mystical experiences, the kind of experiences William James described as religious and Sigmund Freud called oceanic. The oceanic feeling is a sense of limitless horizons, an opening of vision, the feeling of being simultaneously more powerful and also more helpless than ever before. It is the feeling of great ecstasy, wonder, and awe. It may include the loss of one's place in time and space; yet this is accompanied by the conviction that something extremely important has happened. One becomes transformed and strengthened. Daily life takes on new meaning and power. Maslow began to refer to these moments as "peak experiences" and saw them as important in the self-actualization process. Rather than draw a sharp line between the mystic experience and daily life, Maslow sought to see them on a continuum that stretched from intense to mild experience.[7]

In 1964 Gestalt therapist Fritz Perls took up residence at Esalen and began the era of encounter groups. War broke out between thought and feeling. Rational thought had to be conquered to liberate one's inner feelings. Avoidance of feeling Perls dubbed a "head trip." His slogan was "Lose your mind and come to your senses." His Gestalt Prayer gave us the epigram of the 1960s, "I do my thing, and you do your thing."

A bit later Will Schutz moved to the Esalen campus with his program of "open encounter." He reformulated René Descartes's famous axiom "I think, therefore I am" to read: "I feel, therefore I am." Schutz's eclectic approach to group therapy included a variety of elements such as psychodrama, Gestalt, sensitivity and T-group methods, nonverbal trust exercises, nudity, body wrestling, and psychosynthetic imagining. His aim was to achieve joy in life, and his means for achieving it was "expansion."

> Joy is the feeling that comes from the fulfillment of one's potential. Fulfillment brings to an individual the feeling that he can cope with his environment; the sense of confidence in himself as a significant, competent, lovable person who is capable of handling situations as they arise, able to use fully his own capacities, and free to express his feelings.[8]

Despite their exalted promises of actualizing human potential in the numerous guests attending their seminars and group therapy programs, the professional psychologists themselves sank into a pattern of petty rivalry. In his *Facing West from California's Shores*, David Toolan describes how Perls referred snidely to Schutz and company as the "Joy Boys" and spoke of Maslow's concepts of "being motivation" and "peak experience" as just so much "elephantshit."

In the early 1970s Esalen added the influence of Italian psychosynthesist Roberto Assagioli. Using fantasy and imaging techniques to sort out the various subpersonalities within, Assagioli sought a method to help us to get in touch with the higher self, which would be capable of orchestrating our internal multiplicity.[9] The adoption of the higher-self orientation eventually led Esalen beyond personal and interpersonal relations into transpersonal or metaphysical psychology. This, it turns out, has become central to new age cosmology.

est

One of Mother Esalen's prodigal children, so to speak, is est, an acronym for Erhard Seminars Training. It refers to an organization called Werner Erhard and Associates, known more recently as the Forum. Since est's founding in San Francisco in 1971, hundreds of thousands of business executives, educators, homemakers, and others have taken the two-weekend training course in order to shed weight, overcome shyness, increase personal energy, establish a positive self-image, or improve their love life. All have been seeking greater "aliveness."

The est Standard Training is a kind of participatory theater in which the trainer uses a form of Socratic method to interrogate the trainees and draw forth personal transformation. The training seeks to evoke a catharsis, even a peak experience if possible. The aim is to dislodge past conceptual patterns of behavior dictated by the mind—that is, to "blow one's mind." Mind blowing supposedly aids the trainee in opening up to daily experience, in really *experiencing* experience. This is the path to higher consciousness.

Werner Hans Erhard, founder of est, seems to be perpetually trying to clean up the mess that is his life. Born during the Depression to an Episcopalian mother and a Jewish father who converted to Evangelical Christianity, Werner was first named Jack Rosenberg. He changed this name, just as he changed so many other things in his life, after deserting his first wife and four children on May 25, 1960, secretly fleeing Philadelphia with his paramour to take on new identities in St. Louis. While riding in the airplane and reading an *Esquire* magazine article on West Germany, he chose to call himself Werner after Werner Heisenberg, the physicist known for the indeterminacy principle; Hans in honor of Hans Lilje, the Lutheran bishop incarcerated by the Nazis; and Erhard after Ludwig Erhard, West Germany's economic minister who later became chancellor. His companion and new wife, formerly June Bryde, changed her name to Ellen Erhard. With new names in hand, the two began to search for a new identity, a search that took them eventually to California.

Erhard is a salesman. He sold used cars, the Great Books, and educational materials produced by Parents Magazine Cultural Institute before creating est. An autodidact, unable to attend college because he got his high school girlfriend pregnant and married her at age eighteen, Erhard has since read and studied books dealing with motivation technique. The two books that most influenced him early on were Napolean Hill's *Think and Grow Rich* and Maxwell Maltz's *Psycho-Cybernetics*. Then he made contact with Esalen. The principles of success he had previously found in the Hill and Maltz self-help books were reinforced by the principles of personal growth he encountered when reading Rogers and Maslow, as well as in a

Fritz Perls seminar he attended at Esalen. What he learned he adapted to his work of motivating the sales staff at Parents Magazine Cultural Institute to communicate well in their selling.

Erhard is eclectic. He augments and integrates. He begs, borrows, and steals good ideas, and has gone well beyond the original combination of self-help and Esalen. During the latter 1960s, Erhard imbibed and transmuted the principles of Zen Buddhism that he learned at the feet of Alan Watts in Sausalito, Dale Carnegie's personality development course, training in the martial arts, the notion of inner stillness in the teachings of Subud, and the doctrine that the mind is the root of all our trouble as promulgated by L. Ron Hubbard's Scientology. All have gone into the planning of est.

Werner Erhard claims to have had a peak experience. It occurred in October 1963 while he was in the San Francisco office of Parents Magazine after his staff had gone home. He was sitting alone, looking out the window. What he experienced was more focused than the generic oceanic feeling; it was focused on Erhard's sense of self and a conversion of values.

> The peak experience that I had in 1963 was a peak experience of what I call Self. . . . I truly experienced *the* Self—not *my* Self: the word "my" belongs in the world of *concept* about Self, not *experience* of Self. I was carried out of my ordinary state, not merely to another state, but to the context for all states, the context of all contexts. . . . The experience was truly a conversion experience. The word "conversion" is often applied narrowly to religious experience—whereas in fact it belongs across the spectrum. Chiefly, it is a death of one's old values, and a rebirth with new values. Those things that previously were important are no longer so. I could still enjoy material things, but they no longer held any meaning for me for their own sakes.[10]

For Erhard the peak experience signaled the death of his previous value system centered on becoming a success in business. What was rising was a new set of values centered on personal growth, on self-satisfaction, on becoming whole and complete.

This led to a central doctrine of est: climbing the ladder to the Self. Borrowing the concept of the ladder of philosophy from Ludwig Wittgenstein's *Tractatus Logico-Philosophicus* and combining it with the distinction between the mind and the self in Zen, Erhard teaches us to pursue identity by recognizing that the Self is what one truly is. But the true Self is not *my* Self. The true Self stands beyond any individual, identification, form, process, or position; yet it gives rise to them. The Self is not one's conscience. Nor is it one's mind. Rather, the Self is the context of all contexts in which the activities of our conscience or mind take place. Rather than identify ourselves as this or that person, ego, or mind, Erhard recommends we think of ourselves as the space in which this identity takes place. Once one has climbed the ladder to this insight and been transformed by it, then creativity, vitality, happiness, and true self-expression will arise spontaneously.

est disciples are certainly convinced this is the case. One of my graduate students and friends, Tom Ross, has experienced a dramatic personal renewal and growth in self-confidence as a result of est. He began with the two-weekend standard training seminar and then followed this with the Forum, a program explaining the underlying est principles, which incorporate much of Heideggerian philosophy. This led to the six-day advanced course and the Mastery of Empowerment course at a site near Santa Rosa, California. Included in this are the rope exercises, such as flying down a 400-foot-long zip line from a height of 150 feet. The purpose of such exercises is to face what one fears. The key here, Tom tells me, is that you promise to follow instructions no matter what. The rappeling exercise begins by leaning backward over a 70-foot cliff. With rope in hand you are instructed to let go and fall. "This was hard," Tom told me, "but once I let go and began to bounce down the mountain it was fun. It was exhilarating."

In the Tyrolean traverse exercise, one crosses a canyon while hanging on to a combination of ropes. The initial fall carries one quickly to the middle, where one hangs in midair over the center of the abyss. The second half is an upward pull dependent entirely on the power of one's own arms. Your friends who are watching shout encouragement: "Keep your promise! Don't give up!" They encourage, but they do not help. You have to pull your own weight.

The physical exercises have their counterpart in mental exercises, in group conversation where you are encouraged to pursue your true Self in the company of others who are pursuing the same thing. Frank discussion takes place about one's past griefs or sexual experience, asking about the possible constrictions they might be putting on daily life. "We place unnecessary limits on ourselves," Tom says. "What we need to do is let go of the self-imposed limits." Tom is a Presbyterian minister and no longer is involved with est. Yet when reflecting on his experience, he says, "I wish the Church could have done for me what est has, but it hasn't."

Such programs have been subject to criticism. The human potential movement and its accompanying impact on the wider culture has undergone considerable attack on the grounds that it is essentially narcissistic. It is inward looking and self-centered. It indulges in self-pleasure, whether in an individual or in a social form. Movements such as women's liberation and gay liberation, which borrow new age consciousness and awareness techniques, are accused of donning the banner of "liberationist critiques of modern society" only as a smoke screen designed to hide their underlying hedonism. Most noted among the critics is Christopher Lasch, who describes what is happening as a form of decadence that has carried "the logic of individualism to the extreme of a war of all against all, the pursuit of happiness to the dead end of a narcissistic preoccupation with the self."[11] W. W. Bartley III, defending Erhard's est from such charges, responds by saying,

> The charge of narcissism has to do with a verbal misunderstanding. Some writers have been led astray by a technical use of the word "self." "Self" as used by Werner has nothing to do with "selfish"; it has no connection to the accidents of individual biography or history, personal appearance, achievement or possession. There is nothing narcissistic about attempting to transcend those things in life that lead people to narcissism.[12]

The Esalen leaders of today are not particularly proud of the accomplishments of est and other similarly packaged psychotechnologies. They think of such mass programs as distortions. Erhard is called a "shameless raider" of the Esalen "pot of gold"; and he is lumped together with other prostitutions of the new age such as the cult of Baghwan Rajneesh and L. Ron Hubbard's Scientology.

To be sympathetic, we must be alert to covert classism in critiques of Erhard. He is self-taught and eclectic. He does not have a college degree from Stanford. He does not belong to the credentialed class of the educated bourgeoise who make up the primary clientele at Esalen.

And then there is the California factor. This is frontier country. Once we give ourselves permission to cross the frontier that previously has bound our minds and spirits, anything can happen. We open ourselves up to creativity. We also open ourselves up to chaos. We open ourselves up to the packagers and distributors such as Werner Erhard and Terry Cole-Whittaker. This is the risk. This is the excitement. David Toolan says it nicely.

> Since pioneer days, California has served as the test range for America's mythic boundaries. The state has no doubt also teased its current inhabitants to imagine they ought to look and feel as good as the scenery and weather. . . . No question, Esalen seeded the U.S. landscape with its catalogue of body, mind, and soul arts that other networks and institutions with former sociological roots and longer historical memories continue to harvest. And I am grateful.[13]

Holistic Health

Modern medicine is under attack. The new age is promoting a postmodern approach. It is called holistic (sometimes spelled *wholistic*) health.[14] Although recognizing the achievements of the scientific approach to medicine that has dominated the West during the modern period, new agers attack it for its limitations. Scientific medicine has worked with a mechanistic model of the human being, a model that treats the body as a machine separable from one's emotional and mental nature. It fragments the human person. Consequently, the model of health with which modernity works is only partial. The emerging postmodern understanding, in contrast, treats the person as a living organism replete with body, mind, and spirit. It seeks to be comprehensive, treating us as *whole persons*.

Holism can mean many things. The holistic approach to medicine and mental health includes three distinct yet complementary components. First, each person is treated in context. Each of us is more than an individual with a body. We belong to families, and our family life can contribute to our becoming sick or enhance our ability to become well. Similarly, we work at a job; we embody the values of our respective ethnic group; and our daily routine involves an identifiable urban, suburban, or rural environment. All of these factors need consideration when we seek to promote health, prevent illness, and encourage healing.

Second, each person is treated as a living organism, not a broken machine. This represents a change in models. Modern medicine has been working with the model of the human being as a machine that operates according to certain identifiable principles. Doctors go to medical school to learn how the machine works and how to fix what is broken. When a patient appears in the hospital with an illness or injury, he or she is treated like a machine that needs repair. Cure comes from the outside, through medicine or surgery or guided therapy. The holistic model, in contrast, presumes that the powers of healing come first from within the so-called patient. We have within us the capacity to stimulate our innate healing processes and to make the changes in our lives that will promote health and prevent illness. Mental attitude is extremely important, because a close link between body, mind, and spirit is assumed. Self-healing is important: the holistic attitude emphasizes the self-responsibility of the person in addition to any treatment that comes from the outside.

Third, treatment may include alternative medicines and therapies. The holistic approach is not limited to what is prescribed by the American Medical Association. Beyond the standard *materia medica* we find homeopathy, acupuncture, biofeedback, hypnosis, meditation, psychic healing, touch therapy, shamanism, root medicine, and maybe even prayer. What is being sought is a synthesis of science and spirit.[15]

An important shift in basic assumptions is going on here. Holistic medicine begins by thinking of health as a positive state in its own right, not merely as the absence of disease. The problem with modern medicine is that it has assumed its responsibility is basically negative: to rid people of diseases. What has not been addressed in any comprehensive way is the criteria for determining good health. The holistic approach aims at discerning just what constitutes good health and moving directly toward it.

One of the key words has become *wellness*. Holistic health advocates climb a ladder that ascends from clinical disease to the absence of disease, then higher to what the World Health Organization calls "complete physical and mental well-being," to something still higher: a state of extraordinary vigor, joy, and creativity. Some call this "super health," others "high-level wellness."[16]

Fritjof Capra calls health "dynamic balance." So understood, health is an experience of well-being that involves the physical and psychological aspects of the organism, and also its interactions with the natural and social environment. This opens the door, Capra believes, to shamanism. The shamans or root doctors among American Indians and elsewhere took, and still take, a systems approach to health. Human beings are assumed to be integral parts of an ordered system—specifically, the system we know as the cosmic order. Illness, then, is thought to result from a disharmony with the cosmic order. Even minor things such as sprains or fractures or snakebites are seen as being due not simply to misfortune, but rather to a disharmonious relationship with the larger world system. Accordingly, shamanistic therapies emphasize the restoration of harmony, or balance, within nature, in human relationships, and in relationships with the spirit world. We can learn from the shamans, argues Capra, to see human health in this overall cosmic context.[17]

Holistic health proponents by no means advocate avoidance of doctors or the medical establishment. Rather, they seek to modify if not transform current practice. Among the modifications is the emphasis on the manner in which the physician ought to relate to the patient. The physician ought not to look at the patient's body in isolation from its psycho-socio-economic context, but rather should take this context into account. Also important is physical touch. The doctor's soft, patting touch, the careful dressing of wounds, the hand on the laboring woman's belly—all function to connote intimate communication and give reassurance. Touch is therapeutic.

Because wellness is the objective, holistic health emphasizes nutrition and exercise. Health food stores have become new age centers in many communities. Jogging and aerobic exercise have become prescriptions for overcoming depression and enhancing psychological balance. Eastern practices such as the martial arts, deep breathing, and tai chi give self-control and emotional flexibility. All capitalize on the "wisdom of the body," which is alleged to be innate.

Aquarian conspirator Marilyn Ferguson wishes to reinterpret disease and illness in a positive, rather than a negative, fashion. Dis-ease means dis-harmony. As such, it is a sign that a change is warranted, that an opportunity for transformation is nigh. We should look upon illness as potentially transformative because it can cause a sudden shift in values, an awakening. Each of us just might be keeping secrets from ourselves—unexamined conflicts, suppressed yearnings—and illness may force them into awareness so that we can deal constructively with them.

This positive interpretation of disease and illness is part of what Ferguson calls "the new paradigm," the postmodern paradigm that she hopes will replace the modern one. She contrasts the modern or scientific paradigm, which focuses on symptoms, with the new holistic paradigm, which focuses on good health. Whereas the modern view sees the body as a broken machine in need of repair, the holistic view sees it as a dynamic system of energy interacting with other fields of energy. Whereas the medical approach is specialized, the holistic approach seeks integration; it is concerned with the whole person. Whereas the professionalism of the medical establishment strives to be emotionally neutral, holistic health advocates believe caring is an actual component in healing. Whereas medical treatment is based upon intervention through drugs or surgery, holistic practice reduces intervention to a minimum by employing noninvasive techniques such as psychotherapies, diet, and exercise. Whereas hospitals make the patient dependent, holistic therapy presumes the patient is autonomous.

The key to this new paradigm is the assumption that the power of healing comes from the inner person. We can no more manipulate the body into health by external ministrations than we can manage the ebb and flow of the tides by an organized system of mops. The greatest outside effort cannot do what the central power within us does easily and with unerring grace and providence. Healing comes from the body-mind matrix, from our innate somatic and psychological harmony. There is a healer inside us. In a sense, Ferguson says, there is always a doctor in the house.[18]

Holistic medicine is by no means strictly an internal affair, however. It also promotes a vigorous social ethic. It includes a strong commitment to change those social and economic conditions that perpetuate ill health. This is an expansion of the assumption that the individual cannot be isolated from his or her social, economic, and ecological context. Treatment of a lead-intoxicated child includes pressing for legislation to keep lead-based paint off babies' toys. It includes advocacy for other kinds of political activities leading toward the elimination of hunger and malnutrition, and of the poverty and political oppression that create hunger and malnutrition. Groups such as the Medical Committee for Human Rights and Physicians for Social Responsibility, for example, argue that such things as industrial pollution, nuclear development, and international war are bad for our health.

Capra presents a political platform for advocacy that includes (1) restrictions on advertising of unhealthy products; (2) "health care taxes" levied against corporations that pollute the environment or create similar health hazards; (3) increased incentives for industry to produce more nutritious foods, including restrictions on vending machine companies so that they may sell only nutritional products in schools, hospitals, prisons, and government cafeterias; (4) legislation to support organic farming; and (5) general social policies aimed at aiding impoverished people through better education, employment, civil rights, family planning, and, of course, health care.[19]

Some church leaders are seeing the health in holistic health, taking cognizance especially of the reintegration of the spiritual with the physical. One of the leaders for a generation now is Granger Westberg, who has been developing wholistic health centers that coordinate doctors, nurses, and parish pastors. The first was the Neighborhood Church Clinic in southern Ohio, opened in 1969 to serve low-income people who have only limited access to otherwise costly medical services. In 1979 Westberg opened a similar program in Hinsdale, Illinois, a wealthy Chicago suburb that has more doctors per square mile than almost any other community. When challenged on this, Westberg responded that he was seeking to demonstrate the principle that the wholistic approach is valid for everybody, regardless of income level. Similar centers can now be found in Minneapolis, Cleveland, and Washington, D.C.[20]

Westberg, along with Rev. Jack Lundin, formerly of Chicago and now San Jose, have been developing what they call the "parish nurse" program. The way it works is that nurses and doctors and other health professionals in a given congregation come together and formulate their own philosophy of health in the church setting. Then they plan ways to meet the needs of their congregation through programs that complement—not replace—the normal care given by physicians, clinics, and hospitals. This may include blood pressure tests during coffee hour after worship on Sunday morning, referrals to appropriate agencies, educational programs in the church regarding nutrition or disease prevention, and such. Whatever is done integrates physical well-being with emotional health, medicine with prayer. Westberg calls it "wholism," and by it he intends to treat each person wholistically in a way that combines body, soul, and spirit.

I have spoken with some of the nurses who head up such a program in a local congregation. They tell me they are extremely excited about it. One nurse told me, "Now I can do what I wanted to do when I first went into nursing: care for people! Here at the church I don't waste my time charting or waiting for doctor's orders. I couldn't be happier." What she does at the church is part-time, voluntary, after she leaves her nursing shift each day at the hospital.

New Age Music

Not only do trade bookstores have new age sections, so do the music stores. What we find on the tapes and records sold there, to mix the metaphors of eyes and ears, is *visionary music*. While reading or driving I frequently put into my tape deck *Natural States* by David Lanz and Paul Speer, or a selection by Steven Halpern. What I hear directs my mind's eye to the beauty of the forest, to the depth and distance of the mountains, or to the calming eternity of ocean waves washing upon the beach.

How does one describe new age music? It emits an ethereal sound that opens up a space in your schedule and permits your mind to wander. It is a healing sound: contemplative, mellow, introspective. By echoing the ambience of the natural environment, it seeks to be unfrenetic and conducive to meditation. It calms, reduces stress, and seeks to elicit a more peaceful state of being. At its heart, new age music is meditative.

Originally solo keyboard music with accompanying experiments in acoustical sounds, new age music has developed and now includes a wide variety of traditional and electronic instruments. It was pioneered by artists like Paul Horn and Paul Winter. Once the name "new age" caught on, it has become an encompassing category that includes many musical styles that do not fit elsewhere, such as fusion, minimalist, and world music. Nevertheless, its simple meditative core still distinguishes it from jazz, rock, or classical music.

It is a commercial success. New age music now accounts for 2 percent of all record and tape sales. Windham Hill records, specializing in new age sounds, brought in $35 million in 1987. RCA, A&M, MCA, and Capitol Records have contracts with new age artists such as George Winston, Andreas Vollenweider, and Kitaro, whose recordings make it big on the charts.

New age music does have its critics. It has been accused of being wallpaper music, audio Valium, yuppie Muzak, and just too boring to take seriously. In its defense, we need to note that new age music is not meant to be listened to intensely or critically, as we might do with a classical symphony or when dancing to rock. In fact, listening to it intensely would defeat its purpose. Rather, the beauty of new age music is its subtlety, the surprising combination of instrumental sounds that trigger your imagination to take flight in its own direction.[21]

Crystal Consciousness

As we noted earlier, Jonathan Adolph, senior editor of *New Age Journal,* distinguishes between the essential philosophy of the new age movement and what he calls "fringe issues—distractions from the largely practical and down-to-earth matters that lie at the center of new age thinking."[22] What does he list as fringe distractions? Two things: crystals and channeling. Yet, interestingly enough, advertisements for crystals and channelers appear on the pages of his magazine.

Fringe or not, crystal consciousness certainly resonates with the techniques and teachings of the other components of the new age movement. It prescribes deep breathing exercises and mental imaging of new states of existence as a means of personal transformation. Use of crystals can supposedly heal hurts in human relationships and change other unwanted circumstances. Placed on the body at points of pain, crystals allegedly have physical healing power. Crystals also aid in developing psychic abilities such as clairvoyance, clairaudience, and travel on the astral and mental planes.

The power to do these things comes from a higher level of self, a source that transcends the ego. Uma Silbey, a West Coast instructor in meditation and a crystal jeweler, says we may call this transcendent source by any name, such as Spirit, Higher Order, or God.[23] According to Uma, if we do not feel this higher power, it is due to our own self-imposed boundaries. We tend to build mental fences. We unnecessarily constrict ourselves through limiting ideas. If we are willing to drop our fences and open ourselves to the higher potential available, then we can and will receive unlimited energy, vision, love, creativity, contentment, and wisdom.

This is where crystals come in, explains Uma. They help to open us. They are not good luck charms or amulets. Rather, they are a meditative device. Energy, in the form of vibration, is projected from each crystal and forms a field around it. It is through manipulation of this vibratory energy that the crystals aid us in effecting transformation. Uma says, "The entire universe is a state of mind . . . change your mind, change your universe." The crystal does not perform magic in itself; rather, it assists the mind in its work of changing things.

What kinds of crystals are we talking about? Quartz crystal stones, either clear or colored, are the most widely used. Both quartz and human beings are largely comprised of silicon dioxide, which makes us cousins among the chemical families on Earth. Katrina Raphaell argues that clear quartz has the advantage of vibrating with clear light that contains all the other colors. Clear quartz radiates divine white light and by seeing, touching, wearing, using, or meditating with these crystals one can allegedly work with that light to increase the positive vibrations in one's life. Each color has its own rate of vibration. As for myself, I have chosen an amethyst crystal, partly because of its beauty and partly because its pink color is associated with healing.

Shape is important. The sides of the quartz crystal symbolize the chakras. Chakras, according to the Indian practice of yoga, are points along the human spinal column that transmit divine energy. The flat base represents the crystal's source in the earth. Rising up from the earth, the obelisk-shaped crystal is topped with a miniature pyramid that terminates at the point. This is the crown alleged to connect us with the infinite. Oftentimes a crystal is cut with a cloudy or milky section at the bottom, gaining more clarity as it reaches the peak. This symbolizes growth in consciousness, beginning with the dullness of our preawakened state and rising in awareness to the point of union with the infinite. In this way crystals aid in the realization of our cosmic self, say their proponents. They represent the material plane of existence in its state of perfection.[24]

Crystals need to be cleared and charged. Salt water cleansing helps clear them of old energies. They can be charged by blowing into them. Through the use of the imagination, we can take a negative feeling such as anger, exhale, and blow the vibrations of that anger into the crystal. Then we can bury the crystal in the soil, where Mother Earth will neutralize and transmute it. The result is that we ourselves feel relaxed, cleansed, calmed.

As an exercise in transformative meditation, Uma Silbey asked me and the workshop group I was with at the time to close our eyes and breathe deeply three times. Then, step by step, she talked us through an imaginative sequence. First, we imagined that we were surrounded by crystals, that we were within a crystal energy matrix. Then we were asked to see ourselves inside a crystal, to feel its hardness and its cooling surfaces. Once we were fully relaxed, Uma began to repeat: "You have a right to be happy." Then she asked: "Are you happy? Why not?" We then constructed in our vision the situation that was making us unhappy. To this we added a picture of the steps necessary to change unhappiness into happiness. This was followed by another step in which we imagined a transformed situation in which we were truly happy. As the vision proceeded we were asked to see ourselves bathed in golden light, a light that we inhaled and ingested and that filled us with wisdom and truth.

The purpose of all this is empowerment so that we can better control out lives. The act of centering through paced breathing and meditative concentration is already a form of self-control. Uma Silbey employs an inspiring metaphor here. If our mind is uncontrolled, she says, then it resonates with the vibratory states around us. If people around us are angry, we become angry. If they are happy, then we are happy. If the sky is overcast, then we may feel depressed. Under these conditions, we are slaves to our minds. But, says Uma, we should be masters, not slaves. Crystal guided meditation can aid us in focusing the mind and in gaining mastery. Once we have developed this capacity, then our mind will be like a body of deep water. Thoughts, like waves, will cross its surface. Yet the depth of the water will not be disturbed. Thoughts, stimulated by external vibratory forces, will come and go; but they will not ruffle the mind. The mind will rest in a state of peaceful awareness.[25]

Channeling

The occult and the new age share much in common. The word *occult* comes from the Latin *occulere,* "to conceal," and refers to magical or mystical knowledge shrouded in mystery. What is required to obtain this special knowledge—this esoteric knowledge—is a teacher, an enlightened one, a medium. This is vividly demonstrated in channeling. Channeling not only teaches the occult, it also presupposes it.

The word *channeling* refers to a family of alleged phenomena in which a nonphysical entity communicates through a human medium, through a channel who links the spiritual and physical worlds. It traditionally includes necromancy: communicating with the spirits of departed loved ones in a séance. In the new age, however, it refers more often to the process whereby a disembodied teacher communicates occult doctrines to a discipleship. Ruth Montgomery, for example, claims that a spirit entity "takes over" her body—her typing fingers—and communicates through automatic writing. Judith Z. Knight goes into a trance on stage, and a spirit entity named Ramtha then speaks to the assembled audience through Mrs. Knight's voice. Channeling is the communication of information to or through a physically embodied human being from a source that is said to exist on some level or dimension of reality other than the physical.[26]

Channeling is by no means new. We can find a salient example of it in the Bible. King Saul, fearing war with the Philistines, wanted divine counsel and comfort. So, even though he had previously outlawed necromancy, he sought out a medium at Endor to raise the spirit of the dead prophet Samuel in order to ask his advice (1 Sam. 28). This led to tragedy. In general, the Bible strongly discourages trading in spirits.

Carl Jung reports a fascinating series of séances during the winter of 1899–1900 with a relative of his, a fifteen-year-old girl. Going into a trancelike sleep Jung called "somnambulism," she would speak with the voice of her deceased grandfather as well as the voices of many other dead relatives and friends. Her vocabulary and dialect would change to fit the style of German appropriate to each voice. She embarrassed those attending the séances by revealing vivid details of family romances and passions. Significant for the new age nearly a century later, the channeled spirits taught a cosmology that included reincarnation and posited the existence of star-dwellers. There are people living on the planet Mars, she reported. Mars is covered with canals, which are in fact artificial lakes and are used for irrigation, and Martians travel in flying machines, she told everyone. She added that there are no wars on Mars or among the star people, because no differences of opinion exist.[27]

At the turn of the twentieth century, there seemed to be a widespread association between séances, reincarnation, and star traveling. These themes fit together in the popular 1915 novel *The Star Rover* by American author Jack London, whose mother had been a spiritualist.

Thus, what is going on today has a history. Toward the end of the nineteenth century, Madame H. P. Blavatsky channeled volumes of her *Secret Doctrine* on the origin of the cosmos and the genesis of the human race. In the 1920s Alice A. Bailey claimed to be transcribing twenty-five books' worth of the thoughts of a former Tibetan teacher, Djwhal Kuhl, nicknamed D. K. In a similar manner, miracle healer Edgar Cayce, who died in 1945 at the age of 67, is said to have channeled teachings that lead to an "attunement with God." The Cayce doctrines are actually an occult philosophy that looks like a piecing together of elements from Christianity, Theosophy, and pyramidology. More recently, Jane Roberts's 1972 book *Seth Speaks* began a series of best-sellers through which occult teachings have spread to a mass audience. Jack Pursel, a Los Angeles–based channeler of an entity named Lazaris, claims he can lead us through the steps to meet our own Higher Self; and this will change our life. Penny Torres Rubin channels an entity named Mafu, who says to those listening: "You are God. You must touch that and know that before ascension occurs."

Necromancy became a challenge to the Christian churches in the 1960s when the enigmatic Bishop James Pike sought to make contact with his deceased son in a séance. The eccentric and energetic Episcopal bishop of California and dean of Grace Cathedral in San Francisco always seemed to be in trouble. He was tried for heresy over his denial of Jesus' virgin birth and of the doctrine of the Trinity. He struggled with alcoholism, three marriages, and difficulties with his four children. He lost his son, Jim Jr., first to the hippie drug culture of Haight-Ashbury, then to suicide, a gruesome 30-30 rifle shot through the head in a New York hotel room. The body was brought back and his ashes thrown to the winds of San Francisco Bay from the Golden Gate Bridge.

Deeply saddened at the tragedy, Pike, having gone to Cambridge, England, sought out medium Ena Twigg. Twigg went into a trance and the voice of Jim Jr. purportedly spoke, referring to his father as "Dad" and speaking of his own failures in life. He confessed to being responsible for certain poltergeist phenomena in the Pike home. Then he concluded by saying, "I love you very much. So much love and no means of giving it!" After returning to the United States, the bishop continued conversations with Jim through a Santa Barbara medium, George Daisley. Then in 1967 he participated in a dramatic television broadcast in which medium Arthur Ford allegedly brought the voice of Jim Jr. to the viewing public. Jim Jr. brought greetings from many deceased in the Pike family as well as other known clergymen and theologians. "Everything matched," Pike told a *Newsweek* reporter. "The whole thing is sufficient for an affirmation that there is continuity with people who have passed on."

Newsweek was sympathetic yet caustic. In its reporting, the national magazine described the séances as unconvincing, noting how Jim time and time again told Pike exactly what a grieving and guilty father wants to hear—that Dad is an OK fellow and in no way responsible for the suicide. Negative repercussions followed. Anglican Christians began to lose respect for their California bishop and stopped inviting him for speaking engagements. Conservatives became hostile and vitriolic. In an attempt to quell the rising opposition, Pike published a book to express his views, *The Other Side*. It sold seventy-five thousand in hardcover and two million in paperback. In its review, *Time* magazine drew out a touch of irony by telling readers to ask themselves why a bishop who had been so skeptical of the received Christian tradition should so readily accept the assurance of asserted spiritualists that there are cats in the afterlife. As for the dead Jim, the *Time* review said he appeared in the book to be so vague and formless as to seem nothing more than a loving father's wish fulfillment.

With his third wife, Diane Kennedy Pike, the bishop withdrew from the Episcopal church and started a foundation to assist others who find themselves in religious transition. Then in 1968 the ex-bishop's stormy career came to a stormy conclusion. Having gone out with only two Cokes into the desert two miles west of the Dead Sea in Israel, Pike and his bride became lost. He, then age 58, became tired and could walk no farther. She, then 30, ran on for help. Six days later his body was found on a ledge beneath an overhanging rock. It was in kneeling position, as if he had died in prayer.

Since James Pike's death, Diane has been working with a new age self-help group in San Diego called the Love Project. In a 1988 interview she said of her former husband, "They called him crazy—when he was, in fact, ahead of his time." She says of herself that her present work is not primarily concerned with continuing her interest in psychic phenomena. "In a way, it's a shame," she remarks, because "I could have been channeling Bishop Pike all these years and making a fortune."[28]

In addition to channeling contact with deceased relatives and friends, new age mediums receive and transmit the esoteric teachings of supraphysical philosophers and gurus. What is significant is what these supposed disembodied entities teach. They teach a version of the perennial philosophy, and in some cases unadulterated gnosticism. (We will define perennial philosophy and gnosticism in more detail in chapter 2.) The invitation they offer is to follow a path that leads to one's own true self. Once the true self is found, the whole universe opens up. Why? Because, they say, the self and God are one and the same.

Take Ramtha, for instance. Ramtha is the name of an alleged master who lived on the lost continent of Atlantis some thirty-five thousand years ago. Ramtha's channel is a former housewife, Mrs. J. Z. Knight (née Judy Hampton) of Yelm, a farming community just south of Seattle, Washington. According to Ramtha, there seems to be a three-step movement whereby the connection is made between the sublime divine reality and the true self. The middle step is Ramtha, the mediator who links the two. Ramtha begins by referring to himself as "the Enlightened One" and comforts the audience by affirming belief in the Christian Trinity. The Father is the source or principal cause of all that exists, he says. He is the most superlative being. The movement of the Father became the Son, the Christus, and what the Son has accomplished the Father has accomplished. Once this is clarified, then Ramtha identifies himself with God the Father in parallel fashion. He applies here a phrase that clearly connotes Jesus, "I and the Father are one" (John 14:10–20). The final step is to identify the self of Ramtha with one's own higher or true self. This leads to the realization that each of us is essentially divine and, as divine, that we have untold creative powers available for exercise. The key is the "attitude of unlimitedness," an attitude we gain when we think of ourselves as God.

> He [Ramtha] has also realized his own unlimited nature and the truth of the saying, *I and the Father are one.* Knowing he is a perfect reflection of the Father he feels that all kingdoms are within his own dominion, and he is able to manifest on any level in any way that he chooses at any time because he doesn't subscribe to the idea of limitation; he is at onement with all things, with all the elements. He is a totally manifesting and manifested God.[29]

It is the attitude of unlimitedness that has therapeutic power for Ramtha's disciples. According to Ramtha, what limits us is the great whore, fear. Fear inhibits our creative living by stagnating our emotions and retarding our thoughts. It does not permit love to bloom. This leads to underachievement and boredom. The reason we find ourselves fearful is that our ego has been altered. We live with "altered egos"—that is, our innately divine and fearless ego is encrusted and encumbered with alien fears and inhibitions. What we need to do is follow the pathway to unlimitedness, the road to the kingdom of heaven. This is the road of becoming; *becoming* means becoming "unaltered."

According to the Ramtha philosophy, central to becoming unaltered and unlimited is gaining a sense of self-love. The problem is that we are fallen creatures. The nature of the fall is that we have thought of love in terms of service. The ideal of service, especially as reinforced by religious teachings, is limiting and even damaging to authentic self-expression. "I realize now how incredibly limiting it was," writes a Ramtha disciple, "how it kept me in a certain position, in a certain place that never fully allowed me to appreciate the totality of my own being." Once the disciple came to see herself as God and could thus love herself, then she could have "the full experience of what *mastership* means in my life."[30]

The Ramtha soteriology—the method of salvation—is based on achieving self-love. Before one can love the world, says Ramtha, one must first love one's self. "You learn to love all people, but you learn to love yourself first, and first meaning, the first priority in life is *you*."[31] This leads to a greater sense of freedom, a release of creativity, and the experience of mastery. Working with the assumption that thought and feeling produce reality, Ramtha tells us

> If you change your words from Self-doubt, Self-damnation, and Self-*hate* into Self-*love,* into *is,* and cease asking the opinions of everyone else, you will find your fortunes and your knowingness will accelerate with great vigor. You are simply taking the law that you yourself created and bringing it into that which is termed the purpose for good by designing what *you* want. All you have to do is think it and feel it into emotion; then it is set, it will come to pass.[32]

There is power here. To think that my daily problems are the result of limitations I have put on myself—I have imbibed the constricting ideals of my religion and the limiting roles of my society—offers me a way out. If I think of myself as my God, as the author for good or ill of all that I am, then I am in a position to take control of my life. I can become the captain of my soul, the master of my fate. All I need do is identify myself with Ramtha's self, which in turn is identified with the self of God the Father, the principal cause and source of all that is.

Ramtha's philosophy appears to be appreciated by large numbers of people. J. Z. Knight channels Ramtha's ideas into books, tapes, lectures, and seminar programs, all of which seem to be selling very well.[33] In 1988 she held thirty-one seminars in Yelm plus additional programs in New Zealand, Australia, England, Canada, and in cities across the United States. People from all over—one estimate is four thousand—have pulled up stakes and moved to the region around Yelm just to live near the channel.[34] In addition, J. Z. Knight has become a channel to the stars—Shirley MacLaine, Burt Reynolds, Clint Eastwood, Richard Chamberlain, Joan Hackett, Shelley Fabares, and Mike Farrell.[35]

What is the credibility of such new age teachings?[36] If Ramtha teaches us to overcome our fear through the enhancement of self-love, this may be empowering advice. After all, the New Testament says "love casts out fear" (1 John 4:18). Unfortunately, however, it appears that Ramtha and the Bible differ somewhat on how this love works. For Ramtha, self-love is directed at the self, the self that has virtually become one's God. This excludes service to others, because the idea of service to others as taught by the world's religions limits our self-expression. The New Testament, on the other hand, understands love fundamentally as *love for the other*. God—not our own self, but rather the God who created and plans to complete the world—loves us, and this love frees us to love one another. The passage just cited continues by saying: "We love, because he [God] first loved us. . . . The commandment we have from him is this: those who love God must love their brothers and sisters also" (1 John 4:19, 21).

From the point of view of the critics, channeling is one of the most suspect of the new age phenomena. Perhaps this is due to the precedent set by the three Fox sisters, who started the spiritualism movement in 1848 and then four decades later, in 1888, confessed that it had been a fraud from the beginning. Perhaps the logic is this: if channeling was a fraud in the nineteenth century, then it probably is in the twentieth century as well.

Yet, more is said. In those cases where fraud can be ruled out, skeptics suggest that channeling is due to divided consciousness. An automatism such as automatic writing produces communication from a dissociated portion of the mind, from the unconscious. Experiments by Stanford University professor Ernest Hilgard show that channeling-like phenomena can be induced hypnotically.[37] In short, channeling can be explained as a purely psychological phenomenon.

Channeling may even have a sinister side. This is what Ted Schultz thinks. He says Ramtha's morality is potentially dangerous, because he does not "abhor the act" of murder. Schultz points out that a large number of murderers attribute their actions to the orders of channeled spirits. The famous Son of Sam serial killer of six women, David Berkowitz, claimed he did so at the behest of a six-thousand-year-old entity who spoke to him through his neighbor's dog. Britain's Yorkshire Ripper, killer of thirteen prostitutes in 1975, and Mark David Chapman, the murderer of John Lennon, make similar claims. Schultz is willing to explain this psychologically. Although normally harmless, channeling as an expression of our dissociated unconscious mind may, in some instances, lead to destructive consequences.[38]

UFOs

For some time now trade bookstores have displayed their materials on unidentified flying objects (UFOs) on the shelves marked "Occult." Now they can be found on shelves with new age books. This used to aggravate me. I thought they belonged among books on science or some similar nonfiction section.

I have been a serious UFO researcher for a decade and a half, and the other researchers whom I have come to respect are scientific types. My fellow investigators who belong to the same research organizations I do tend to come from scientific and technical professions such as astronomy, engineering, chemistry, and computer science. They are screened for their credentials so that we don't send the town fool out to investigate a reported UFO sighting.

We have been treating the UFO phenomenon as a mystery to be solved. We have employed systematic investigative techniques for interviewing witnesses, laboratory tests of physical evidence, statistical analysis of cases, and in general have sought to make Ufology a respectable discipline. We have treated the subject matter with the assumption that we are possibly dealing with machines of some sort, either terrestrial or extraterrestrial in origin. One research group with which I am proud to be affiliated, the Mutual UFO Network (MUFON), has even had a small study group working on the problem of UFO propulsion between planets.

This means we have shied away from claims that associate UFOs with paranormal phenomena such as mental telepathy, clairvoyance, astral travel, dematerialization and rematerialization, and spirit guides. So at first I was slow to admit that Ufology is a topic that should be associated with the new age. It belongs to the modern age, or so I had been assuming. But now I am beginning to change my mind. More and more, the public, due especially to the lead of publishers, is working with the assumption that belief in UFOs is an integral part of the occult and the new age. Many new age gurus such as David Spangler are incorporating a UFO faith into their

planetary and interplanetary vision.[39] Hence, the connection between the topics must be acknowledged. My only worry is that this
association may tend to reduce the credibility of authentic UFO
research; but, then, perhaps this is unavoidable.

The best example of the connection between the new age and
UFOs is the belief that entities from outer space have been infiltrat-
ing human society on Earth. Significantly, the form this infiltration
takes is that of thoughts entering into the consciousness of various
individuals, becoming part of their mental world.

In his best-selling book *Communion*, New York City journalist
Whitley Strieber reports that while asleep during a vacation at his
country cabin, he was abducted by a group of gray-skinned creatures who moved in an insectlike manner, taken aboard some kind
of craft, and then returned to his bedroom before awakening. In
fact, he reports that he has been contacted frequently throughout
his entire life by aliens. As Strieber reflects on these alleged experiences, he considers two possibilities: the aliens may come from the
outside, from space, or they may come from inside, from within his
own terrestrial consciousness. He is not suggesting that UFO abduc-
tion accounts are fictions. Rather, he suggests that a form of higher
consciousness is communicating with us through such contacts.[40]

During a coffee break at a recent UFO meeting I attended, the
woman who sat next to me said a space alien was living in her mind.
The space entity had come to earth via a flying saucer and had
entered her consciousness two years before our conversation. She
told me it all began at a particularly depressing time in her life. She
had done something terribly wrong that harmed another person.
For a period of ten days she was immobilized by feelings of guilt.
Then she heard a voice from within say, "You are forgiven." She
began a conversation with this voice who told her of its extraterrestrial origin. The two have been living together ever since. They con-
verse daily, and the alien intelligence offers frequent advice and
consolation.

At the same meeting I met Joseph Ostrom, a contactee. He
reported that while he and his girlfriend were vacationing together
at Ayia Galini on the island of Crete, he was abducted aboard an
alien spacecraft. The gray-skinned aliens laid Joseph out on a table
and examined his body. What Joseph felt was "heartfelt warmth,
love." Then they announced that they had chosen him to be a mes-

senger to the human race on Earth. He was, shall we say, commissioned to be a prophet of heavenly truth. He is now a channel through which space beings can send messages for the benefit of humankind. What is the message? It is this: "Everything is one thing; it is all God."

Psychic Ruth Montgomery proffers a whole system to explain it all, both the extraterrestrial aliens as well as the internal psychological experience. Montgomery begins with the doctrine of reincarnation, meaning that our souls bounce from body to body not just on Earth but also from planet to planet. Through death and rebirth these disembodied souls can travel from one star system to another. Many individuals who presently live on Earth were, in previous incarnations, residents of planets orbiting Sirius in the constellation Canis Major. They are able to travel by dematerializing and rematerializing in their new locations. Therefore, they really do not need spacecraft, even though they occasionally use them.

How does Ruth know these things? She is the recipient of revelation—that is, her Guides tell her. She tells us that Guides are souls like ourselves who have had many previous lifetimes but are currently in the spirit plane, as we will be when we pass through the mysterious door called death. She was introduced to these Guides by Arthur Ford, the same medium who spoke with Bishop Pike's son on Canadian television. Since then, the Guides have been available to give answers to questions Ruth poses regarding the nature of the UFO phenomenon.

Why are they coming to Earth? To help us. To save us. One space being named Rolf has spoken to Ruth through the Guides, declaring: "Ruth, it is vital that you get the message across to others that we are coming in great numbers, not with any intention of harm, but to help rescue earth from pollution and nuclear explosions. We want all to live in harmony."[41] This message—that earthlings need to be protected from the threat of nuclear war and establish planetary peace—has been the message associated with the UFO phenomenon since the early 1950s. In another book I wrote a decade ago, I did a study of just this message, referring to it as the "celestial savior" model for understanding the purpose of UFO visitation.[42]

The bottom line here is that Ruth Montgomery sees herself—as do other contactees—as a channel for supraterrestrial teaching.

What is the content of this teaching? By this time it is probably becoming predictable. It is an amalgam of Hinduism and gnosticism. The Guides tell Ruth, for example, "that each of us is something of God, and that we are all one. Together we form God, and it is therefore essential that we help each other, so that all may advance together."[43] Each of us is born with a spark of the divine within us, and our spiritual quest as we move from incarnation to incarnation is to realize fully this cosmic oneness with God. The teachings revealed by the Guides are quite obviously new age.

By positing metaphysically that all things are really one thing, it is easy to draw a connection between the inner life of the psyche and the outer stimulus brought by space visitors. One New York man whom Ruth says embodies a soul formerly from the star Arcturus is quoted as saying, "I have the ability to tune in to inner forces and to understand how extraterrestrial forces work."[44] This means that the physical presence of UFOs as a visual phenomenon is less important than their psychological impact, their presence in the dimensions we ordinarily associate with mental telepathy and spiritualism. The space beings live within us.

Astrology Is Back

Astrology is back. Of course, it never really went away. To our knowledge, astrological systems of belief go back four thousand years to the ancient Mesopotamians; they spread from there both east and west. Claudius Ptolemy codified what would become the Western system of astrology in his book written about A.D. 140, *Tetrabiblos,* and the horoscopes in today's newspapers continue this ancient tradition. Parallel systems were developed in India and China; and in the most sophisticated urban centers of today's Orient, business ventures and weddings are planned only after an astrological reading to determine if the timing is auspicious. If there ever was a transcultural belief system, astrology is it.

In the spring of 1988, Donald Regan, former secretary of the Treasury and White House chief of staff, shocked the nation by revealing that the president's wife, Nancy Reagan, had been consulting an astrologer and actually influencing the chief executive's decisions on the basis of astral predictions. The first lady had been dabbling in the occult as early as 1967, when her husband was governor of California, by relying upon the advice of prophetess Jeanne Dixon. Later she lost confidence in Dixon's powers and switched her allegiance to Joan Quigley. Joan Quigley is a San Francisco astrologer and author of three books on the subject. She convinced Mrs. Reagan of her abilities by retroactively forecasting danger on March 30, 1981, the day John Hinckley, Jr., tried without success to assassinate the president. Having become converted, Nancy Reagan consulted Quigley regularly and even persuaded her husband to plan the all-important Washington-Moscow summit on the basis of the astrologer's advice. Mikhail Gorbachev is a Pisces and Ronald Reagan an Aquarius, and Quigley had determined that 2:00 p.m. on December 8, 1987, would be the most propitious moment for the superpower leaders to sign the intermediate-range nuclear forces treaty. At Nancy's behest, this is the way it happened. So Donald Regan writes, "Virtually every major move or decision the Reagans made during my time as White House chief of staff was cleared in advance with a woman in San Francisco who drew up horoscopes to make certain that the planets were in a favorable alignment for the enterprise."[45]

Nancy Reagan is not alone. In contemporary North America an estimated fifty million people read their daily horoscopes, some casually, some in earnest. Astrology is in revival. This would be the case with or without the new age movement. Educated people began to discard astrology in the seventeenth century when the science of astronomy rose up to take its place. Once Copernican astronomy had dislodged a major Ptolemaic assumption—namely, that the Earth is at the center of the universe—it was only a matter of time before disenchantment set in. So astrology went underground in Europe during the eighteenth century, reappearing briefly during the French Revolution in the 1790s. In the 1890s, however, a revival began in England and France that spread to Germany; and it has continued to the present time. Carl Jung commented, "I can point to the easily verifiable fact that the heyday of astrology was not in the benighted Middle Ages but is in the middle of the twentieth century, when even the newspapers do not hesitate to publish the week's horoscope."[46]

The revival of astrology as well as many other occult teachings is most likely due to the widespread influence of one of Madame

Blavatsky's associates, Alan Leo (1860–1917). Calling himself a theosophical astrologer, he published a series of popular textbooks and invited the populace into the mysteries of esoteric knowledge. It is likely that the connection we see today between astrology and the new age was a connection already made by the theosophists nearly a century ago.

The underlying assumption of the astrological belief system is that the universe manifests an overall order, and this order directly influences our personality makeup as well as the day-to-day course of our life. The two momentous events in a person's allotted time are birth and death, and astrology claims that these significant personal events are also significant cosmically. The way to apprehend this significance is to draw a horoscope. A horoscope is based on the location and the date, including the time of day if possible, of one's birth, from which a birth chart can be constructed. Into the construction go the relative locations of the planets plus the location of the sun in relation to the twelve signs of the zodiac and the twelve houses. The relative location of these heavenly bodies at the moment of birth is said to determine a person's basic character.

Astrologers forecast the future based on the assumption that the angular relationships between good and bad aspects of two or more planets have an effect on what happens to us here on Earth. For example, a conjunction of the moon (which symbolizes the soul or psyche) with Venus (which symbolizes love and sex) could indicate a period of intense emotional life and even love. This would be a good time to pursue a courtship. Earnest readers of horoscopes and visitors to astrologers are looking for an auspicious moment to execute certain plans or pursue certain goals.

This is the way astrology works in almost every part of the world where it is practiced. Under the influence of new age ideals, however, it is undergoing some modification. It is being pressed into the service of self-realization. It is becoming one more means for pursuing personal healing and wholeness.

Gregory Szanto, for example, is developing what he calls "astrotherapy," combining astrology with Jungian psychology. He assumes the stars are united to the psyche. The key is the birth chart, which Szanto believes encapsulates the whole—the original essence—of who each person is. He believes that "the Horoscope is the reflection of the individual in his wholeness. All that is within the individual, conscious and unconscious, is contained in the wheel of the Birth Chart."[47] He assumes that the process of individuation whereby the human ego becomes distinct represents a loss of personal-cosmic unity; and therefore what we need to do to achieve transformation is to retrieve the latent wholeness revealed in the horoscope: "The goal of astrology when used as therapy is to provide the means to see the psyche as a whole so that the individual can experience his true nature and transform the conflicts within him."[48]

Astrology seems to be one more wonder of antiquity that has been mixed into the optimistic brew that is the new age elixer.

But there are skeptics. There are those who argue that astrology is a premodern anachronism and should not be taken seriously by any modern person. The Committee for the Scientific Investigation of Claims of the Paranormal (CSICP) centered in Buffalo, New York, for example, is a reactionary group of science-minded intellectuals who are dedicated to stamping out all forms of superstition, pseudoscience, and religious folderol. In their excellent journal *The Skeptical Inquirer,* they regularly attack parapsychology, new age cults, and belief in such things as UFOs and the Loch Ness monster. They also attack astrology. The chief weapon they employ in the attack is the controlled experiment. In case after case these scientists can show that the predictions of astrologers are never better than one could achieve by random chance.[49]

The stars told Joan Quigley that an earthquake would rock San Francisco on May 5, 1988. When the date came she was out of town, perhaps indicating how seriously she takes her own astral calculations. Those who remained in San Francisco felt no tremors, however. The day came and went without incident. Most critics are likely to place such a prediction in the category of a mere guess. The chances of her guessing the precise day on which an earthquake will strike a particular location are probably infinitesimal.

The scientific criticisms of astrology are many. CSICP member and humanist philosopher Paul Kurtz offers six.[50] First, we know now that the Earth is not the center of the universe. All the planets orbit the sun. Only the moon orbits the Earth. Thus the horoscope, which assumes earth centricity, is based on a fundamental astronomical error. Second, in the eighteen hundred years since Ptolemy codified the astrological principles, the shift in equinoxes due to the

Earth's spin has changed the location of the so-called fixed stars by approximately thirty degrees. This means that the signs of the zodiac no longer line up with the constellations that once gave them their names. Virgo, for example, is now in the constellation of Leo. The tropical and sidereal schools of astrology must keep chasing the movement of the constellations to reorganize their methods of calculation. Third, the actual influences of the heavenly bodies on Earth—gravitational, electromagnetic, nuclear—are so indiscriminate as to be virtually irrelevant to the formation of personality traits in the delivery rooms of our hospitals. The obstetrician or nurse hovering over mother and child exerts a far greater influence than Mars or Jupiter. Fourth, the definition of the moment of birth is not fixed. What does it refer to? The emergence from the womb? The first breath? The cutting of the umbilical cord? Such things as induced labor and cesarean operations make the question of the time of birth moot. Fifth, do not our genetic makeup and social standing become far more significant factors in determining our lives than star movements? Kurtz notes how St. Augustine became a critic of astrology when he noted that a slave and his aristocratic master were astral twins but led entirely different lives, given their different roles and circumstances. Sixth, astrology lacks a coherent conceptual framework. Astrologers cannot describe how determinism works without entering into contradictions. On the one hand, the stars are determinative; on the other hand, horoscopes give counsel and advice. They impel rather than compel. This leads astrologers such as Joan Quigley to remark, "I advise them [Ronald and Nancy Reagan] to be careful; I don't make decisions for them. . . . It is like being in the ocean: you should go with the waves, not against them."[51] Kurtz can only ask: is this a kind of weak deterministic theory? If so, then how much confidence can we have that the planets at the time of birth actually imprint individuals and even outline their destinies? Kurtz concludes that there is insufficient scientific evidence to show any reason why one could with intellectual honesty believe what astrology teaches.

Astronomers, who represent the position of modern science, tell us to look at the stars and to enjoy their beauty. They tell us in addition that the stars have no direct influence on our love life, on whether or not we will get a promotion on the job, or whether earthquakes will hit our region. The stars and planets and other celestial bodies simply do not care!

Why then do modern people believe in astrology? Kurtz hypothesizes that astrology must have some sort of psychological function. It reinforces the longing each of us has within us, in some mysterious way, to be related to the cosmic scene over and beyond our comprehension. It gives our otherwise puny life cosmic significance. It is this desire for expansive significance that, despite negative evidence to the contrary, keeps people looking again and again at the stars for the answer to their problems.[52]

What are we to think from a Christian point of view? It is no accident that the author of Genesis 1:1–2:4 reports that God created light on the first day and then waited until the fourth day to create the sun, the moon, and the stars. Light comes before the heavenly bodies that give off light. Objects we see in our skies, then, are there because God put them there. They serve God's purposes. Genesis makes a point that is absolutely decisive regarding the place of astrology: the heavenly bodies are the creation and servants of the God who is prior and beyond them. Furthermore, our destiny is in the hands of the very God who has power over the planets and stars. Whatever influence the astral lights have on our lives is at best indirect, subject to a yet higher influence. By whatever impersonal celestial forces we on Earth are affected, we are affected all the more by the personal God who is their author and ruler.[53]

In the controversy between astronomy and astrology, then, it makes little difference to the Christian who wins. It matters little whether in the final analysis the stars care or do not care about our daily life. What matters is that God cares. And this we are assured. Therefore, it is superfluous to seek astrological counsel to determine whether or not a given moment is auspicious enough to take a contemplated action. It is not in our birth chart that we find an elusive wholeness; but rather we find our genuine wholeness when anticipating the new creation promised by God. The Holy Spirit has promised to take up residence within us. Once the Spirit enters, we discover the miracle that the Spirit had been within all along. Once we realize this close relationship with the God who created and ordered the stars and galaxies in the first place, then plotting our lives according to the celestial functionaries becomes an unnecessary extra.

Ecofeminism

Women play an important role in every aspect of the new age sub-culture. Sometimes this special role becomes the focus of attention. When it does, it is abstracted into a more general principle, the principle of the feminine. To the fore come feminine themes such as intuition, receptivity, embodiment, attunement with nature, and a sense of oneness with the whole of planet Earth.

Such themes are visible in the artwork of Joan Marie of Sedona, Arizona. Characterized by soft hues such as blues, pinks, yellows, and greens, her drawings have a surrealistic style and provide visual symbols for new age teachings. In her *Receiving the Light to Expand,* we see an outstretched cosmic hand holding a glowing crystal set against a backdrop of winged planets. Emanating from the crystal are beams of energy. Joan Marie's accompanying interpretation is that she has received the light, the knowledge of how the universe operates. This is the knowledge given us by Mother Earth. If we will but open our minds to "unlimited positive thinking" and receive these gifts, we can make our dreams come true.

In another piece titled *In Control of My World,* Joan Marie offers a sketch of a hand holding the entire planet Earth in its grip. Yet it is a peaceful grip, exuding tranquillity through the blues and greens of the oceans, skies, and forests. What is important for feminist consciousness in an age of revolution against patriarchy is to feel "in control of my life, symbolized by the world held in my hands."[54]

Jungian analyst Marion Woodman believes that a hitherto repressed feminine force is beginning to exert its power in our culture. This force is best symbolized by the Black Madonna, and she is making her initial appearance in the dreams of people reflecting on the inner world. She is dark because she is as yet unknown to consciousness. Our task, says the psychologist, is to make this feminine principle conscious. "We have to connect to her" when attacking our male-dominated society and defending the Earth's ecology, says Woodman, "because the power that drives the patriarchy, the power that is raping the earth, the power drive behind addictions, has to be transformed. There has to be a counter-balance to all that frenzy, annihilation, ambition, competition and materialism."[55]

In some instances, consciousness raising goes well beyond a mere psychological process to the point of reevoking the female goddess of former times. The result is a form of neopaganism that centers on worshiping the Mother Goddess. Referred to by some as the "Gaia Hypothesis," the neopagan view is that the Earth itself is a living and sacred being. The importance of this concept, stresses the California Institute of Integral Studies, is that the concept of the Living Earth marks an attitude shift toward a holistic vision that will help us to solve our ecological problems. Moreover, new age feminists greet the return of the goddess with applause, hoping that it will liberate women from patriarchy as well as save the earth from destruction by modern civilization.

A microcosm-macrocosm correlation seems to be assumed here. At the level of the microcosm, we as individuals need to engage in consciousness raising to release in ourselves hitherto untapped feminine powers. At the level of the macrocosm, our entire culture needs to return to the premodern period and retrieve the now-forgotten feminine vision of an Earth at peace and a humanity in harmony with nature.

Vickie Noble provides us with a good example. She says that the Goddess is buried in the depths of the collective and personal unconscious, so that if we seek to unlock the unconscious she will eventually be seen. In her book *Motherpeace: A Way to the Goddess Through Myth, Art, and Tarot,* Noble names this matriarchal consciousness Motherpeace. Centering in the heart rather than the head, feminine consciousness requires a nonrational means of approach. It is creative and intuitive in contrast to the logical mode in which we usually function. It requires a surrender of our daily waking consciousness and an opening to receive the power of the feminine force. As a means for facilitating this opening to the power of the Goddess, Noble recommends the use of tarot cards.

Tired of the previous tradition of tarot cards designed by male artists and reflecting the patriarchal mind-set that is ruining the world, Vickie Noble along with a friend, Karen Vogel, have created their own set of pictures for tarot reading. The colorful Empress card pictures the Earth Mother goddess lying in a seductive pose on grass, covered in part by a leopard skin and tenderly sniffing a rose. This is the Great Mother who promises abundance, birth, growth, harmony, community, and relationship. In the form of archetypes such as Ishtar and Aphrodite, the Babylonian and Greek goddesses of love, the Empress represents the Earth from which all life is born and to which it returns at the end of its natural cycle. What the Empress can do for each of us is draw out our artistic side, open us to love of beauty, and heighten our aesthetic appreciation.

Noble, like many others who are dissatisfied with the destructive impact of the modern world on the environment, works with a mythicized picture of world history divided into three stages. First, according to this emerging postmodern myth, was the period of the Empress when matriarchy was dominant, the golden age, the primeval paradise, when all things existed in peace and harmony, and there was a wholistic integration of body and spirit, humanity and Earth. Then, second, the human race fell. The fall resulted from the rise of male dominance in society, the rise of patriarchy, which uses logical thought and technology to gain mastery over the Earth. What we are looking for now, third, is healing transformation. This transformation consists in a revival of the premodern, prepatriarchal wholism of the Goddess. In ancient times

> religion, science, and measurement of time were not separate from the body and the biological fertility mysteries of sexuality and re- production; they were one body of knowledge. It is from this an- cient holistic framework that we have fallen away, and which we are just beginning culturally to rediscover. The return to the Goddess implied by contemporary interest in astrology, Tarot, and other "right brain" activities . . . is the start of healing.[56]

In short, the Goddess has saving power if we will but open ourselves and permit the feminine principle to operate in us both individually and globally.

In general, the new age honors revived sensitivity to things natural, to the forces of nature and the beauty of the Earth that gives us life. It opens the door to a wide variety of premodern prac- tices such as shaminism, root medicine, witchcraft, and magic. Through this door has walked the side of the feminist movement that identifies with nature. *Witch* and *magic* are now good words, not bad.[57] The nature religion of the practicing witch is welcomed into the new age fold.

Yet, it would be a mistake simply to equate feminism with the new age. The women's liberation movement of the 1960s was first and foremost a political movement aimed at achieving economic equity and cultural enfranchisement for women. It turned religious in the 1970s, as did so much of the rest of our culture. The rejection of male dominance in the workplace became rejection of male dominance in the priesthood and finally rejection of male images of the divine. Hence, even had there not been a new age movement, the feminist trajectory would probably have still followed this course. It is driven largely by energies unique to the woman's struggle. Nevertheless, there is some overlap between feminism and the new age, in the form of goddess worship.

Theosophy

As we have seen, a wide variety of quite different things gets painted with the new age brush. But where does the phrase "new age" come from and why is it identified with a certain set of ideas? I have been researching the matter, and to the best of my knowledge the contemporary use of "new age" and the accompanying phrase "age of Aquarius" comes from the work of Alice Bailey (1880–1949). Originally an English theosophist, Bailey broke from the society in 1920 yet continued her own version of theosophical teachings until nearly midcentury.[58]

At the root of the matter, then, lies the importation of Asian ideas to Europe and America by the Theosophical Society at the turn of the century, and particularly by Helena Petrovna Blavatsky (1831–1891). We mentioned her earlier in connection with channeling and astrology. Mme Blavatsky was an adventurous Victorian hippie who at the age of seventeen ran away from her husband after only a few months of marriage, supporting herself by riding horseback in a circus in Constantinople and by giving piano lessons in London and Paris. She studied snake charming and spiritualism in Cairo in the 1850s, where she was seen dressed as an Arab and smoking pot. She came to America in 1873 to pursue spiritualism and, with the help of Colonel Henry Steel Olcott, became known as a medium. Olcott and Blavatsky conducted numerous discussion groups called "at-homes," which led to the establishment of a formal society in 1875. Searching the dictionary for a suitable name, they came across and elected the word *theosophy,* meaning "wisdom of God." Blavatsky's first book, *Isis Unveiled,* was published in 1877; the writing was influenced by healthy doses of hashish and a vision of the goddess Isis herself. Through contacts with the Arya Samaj movement in India, Blavatsky and Olcott moved the Theosophical Society to the sacred soil of that Asian land in 1879, setting up their headquarters on the Adyar River near Madras.

Mme Blavatsky shared with her followers occult wisdom that she claimed had been communicated to her supernaturally from the Mahatmas or great souls, also referred to as the Hidden Masters or Secret Brothers, living in the Himalayas. When this was exposed by a disgruntled employee as a fraud, Mme Blavatsky, fearing further exposure in a court trial, fled India for Europe in 1884. Eventually, while staying in England, she wrote her masterpiece, *The Secret Doctrine.*[59] The Society for Psychical Research studied Mme Blavatsky's claims and did her the honor of dubbing her "one of the most accomplished, ingenious, and interesting imposters of history."[60]

The Secret Doctrine combines a number of ideas drawn from Indian philosophy and the occult, especially ideas like monism, karma, and reincarnation. It teaches that all persons participate in a single divine consciousness and that salvation on earth will be accomplished gradually through a further evolution of this consciousness; and this evolutionary advance is being guided by a divine plan and paced through a history of what are called "root races." This divine plan is being supervised by perfected individuals called the Masters of the Wisdom, masters who channel this wisdom to humanity through their chosen medium, Mme Blavatsky. When Annie Besant took over the presidency of the Theosophical Society in 1907, she added a healthy dose of millennialism, the expectation that a messiah or World-Teacher would soon appear and usher into the world what she called "the new civilization."

Although raised an Anglican and married to an Anglican priest who was evidently too dull, the young Annie Besant (née Wood, 1847–1933) left her husband and daughter and became for a while an outspoken atheist engaged in a public repudiation of orthodox Christianity. As a social reformer, Mrs. Besant took up causes such as dissemination of birth control information, women's rights, and labor reform. She was a utopian idealist. She wanted a new and better world. She became attracted to the work of Auguste Comte and the idea of founding a new religion dedicated to serving humanity, one that would produce on earth what the Christians called "the kingdom of God," but which she preferred to call "the kingdom of man." Mrs. Besant converted to Theosophy in 1889, thinking this would be the religion that would transform the world.

Her view has been described by one scholar as "progressive messianism," which holds that terrestrial salvation will be accomplished gradually through an evolutionary advance led by a messianic figure.[61] Here she was expanding on what Mme Blavatsky had taught. *The Secret Doctrine* had introduced the notion that a "sixth root race" would eventually arise, originating most probably in southern California, and would develop a new human faculty—called in Sanskrit the *buddhi* quality—that would enable these people to perceive the truth that everything is God. This sixth root race would then lead the peoples of our planet into a new civilization that would be characterized by brotherhood, love, and peace. What Annie Besant added to this scheme for salvation on earth was the idea that the beginning of the new root race would be heralded by the appearance of a *jagadguru,* the World-Teacher, also known as the Christ or the Bodhisattva. This messianic teacher would embody the spirit of the Lord Maitreya prophesied by certain Buddhist traditions; he himself would demonstrate the quality of buddhi and would be able to help each of us activate our own buddhic faculty.

In 1908 Mrs. Besant adopted a twelve-year-old boy from India, Jeddu Krishnamurti, and raised him to fulfill this messianic role of the World-Teacher. In 1926 she purchased land in the Ojai Valley in California, where she hoped to establish a model in miniature of the coming world civilization to help in the training of the new human type. Krishnamurti himself was understandably ambivalent about his chosen role, wavering between making his mother happy and outright rebellion. On occasion he assumed the role of Maitreya's incarnate voice. Yet his teachings gradually diverged. He downplayed the significance of the channeled masters, saying that rather than rely upon them each individual should seek liberation by himself or herself. He advised theosophists not to puzzle over his messianic identity but to turn their attention to his message, to find truth for themselves apart from his or any other authority. By 1929 it had become clear that Krishnamurti would not accept the role of the world's messiah, much to the disappointment of his mother. Due to the disappointment over Krishnamurti, although today's Theosophical Society continues to propound its Indian mysticism, it has lost much of its emphasis on progressive messianism.

The shocking disavowal of messiahship by Krishnamurti deflated much of the energy and verve of the Theosophical Society. Since the 1930s it has taken a low-profile role, concentrating on preserving its wisdom through publications and conferences. Into the void, however, have jumped other more flamboyant leaders. Worthy of note here are Guy and Edna Ballard, who founded the "I Am" movement in 1934. Like Mme Blavatsky, they claimed contact with ascended masters. One of these was said to be Master Saint-Germain. The "I Am" movement became "it was" in 1939 with the death of Guy Ballard, who had been predicted to ascend to heaven rather than to die. The Ballards were replaced in the 1960s by another married couple, Mark and Elizabeth Clare Prophet, who claimed contact with the same ascended masters, especially Saint-Germain. Mark passed away in 1973, yet Elizabeth Clare Prophet has continued on to become one of the most articulate and powerful leaders of the new age.[62]

Meanwhile, the messianic theme of the new civilization has followed another parallel track with Alice Bailey in England. In addition to the phrase "new age," Bailey has bequeathed to our era "The Great Invocation," a prayer designed to invoke the presence of the combination Maitreya-Christ figure now used by many new age groups. A successor to Alice Bailey, Benjamin Creme (b. 1923), has taken up Annie Besant's role of John the Baptist preparing the way for the imminent coming of the messiah. He says he is telepathically in contact with the Lord Maitreya, and when the world becomes ready, the Lord will reveal himself.[63] Creme lectures around the world and maintains communication with his followers through his magazine, *Share International,* and an organization called the Tara Center with offices in New York, Los Angeles, Amsterdam, and London.

What this brief history of the theosophists shows, I think, is that what we have here is a curious hybrid of ancient Asian mysticism and nineteenth-century Western progressivism. With the traveling of missionaries all over the globe and the expansion of the British Empire, new information about exotic religions poured into Europe in the early nineteenth century. The English especially became fascinated with India. German idealism seemed to have an affinity with Indian Brahmanism. A connection was made. Even in America, the transcendentalists such as Ralph Waldo Emerson began to experiment with Hindu mysticism. The theosophists were riding the crest of a wave of Western curiosity toward things Eastern, a curiosity revived in the late 1960s.

Yet this is a distinctively *Western* version of things Eastern. We in the West are still reeling from that powerful biblical symbol: the kingdom of God. This symbol communicates that it is God's intention that this world be different from what it is. Instead of strife and war, there should be love and peace. Instead of material indulgence and greed, there should be spiritual insight and charity. This vision of what the world should be but isn't is the driving force behind those movements that seek to harness the power of the industrial revolution and the democratic revolution in the service of humankind by transforming our society into utopia. This was the driving force behind Christian postmillennialism and the movement to abolish slavery a century ago. It is now the driving force to establish a global society that will put an end to poverty, oppression, and war.

What we have in Theosophy, and in the new age as well, is an attempted marriage of East and West.

Conclusion and Prospect

In our brief tour through a number of sites where the new age is happening, a few common themes emerge. The direction is becoming clear: one moves in the direction of the inner life, but this eventually opens out onto the whole of the cosmos. It leads to an identification of the self with the whole of the cosmos and with God. It also leads to the idea of transformation, of transforming oneself as well as the whole of society. Such a world view is bursting with theological implications. But before we begin to subject this to theological evaluation, we need to clarify further just what is being taught by the new age. In the next chapter we will focus more directly on the basic axioms of the new age world view. We will follow this with a review of some religious reactions to new age teachings plus a careful examination of the developing new age interpretation of natural science. This will prepare us for testing the spirits in the concluding chapter.

Chapter Two

The Eightfold Path:
What the New Age Teaches

 "Ted, what I would like to see you do in California is get into the spirituality. Reflect on it theological-ly." We were sitting by the window in a coffee shop at Chicago's O'Hare Airport. Speaking to me was Bill Lesher, then president of Pacific Lutheran Seminary in Berkeley. He was encouraging me to leave my post at Loyola University in New Orleans and come to teach theology at the seminary and the Graduate Theological Union. More than teach, he wanted me to continue my research on the relationship between theology and culture, looking especially at the burgeoning religious consciousness on the West Coast. Bill was convincing. My family and I arrived in Berkeley in late summer 1978.

Our two oldest children began attending the Cragmont Elementary School a few blocks from the seminary. After a week or so, our son Paul told us he had made a friend named Dillan. "Can I go to church with Dillan?" he asked. "Sure," we told him, hardly questioning why it was they were going to church on Wednesday evening. "Perhaps it is a Methodist prayer meeting," I thought. When he returned, I asked him how it went. He told in his own words of the meditating, dancing, and chanting. After I quizzed further, I discovered he had visited Swami Muktananda. Muktananda says things such as: "Kneel to your own self. Honor and worship your own being. God dwells in you." A few days later, Dillan's parents invited us over for dinner. Dillan's mother is a lovely woman, a former Roman Catholic and now a devoted disciple of the Hindu guru. She was wearing a colorful sari-like dress and bearing her cult name, Anandi, which is Sanskrit for bliss. Somehow I felt we had arrived in Berkeley.

Berkeley, like the rest of California and the other coastal states, sits on the western edge of North America. It also sits on the eastern edge of the Pacific. To look farther west is to look to the East. The new age also looks to the East. Why? Curiosity, perhaps. But the reason usually offered is that the modern West is spiritually bankrupt and that Asia just might have the religious wealth we have squandered. The assumption here is that in becoming secular the modern world has invested all its spiritual capital in scientism and materialism, leaving our culture religiously impoverished. In short, we can blame the modern antireligious consciousness for the new age turn to the East.

Yet, this does not quite tell the whole story. There is more here than just looking for a religious oasis in a spiritual desert. In addition to an apparent rejection of modern secularism, the new age also finds orthodox religion, especially Christianity, inadequate. The emphasis here is on the word *orthodox*. Anything that goes by the name of orthodoxy is likely to be suspect. The term *organized religion* is almost a bad word. On this point, the new age actually embodies the spirit of the modern secular mind. We in the modern West cannot but be hybrids: both accepting religion and rejecting it while both accepting modernity and rejecting it. It is this hybrid, if not even schizoid, mood that provides the context for looking at the actual teachings of the new age.

The present mood begins with the Renaissance and takes its characteristic form during the Enlightenment. It is characterized by its opposition to Christian orthodoxy and to the institutionalized Church. Historically, it was rebellion against ecclesiastical authority—political and intellectual—that marked the advent of the modern world. This rebellion is not over.

Freedom from ecclesiastical authority is important in the West. What George Gallup has concluded to be "a severe indictment of organized religion" is testified to in a June 1978 poll commissioned by Protestant and Catholic groups, wherein 86 percent of the un-churched and 76 percent of the churched agreed that individuals should arrive at their beliefs outside organized religion. About 60 percent of the churched agreed with the statement, "Most churches have lost the real spiritual part of religion." Citing this poll led Marilyn Ferguson to write that

> the spiritual experience in contemporary America . . . has little to do with religion as our culture has known it. It also has little to do with exotic cults and practices. The grass-roots movement is taking place quietly, manifesting itself in ways unique to this time and place. Most of its adherents are incognito to those looking for conventional symbols of religiousness.[1]

That the new age entrance into the religious arena would continue the anti-establishment tradition is probably to be expected. This may be responsible for two characteristics of the major emerging religious consciousness. First, the new consciousness often denies that it is religious at all, preferring to identify itself as a science or as a personal growth enterprise. Despite whatever label practitioners give themselves, however, the religious structures can be discerned. Second, it seems to emphasize the free spirit of the individual and his or her quest for wholeness. It is allegedly noninstitutional and nonhierarchical, and it often perceives itself to be in competition with so-called organized religion.

This emerging religious consciousness is by no means limited to a single cult, race, ethnic tradition, economic class, nation, or to any single formal organization. It consists primarily of widely accepted beliefs or doctrines that sometimes overlap with the official teachings of one or another religious or political persuasion; but in themselves, these beliefs belong to a common world view that interests and involves millions of people in all walks of life. The new age is reminiscent of gnosticism in the ancient Roman Empire both in what it teaches and in its competitive position vis à vis Christian orthodoxy. Elaine Pagels describes ancient gnosticism as "a powerful alternative to what we know as orthodox Christian tradition."[2] The question will arise again as the postmodern age approaches: what is the relation of what might become the new age religion to the orthodox Christian tradition?

This new age religiosity I call *perennial gnosticism.* It is not identical to the gnosticism of ancient Rome, of course. Nothing could be. But the similarities are surprising. One might surmise, as philosopher Aldous Huxley and other scholars such as Jacob Needleman and Huston Smith have, that there is a certain fund of basic religious insights that simply belongs to the human condition as such, and that these insights keep reappearing again and again. Leibniz named this fund of beliefs the *philosophia perennis,* and Huxley describes it thus:

> The metaphysic that recognizes a divine Reality substantial to the world of things and lives and minds; the psychology that finds in the soul something similar to, or even identical with, divine Reality; the ethic that places man's final end in the knowledge of the immanent and transcendent Ground of all being.[3]

The perennial philosophy as Huxley describes it offers a comprehensive world view that includes a metaphysic, a psychology, and an ethic. It contrasts sharply with the modern world view wherein the divine, if it exists at all, is thought to transcend mundane affairs. The net effect for a modern person is that the everyday world loses its enchantment, loses its religious quality. The new age religiosity, in striying to get beyond the nonreligiousness of modernity, intuitively finds an ally in the perennial philosophy.

Although Huxley and others employ the term *perennial philosophy,* I suggest the term *gnosticism.* I do so because the term *gnosis,* having to do with knowledge, is here the basic category for understanding the nature of the human predicament and for solving it. The knowledge that saves is not strictly scientific, in the postmodern view; it is usually a difficult-to-come-by, deeply internal knowing. It is knowledge in the form of awareness or consciousness. Gnosticism in this general sense is at the heart of a larger body of perennial beliefs. This body of beliefs typifies all the higher religions generally and can be discerned easily in Hinduism, Buddhism, Taoism, as well as ancient gnosticism.[4] Despite the recent alliance of Christian orthodoxy with modern secularism, the West has been unable to smother completely this apparently built-in human religious tendency. But because Christian vocabulary has been robbed of its religious content, the new age is resorting to Hindu words as well as neologisms adapted from the human potential movement.

Carl Raschke uses the term *modern gnosticism* to refer to this set of perennial beliefs that stand in revolt against modernity.

> I maintain that the "new religions" and their psychotherapeutic surrogates are mainly the cresting wave of forces that have been at work in Western culture for at least two hundred years, primarily since the eighteenth century, though the seeds were planted over two millennia ago. . . . Modern Gnosticism encompasses not only the different underground religious communities, but also key attitudes on the part of certain intellectuals toward the nature of man, toward society and history . . . [who] must be understood as taking a rear-guard action against the "progress" of the modern industrial world. They are in revolt against the course of modern history and seek salvation within the sphere of the timeless.[5]

We will accept as our task here delineating the characteristics of the emerging gnostic system as it is being articulated in the current religious consciousness and by new age intellectuals. I believe we can identify eight basic tenets to the new age variant on gnosticism. There is, of course, no confessional statement or any official theologian who represents the movement. Not everyone of this religious bent will necessarily embrace all tenets of this eightfold path. Some important teachings may even have been overlooked here. But after noting differences in terminology and nuance in different quarters, I am confident we will find considerable overlap and common adherence.

1. Wholism

Central to postmodern thought in general and the new age in particular is the doctrine of wholism, sometimes spelled *holism*. Physicist David Bohm likes to point out that our English word *health* is based on the Anglo-Saxon word *hale*, meaning "whole," so that to be healthy is to be whole. Our word *holy* comes from the same root.

What this indicates, says Bohm, is that we humans have "sensed always that wholeness or integrity is an absolute necessity to make life worth living."[6]

The cardinal principle of wholism is that the whole is greater than the sum of the parts. It was first articulated in its present form by the South African philosopher J. C. Smuts in his 1926 book *Holism and Evolution*. To understand what we mean by a whole, Smuts used as his example living organisms, such as plants or animals. An organism is certainly made up of parts such as bones and blood, but it is certainly more than merely the sum of its parts. It lives, and its life is more than the sum of its parts. Its principle for acting is internal, not external. Its internal integrity goes beyond the combination of parts. We know this, because when we break it down it ceases to live; we destroy it. We cannot put it back together again by simply reassembling its parts. A living organism is dependent upon its constituent parts, to be sure, but its identity transcends them.

What is exciting to Smuts is that wholism is the key whereby we can understand the entire evolutionary history of nature in terms of emergent creativity. Nature is constantly creating new wholes. New forms of life emerge epigenetically. Hence, time is important. So is newness. He sees the things in nature as a series of events, as centers of happenings. Evolutionary development is marked by ever more complex and significant wholes. There has been and will continue to be progress as we move from the mere material bodies of the inorganic up through the plant world and then the animal realms to human personality; and in the future it may lead to still higher forms of spiritual existence. We are climbing a ladder, each step of which indicates a progressively higher degree of wholistic complexity. "In wholeness, in the creation of ever more perfect wholes, lies the inner meaning and trend of the universe."[7]

Wholism goes beyond mechanism. It goes beyond the modern perspective that tries to understand nature according to the model of the machine. Smuts is knocking on the door of postmodernity. Although we would not think of Smuts himself as part of the new age proper, he has introduced the world to a very significant concept that has become central to new age thinking.

We can also think of wholism in terms of psychology. This is what Carl Jung does, and Jung's wholistic approach to personality integration has had a direct influence on much of the new age. Here, wholeness is equated with health, and the achievement of conscious wholeness is regarded as the goal or purpose of human life. We humans innately long for wholeness.[8]

Wholeness includes the conscious integration of opposites. It integrates the masculine (*animus*) and feminine (*anima*) proclivities that lie within each of us. It even seeks to integrate our shadow, our propensity for sin and evil, into our dominant personality. It integrates conscious and unconscious dimensions. What will become decisively important for Jung's new age disciples is the press toward an advance in consciousness as the principle of integration. Conscious wholeness becomes the good, and privation of consciousness becomes tacitly bad.

Nevertheless, the integration of the shadow leads Jung to distinguish the whole understood as completion from the whole as perfection. The term *perfection* refers to the ideal of moral goodness based upon our notion of a perfectly good God. Integrative wholeness, however, has to do with completion, not perfection. To be psychologically whole is to be complete—that is, consciously owning one's shadow and acknowledging the positively destructive aspects of one's personality. Health requires that we be in conscious touch both with our conscious striving for goodness and our potential for evildoing. Hence, one can have completion without perfection.[9] This subtle but significant distinction of Jung's is frequently overlooked by his new age disciples who tacitly assume the equation of completion and perfection. As we will see, by equating the self with God, new agers tacitly assume that wholeness and perfection automatically go together.

2. Monism

What we are calling the new age sensibility begins with wholism understood as the dynamic of integrating consciousness. For Carl Jung, wholism was a psychological process. Jung tried to avoid making metaphysical commitments. When new agers articulate what they mean by wholism, however, it quickly becomes cosmic. It takes the form of a cardinal belief in the unity of all being. The new age seeks to foster an immediate or direct knowledge of the whole of reality, an experiential connection with the infinite and the eternal, a metaphysical version of what Carl Jung called the experience of "at-one-ment."[10]

Rutgers University philosopher and former editor of *Re Vision Journal* Renée Weber illustrates the mind-set of the serious new age researcher. Weber is seeking a single comprehensive understanding of nature, an understanding that incorporates both science and mysticism. "I realize that I am a maverick," she writes, "for I can settle for nothing less than the whole. . . . It is the sense of the unity of things: man and nature, consciousness and matter, inner and outer, subject and object—the sense that these can be reconciled."[11] There is a unity to the cosmos, she assumes, and she wants our study of nature—through the disciplines of philosophy, science, and mysticism—to reflect this unity. Mysticism is essential here. She defines mysticism as "the experience of oneness with reality."[12]

The word *experience* is significant here. What the new age consciousness claims to be important is that this cosmic at-one-ment is available to human experience. It usually takes the form of an ecstatic experience, which may or may not be labeled "religious" by the persons involved. Marilyn Ferguson quotes one of the members of her Aquarian Conspiracy, a wealthy real estate entrepreneur.

> It was at Esalen, my first trip there several years ago. I had just had a Rolfing session, and I walked outdoors.
>
> Suddenly I was overwhelmed by the beauty of everything I saw. This vivid, transcendent experience tore apart my limited outlook. I had never realized the emotional heights possible. In this half-hour solitary experience I felt unity with all, universal love, connectedness. This smashing time destroyed my old reality permanently.[13]

This real estate agent is struggling for the words to describe what history of religion scholars have referred to as the "oceanic experience." David Toolan, reflecting on his experience at Esalen, comes up with the words. In Toolan's case the experience of cosmic unity was precipitated by his taking LSD, which gave him the feeling that he was returning to his mother's womb and to a time of harmonious relationship.

The basic characteristics of the psychedelic good womb are transcendence of the subject-object dichotomy, strong positive affect, a special feeling of sacredness and pure being which exceeds time, space, and words. . . . Simultaneously you float in an archetypal pattern of energy, biocosmic unity and the Earth Mother of Hindus, the cosmic "Wisdom, mother of all the living" of the Jews, and the Virgin Mary, coredemptrix of humanity according to Catholics. The "oceanic ecstasy" here can be described as contentless and yet all-containing, a loss of ego and still an expansion of consciousness, that includes the whole universe—that identifies with God-as-Mother.[14]

This sense of one's self being whole and being united with the whole marks the end of an existential quest, the finding of a psychological holy grail. It seems to be something we thirst for, something we hunger for. The combining of psychology with religious metaphysics is producing a new age myth that describes the human psyche as originating in some primeval unity of body and spirit, of self and world. Then, the new age myth alleges, we fell. We fell because of the process of individuation. We left the warm symbiotic unity we once knew with our mother and our environment and entered the cold cruel world of independence, the world of separate ego consciousness. Yet we long to return. We long to overcome our individuality and experience again the wholeness we have lost. Our task is to realize the oneness of self and cosmos.

According to Gregory Szanto's hybrid of astrology and Jungian psychology, there once was a time in which no split existed between our conscious and unconscious natures, between the external world of the stars and the internal world of the psyche. It was a state of cosmic oneness. At that time we saw in the perpetual cycles of the planets and in the daily rising and setting of the sun the principles of eternity. We experienced the manifestation of a divine reality that pervaded every aspect of our life. However, we fell from this primeval paradise; and we have been seeking material security and intellectual security ever since. What we look forward to now is a return to unity, but the return will take our individuated consciousness with it. Szanto says the return can be symbolized by the planet Uranus, which is identified with the ego's conscious break away from the authority of others, and Neptune, which is identified with the unconscious.

the Ego through Neptune with the unconscious. This is the search for union, to be at one with our source, with the absolute, or with the spirit. We want once again to be one, to be whole, to blend ourselves with the rest of the universe and humanity as one drop becomes part of the ocean.[15]

Reflection on this oceanic experience in the higher religions often leads to the positing of monism, the doctrine of an underlying cosmic oneness that incorporates and unifies the apparent plurality of things existing on the surface of reality. Monism affirms a latent completeness or perfection of all things lying below the surface of the apparent incompleteness or imperfections we see. The multiplicity, plurality, and fragmentation of life we perceive is either an illusion—that is, it is unreal—or, if real, then its reality is subtly dependent on a principle of mutual complementarity or balance with the uniting whole.

This position has probably been worked out most thoroughly by the eighth-century Indian philosopher Shankara, whose influence in contemporary India is overwhelming. Shankara's view is a nontheistic understanding of cosmic unity usually named *advaita,* meaning "nondualism." According to Shankara there is an absolute reality, Brahman, and there is no other reality but Brahman. Only that is real that neither changes nor ceases to exist, he says, so Brahman is understood as absolute existence, without qualities or attributes, without distinctions within or outside, beyond the subject-object split and beyond the sense of "mine" and "yours," without change or process. Therefore, the distinction between the human self and the single cosmic reality is a false distinction. My self (my Atman) is identical with Brahman. If I fail in my consciousness to realize this at-one-ment, then I am living in ignorance; I am mistaking the illusory experience of daily fragmentation and plurality for reality, not realizing the genuine unity of all things. Marvin Henry Harper contends that Shankara's *advaita* is the most popular philosophy in India today, and in one form or another it pervades the cults that are making their way west.[16]

In Shankara's nontheistic *advaita* the underlying unitary reality is impersonal; it is supradivine. He distinguishes between Nirguna Brahman, the absolute beyond distinction, and Saguna Brahman, the absolute understood as creator, sustainer, and destroyer, which

Brahman, the absolute beyond distinction, and Saguna Brahman, the absolute understood as creator, sustainer, and destroyer, which many call God. Those who mistakenly believe the world to be real will regard God as the creator; but those who are enlightened will see through this and recognize the more primary supradivine reality.

Not all Indians have fully imbibed a monism that swallows up all distinction, that dissolves all drops into a single ocean. A nineteenth-century Bengal poet, Ramaprasada, protests by addressing the goddess Kali, saying: "Mother! I want to taste sugar, not to become sugar."

An alternative to Shankara who exhibits considerable subtlety on this matter is the ancient philosopher Ramanuja. Ramanuja holds that the divine is itself the absolute. The unitary reality is not the advaitan Nirguna Brahman beyond distinction; it is rather the Saguna Brahman, a divine and personal being. In short, there is unity and the unity is divine; but every distinction is not washed away into the one cosmic ocean. In some cases, it would seem, new agers seem closer to Ramanuja than to Shankara.[17] In the emerging postmodern West, the equivalent of Brahman is quite frequently called God, and God represents a shared consciousness rather than an extinguished consciousness. Feminist and futurist Barbara Marx Hubbard, for example, uses the term this way.

> If there's a God, it's He who unites past with present and future, finite with infinite, truth with falsity, until all are more than a conglomeration, until all is one and that one is far greater than the sum of its parts. That oneness is God's creation.[18]

In J. D. Salinger's short story "Teddy," the ten-year-old Teddy is discussing reincarnation and Indian metaphysics with Mr. Nicholson. Teddy explains that he does not want to be loved by a sentimental God because that would be too unreliable. Then he describes an ecstatic experience he had at the age of six.

> "I was six when I saw that everything was God. . . . My sister was only a very tiny child then, and she was drinking her milk, and all of a sudden I saw that she was God and the milk was God. I mean, all she was doing was pouring God into God, if you know what I mean."[19]

Salinger's Teddy speaks like the twentieth-century Indian philosopher and new age guru Sri Aurobindo, for whom the "universe is a diffusion of the divine All in infinite Space and Time, the individual its concentration within limits of Space and Time."[20] He could also be astronaut Edgar Mitchell, who told the Ninth Annual Mandala Conference in San Diego during August 1983 that God sleeps in the minerals, awakens in plants, walks in the animals, and thinks in us.

Monism simply posits the fundamental unity of all things, a single all-embracing reality. It may be a suprapersonal and supradivine reality such as Nirguna Brahman; or the all-embracing reality itself might be considered divine and personal in character. Salinger's Teddy may be combining them, for his pantheistic god unites all things yet seems to be suprapersonal—that is, nonsentimental. Be that as it may, what is key to the new age consciousness is the positing of such an inclusive whole, whether or not it is identified with the divine personality.

3. The Higher Self

The apprehension of cosmic unity seems to carry with it a notion of a higher or supraindividual self, an inclusive reality within which one's apparent or phenomenal self participates. "When we connect with our own souls," says Jungian analyst Marion Woodman, "we connect with the soul of every human being"—that is, with the "World Soul."[21]

Willis Harman at the Institute of Noetic Sciences in San Francisco contends that we are all connected with one another at a subterranean level of the mind, suggesting that there is a larger supraindividual mind beyond our own egos in which we participate. The real estate man quoted earlier from Ferguson says he discovered "multiple dimensions of self; a newly integrated sense of oneself as an individual . . . a linkage with others as if they are oneself . . . and the merger with a Self yet more universal and primary."[22] Personal integration here takes us beyond the individual or phenomenal self. It connects us to a much larger self, which Ferguson describes as an invisible continent on which we all make our home.

The doctrine of the higher self usually begins by acknowledging that life here on earth is darkness, a sleepy haze. We bumble through life in a sort of hypnotic sleep, not clear on what forces are governing the course of personal events. We feel that our life is a lonely combination of inconsistent decisions, random events, accidental happenings. At times things may appear to be meaningful, but overall life has no visible purpose or unity.

If we could penetrate the haze to apprehend the light of truth, we would realize that a hidden higher and eternal self is directing us. Our life happenings are not simply a series of accidents or random events. There is purpose, direction, and influence from a source of which we are at best only dimly aware. Occasionally the higher self breaks through to the mundane level. When it does, we experience a moment of inspiration. Ferguson quotes pianist Arthur Rubinstein, who struggles to define what he calls "this thing in us, a metaphysical power that emanates from us."[23] Harman quotes Ralph Waldo Emerson's "The Oversoul," wherein Emerson writes, "When it breathes through his intellect, it is genius; when it breathes through his will it is virtue; when if flows through his affection, it is love."[24] Deep intuition is there to be used. We should listen to our inner voices and yield to the inspiration of the higher self.

The higher self for Harman seems to be active; it inspires. Harman says the image of the lightning bolt is appropriate to describe how the higher self initiates a breakthrough into our ordinary consciousness. Our task, he goes on, is to understand the principles of creativity inherent in these breakthroughs in our lives. We will then be ready to "channel" this lightening and enlightening energy as it comes through our unconscious. It originates probably from some external source, divine or otherwise.[25]

The concept corresponding to the higher self in Werner Erhard's est seems to be more passive, functioning as a transcendent receptacle for ego activity. Erhard identifies the lower self as the Mind. Our Mind represents our fallenness, our separation from our higher or true Self. Using the metaphor of the machine, Erhard describes the Mind as an automated warehouse of burdened, encumbered memories that aims at "survival."[26] It seeks physical survival but also survival of the person's ideas, opinions, and self-conceptions. To survive, the Mind tries to convince us it is right and everyone else is wrong. It seeks self-justification and domination. Erhard coined the verb *to ego,* meaning "to perpetuate one's own point of view," and pointed out that this is too narrow and dysfunctional.

est wants more than survival. It wants self-actualization and wholeness. The task of est is to help us to rise out of our "State of Mind"
and into our "State of Self." What est knows as the Self is a trans-
individual self. It transcends our identification with our physical
appearance, the things we believe, our job resumé, our affiliations
and memberships. It consists in the open space at the top of the
ladder of philosophy where such things as ego activity and personal
identity take place.[27]

Holistic health advocates operate with a more active or dynamic understanding of the higher self, often describing it as "the healer
inside us." They begin by assuming that we live in a friendly universe, not one jostled from pillar to post by destructive forces. And
this cosmic friendliness expresses itself in our lives through the higher self, through the God within.

> The basic assumption of holistic health views the Universe as a
> friendly and supportive place. . . . Harmony and resonance are the
> result of vibrations which enjoy one another. Within the assumption
> of a friendly Universe . . . [the] creative intention, emerging from
> within the individual, leads each person to . . . : stand in commun-
> ion with a benevolent universe; seek a personal knowledge of the
> inner vision and spirit of the Higher Self (God within) through cre-
> ative intuition and imagination; perceive and interpret through a
> fearless and clear mind exercising intellectual autonomy and
> integrity.[28]

Here as elsewhere in new age thinking, we find a partnership
between modern Western and ancient Asian thought. Sri Aurobindo,
a twentieth-century Indian sage, says that "beyond mind is a supra-
mental or gnostic power of consciousness . . . [which] is at its source
the dynamic consciousness, in its nature at once and inseparably
infinite wisdom and infinite will of the divine Knower and Creator."[29] This reflects eighth-century Shankara and the ancient Upa-
nishadic teachings of Brahmanism wherein one's true self is
designated Atman. The Atman is never born and never dies. It is
changeless, beyond time, permanent, and eternal. It does not die
when the body dies. In fact, for one who has true knowledge, the
Atman is equivalent to and identical with Brahman, the all, the

totality of reality. Life's goal, according to Hinduism, is to come to this awareness. Carl Jung can say of Eastern thought in general that it "has no difficulty in conceiving of a consciousness without an ego. Consciousness is deemed capable of transcending its ego condition; indeed, in its 'higher' forms, the ego disappears altogether."[30]

It is our task as human beings to become aware of this metaphysical power, this unifying reality that lies within us. Socrates' ancient imperative "Know thyself!" is the starting point of postmodern gnostic consciousness. Those who have joined the Aquarian conspiracy—who are breathing now the spirit of the new age coming—are in touch with their higher self and are vigorously pursuing deeper awareness of it. Sri Aurobindo describes it:

> Our humanity is the conscious meeting-place of the finite and the infinite, and to grow more and more towards that Infinite even in this physical birth is our privilege. This Infinite, this Spirit who is housed within us but not bound or shut in by mind or body, is our own self and to find and be our self was, as the ancient sages knew, always the object of our human striving.[31]

This leads to the notion of the divine spark, which we find in some new age programs. A disciple of the channeled entity Ramtha says: "I really don't feel an apparent separation between Ramtha and myself. . . . He is a spark of the divine just like we all are."[32] The divine spark within us is too often smothered by fear. Fear enslaves, encaptures, and inhibits the creative mind; it stagnates emotions and kills hope. Fear is caused by ignorance, by not-knowingness. Once we gain clarity about the source of our fears, we are free from them. Once we come to know the divine potential that lies within us, we find ourselves caught up in the gloriousness of expanded creativity and genuine happiness. Ramtha teaches: "You Are God, I Am God."[33]

There is precedent for this concept of the divine spark within us. According to the microcosmic-macrocosmic anthropology of ancient gnosticism, the human being consists of three dimensions: body, soul, and spirit. The physical or fleshly body belonging to the material world represents the prison of darkness. The psyche or soul has seven built-in passions that correspond to the seven planes or spheres of reality that separate our mundane world from the transcendent realm of divine light and pure reality. The spirit or *pneuma* represents the divine spark, a tiny piece of the eternal light smothered under the layers of darkness and emotion. Restrained by the life of the flesh, the spirit within us is benumbed, asleep, unconscious, ignorant of its true identity and true destiny.

It is this belief that makes gnosis what it is; true knowledge consists in recognizing the divine within the human being. To know oneself at the deepest level, then, is simultaneously to know God. An ancient gnostic teacher, Monoimus, put it this way:

> Abandon the search for God and the creation and other matters of a similar sort. Look for him by taking yourself as the starting point. Learn who it is within you who makes everything his own and says, "My God, my mind, my thought, my soul, my body." Learn the sources of sorrow, joy, love, hate. . . . If you carefully investigate these matters you will find him in yourself.[34]

For new age prophets in general and the human potential movement in particular, wholeness is sought through a turn inward, and God is sought in the same place. The divine spark doctrine appears to be making a comeback, although it is only occasionally given this name.

4. Potentiality

What little child has not been told by his or her mother that each of us uses only 10 percent of our brain power? What this usually means to the child is that he or she should think harder. This brings us to the human potential movement, a movement that has had an enormous impact on the way of life in North America. As we mentioned in chapter 1, its roots lie in the task of self-actualization advocated by psychologist Abraham Maslow in the 1950s. What Maslow called the "peak experience," an experience of religious ecstasy or inspired clarity or joy, he believed could speed up and direct the process of full self-realization. This was the theory that the Esalen Institute at Big Sur sought to put into practice during the 1960s. Esalen then experimented with countless emendations to the original vision, eventually giving us the primal scream, Rolfing, and Radix therapy. It modified our vocabularies to include phrases such as "human potential," "consciousness revolution," "altered states," and "expansion." Wittingly or not, Esalen has become parent to countless children, some loyal, some renegade. Second-generation therapies and cosmologies live on in such programs as Lifespring, Theta, and others, along with est. These borrowed the goods from Esalen, repackaged them, and sold them under altered labels. Thus the human potential movement, like perennial gnosticism with which it overlaps, is a bit amorphous and is no longer the private province of any single organization or group.

Today the term "human potential movement" refers to a wide variety of activities, all resting on the belief that there is more to most of us than meets the eye, that we have much unrealized potential. It further rests on the assumption that individual change can be brought about through self-help. Primarily, one needs to be open to the possibilities of change, to be educated about some of these possibilities, to experiment with them, and to be determined to have them make a difference.[35]

In brief, the human potential movement teaches (1) that each of us has a great potential lying within us; (2) that this potential can be awakened through education and experimentation; (3) that the individual can change his or her situation dramatically—actual self-transformation is possible; (4) that self-realization and self-fulfillment are the proper ends of life.

In reflecting on his experience at Esalen, Jesuit David Toolan believes that at root the human potential movement is seeking a new cosmology, a new grounding for reality. The key to this new cosmology is the innate connection between self and world. It seeks to overcome the dualism of the modern mind that separates subject and object, the humanities from the sciences.[36] When one presses into the primal dimensions of the self, one finds the whole of the cosmos. Jacob Needleman would agree, seeing in this a reaffirmation of the microcosm-macrocosm correlation; the individual human being is understood as the universe in miniature.[37] What this opens the door to, of course, is finding buried within oneself potentialities that we previously thought were only external and perhaps even impossible.

New age voices now tell us that human potential is limitless. All knowledge and power is ultimately accessible to the mind looking within itself, and all limitations are ultimately self-chosen. Immense untapped resources lie within the dormant 90 percent of the brain.

What we need is a will and a technique for tapping those resources, and once they are tapped the whole universe will be available to us. We will find we have clairvoyant powers to engage in activities such as ESP, precognition, psychokinesis, telepathic communication, and astral travel. At some deep level within each of us we already understand these extraordinary abilities, yet we have chosen by the social conventions of modernity to limit ourselves to conscious understanding of only the ordinary physical laws that preclude such phenomena.

Theologian Sam Keen advocates the use of the holographic model for understanding the relationship between the human mind and the cosmos. For him the mind is actually cosmic in scope and hence cosmic in potential.

> The mind is a hologram that registers the entire symphony of cosmic vibratory events. . . . A star explodes and the mind trembles. Just as any cell in the body encodes all the information necessary to reproduce the entire body, so any mind recapitulates all cosmic events. What we call ESP and paranormal experience may only be our dipping into the timeless dimensions which make up the holographic structure of our minds. Science and mysticism suggest that the self may be ubiquitous. Mind knows no barriers.[38]

The point of contact between the human potential movement and what we are calling perennial gnosticism is the tie between the human and divine. The divine within us can be considered part of our potential. "I am God, you are God" can be heard frequently in the human potential movement. This phrase may not always refer to a metaphysical reality; it may function as a heuristic device, as a prompt to encourage each of us to take charge of our own life. Werner Erhard of est says that the Self is the ground of all that is— in fact, the Self is all there is! To speak of the divine is to speak of one's self. A Theta seminar creed reads:

> The thinker in all of us is the creator of our universe and manifests whatever it believes to be true. Within the dominion of our minds we are surely God, for we can control what we think, and what we conceive to be true becomes the truth.[39]

It is at this point, however, that we can discern a difference between the more widely diffused new age religious mood and the highly concentrated religiosity of the cults. Rather than following an ethic of self-realization and self-fulfillment, cult members are enjoined to lead a life of self-abnegation. There is a return to the ascetic ideals of ancient Hinduism and medieval Catholicism, wherein the adept denies himself such things as loyalty to family, possession of worldly goods, drinking alcohol, or engaging in sexual pleasure. Devotees who live in Hare Krishna temples live according to a rigid daily schedule and are not permitted to eat meat or drink such things as beer, wine, coffee, or even tea. Married couples are allowed conjugal love once per month, not for purposes of enjoyment, but for the sole end of producing Krishna-conscious children. Members of the Children of God are permitted extramarital sex, but membership requires breaking off relationships with one's family and rigorous obedience to one's superiors. The list of ascetic restrictions in the Unification Church is similar, and love and acceptance from other members of the group are conditional on how much a person can give. One must constantly strive to work harder and accomplish more. "Yesterday's 100 percent is today's 90 percent" is a common Moonie refrain. Nothing is more devastating to a Moonie than the words, "You are not giving enough. You are selfish, insincere, evil." It is the conclusion of Lowell Streiker that the key word is *self-abnegation* instead of *self-realization*.[40]

The upshot is that almost every new age follower currently agrees with the assumption that each of us is living with an enormous reservoir of untapped potential, perhaps even a cosmic or divine potential. In addition, every new age disciple agrees that this potential should become realized, even if it means bringing our internal divinity to outward expression. What is curious, however, is that in cult form this realization process becomes an ascetic process, one that draws a distinction between self-realization through obedience to the cult leadership and a selfish happiness based on individual self-gratification.

5. Reincarnation

Reincarnation or metempsychosis, the doctrine that souls migrate from one body into another through death and rebirth, probably originated in ancient India but has been widely held in both oriental and occidental cultures since. Repudiated in the West first by the Christian Church, for which reincarnation is incompatible with its belief in resurrection of the body, and then by modern naturalism, for which reincarnation is mere religious superstition, the doctrine is making a comeback. Each issue of the most widely read periodical in the world, *The National Enquirer,* typically contains accounts of people discovering their identities in past lives. Popular books as well as apparently scientific treatises on the subject are widely read.[41] Reincarnation therapy, wherein with the aid of a counselor the client goes back to a traumatic experience in a previous life, is being practiced in many religious cults as well as in more public new age circles.

Actress Shirley MacLaine, for example, has announced that she now believes in ghosts and extraterrestrials right along with reincarnation. "Our bodies are only the houses wherein our souls reside," she says. "When we leave our physical bodies, our souls become energy until we choose to reincarnate in a different form." Through psychic recession she claims to have discovered her identities in past lives: she was a dancer in an Egyptian harem and also a madam in San Francisco.[42]

Bettye Binder of Los Angeles is one of numerous past-life regression therapists. She claims she experienced a spontaneous revelation of her past life as an eighteenth-century Comanche during February 1980, and this set her on the path of studying the principles of reincarnation. What precipitated the first revelation was the intuitive reaction she had on meeting a man for the first time. "I have known him before," she said to herself. Yes, she says, she had known him as the chief of her tribe back in 1746. After apprenticing herself to another hypnotherapist, Loy Young, Bettye began her own regression work at the end of 1980. Now she travels the country taking appointments and charging $100 for a two-hour regression session.

Bettye says that each of us is an immortal soul inhabiting a body and subsequent to our death our soul will take up residence in another body on either this planet or another one in our galaxy. What happens in our life is governed by karma, the law of cause and effect. Karma teaches, and the process of transmigration constitutes our karmic classroom. As the soul moves from life to life it learns, and at some point in the future it will jump off the wheel of death and rebirth. The reason for past-life regression is to better understand our karma; the better we understand our karma, the faster we learn. We can speed up the soul's learning process: instead of taking many lifetimes to learn something, we can learn it in this lifetime.

Regression is a form of guided meditation, with each session lasting about two hours. In the event that an unresolved conflict in a previous life is uncovered, one can make new decisions regarding it. Bettye calls this "rescripting." By it she is gaining a new perspective and establishing a new direction for this lifetime. This constitutes a healing, and healing is the central function of regression therapy.[43]

Past-life regression constitutes one door among many through which the modern Western mind can gain access to things Asian. Eastern mystical literature in general and the *Tibetan Book of the Dead* (the *Bardo Thödol*) in particular have become common reading material in the West over the past couple of decades. Some new age teachers argue that the spiritually sterile culture of modernity (and Protestantism as well), in conjunction with growing global consciousness, has sent religious seekers to non-Western sources of wisdom. Reincarnation is one of the alleged treasures that they have found. A bit ahead of the crowd and in large part responsible for those who have followed, the great Tibetan scholar W. Y. Evans-Wentz has been seeking a rapprochement between Western science and Eastern metaphysics. He believes the convergence of these two traditions will produce an atonement, an "at-one-ment," that will result in Westerners accepting the notion of reincarnation. He writes enthusiastically in his preface to the first edition of the *Tibetan Book of the Dead,*

> Then, when that long-awaited at-one-ment shall have been consummated, there will no longer be doubt, nor fallacious argumentation, nor unwise and unscientific Church-Council anathematizations directed against that paramount doctrine of pre-existence and rebirth, upon which the Bardo Thödol is based. Then, too, not only will Pythagoras and Plato and Plotinus and the Gnostic Christians, and Krishna and the Buddha be vindicated in their advocacy of the doctrine, but, equally, the Hierophants of the Ancient Mysteries of Egypt and Greece and Rome, and the Druids of the Celtic World.

And Western man will awaken from that slumber of Ignorance
which has been hypnotically induced by a mistaken Orthodoxy. He
will greet with wide-open eyes his long unheeded brethren, the Wise
Men of the East.[44]

Reincarnation is an ancient or premodern doctrine that is being
revived today on a large scale. As clearly reflected in the Evans-
Wentz quotation, belief in reincarnation represents, among other
things, a modest rebellion against Western science. The doctrine of
reincarnation is being pressed into the service of postmodern critics
of modernity. It is only a modest rebellion, however, because many
advocates are in fact seeking scientific verification for this otherwise
metaphysical belief. It is still a rebellion, though, because it represents listening to a spiritual voice that speaks to the human soul on
an issue about which science has been silent too long.

Evans-Wentz goes on to offer general praise for the mystical
insights of Asia, and expresses his hope that the coming new age in
the West will be propelled by a renaissance of Indian philosophy.

In the Aquarian Age, as in the New Age now being entered upon,
India, if she remains faithful to those Great Masters of Wisdom
who have preserved her since prehistoric times, who have enabled
her to witness the passing of Egypt and Babylon, of Greece and
Rome and Spain, shall once more, phoenix-like, arise from the ashes of the present and, strengthened by the realization of the failure
of (scientific) Knowledge, retain the spiritual leadership of the
world.[45]

6. Evolution and Transformation

The notion of the Aquarian Age projected by Evans-Wentz is in one
form or another the eschatological driving force of current new age
thinking. Employing the zodiacal image of Aquarius, new age utopi-
anism projects an outpouring of new life on earth; the manifestation
of new energies; the revelation of new wisdom, new teaching, and new
insight; the appearance of communal and natural harmony, peace, and
oneness. Our present moment constitutes the hinge of history, the door
to psychic and cosmic transformation. Such utopian thinking is usually
accompanied by a theory of evolution and transformation.

"I just love the word *evolution*," says Terry Cole-Whittaker. Then she takes the first four letters, *evol,* and reverses them to get *love.* "Evolution is the revolution of love!" she exclaims. Then she exhorts us, "Mutate today!"[46]

The term *evolution,* of course, ordinarily refers to the theory regarding the multimillion-year train of biological development, a development that consists of genus formation through the continuous genetic adaptation of organisms or species to their respective environments by processes such as selection, hybridization, inbreeding, and mutation. In the new age subculture, however, it refers to change on a much more abbreviated time scale. It may refer to psychological change within an individual's lifetime as well as a revolutionary transformation in human consciousness that could occur within a single generation.[47] Most importantly, it identifies transformation as a moral goal. "I'm a *possible*-ist," says George Leonard. "I think it's possible to alter our course. As long as it's possible, I think we need to keep trying."[48]

The presupposed anthropology in such thinking is occasionally articulated: there is no human nature, if by nature one means fixed characteristics and limitations. Change is real and what is presently thought to be human might very well undergo radical transformation. "Man is a transitional being; he is not final," writes Sri Aurobindo. "For in man and high beyond him ascend the radiant degrees that climb to supermanhood."[49]

To achieve such a transformation is the avowed goal of new age theorists. Edgar D. Mitchell, former astronaut and founder of the Institute of Noetic Sciences in San Francisco, believes that by "accelerating awakening of individual human beings to their own potential" we can "change the course of human history." The human predicament is understood as a conceptual confinement by stereotyped thinking, by the belief that we are limited by material forces external to ourselves. In fact, however, we have unlimited potential, potential even to free ourselves from our material or physical existence in the world. If we choose to embrace new age values such as cooperation instead of competition, we can achieve a quantum leap in evolutionary development and attain personal wellness as well as peace on earth. The transformation of the whole "is no further away than a decision of individuals to transform themselves."[50]

Willis Harman, former SRI (Stanford Research Institute) researcher now at the Institute of Noetic Sciences, describes transformation in terms of a societal metamorphosis based on a fundamental *metanoia*, a religious conversion. The new planetary society would live out of a new paradigm, a new world view in which the emphasis in science would be to understand rather than to manipulate through technology; in which the spiritual order would be explored and an ecological ethic would reign; and in which a teleological view of life would organize human efforts around a single central purpose. What he appears to be describing here is a cultural transformation that in principle could occur within the span of a generation. But in Harman's view such a transformation is part and parcel of the cosmic evolutionary process in which we cooperate but that has a *telos* of its own.

> Evolution is seen to be not a random matter, but directed by a higher consciousness and characterized by purpose. This purpose includes the development of individual centers of consciousness with freedom of choice, gradually moving toward ever increasing knowledge of themselves, of Self, and of the Whole. Knowledge of and participation in this evolution is the supreme value.[51]

The key elements are knowledge and choice. We have the power to choose to be something different from what we presently are. Humankind is a transitional species, a link in a vast evolutionary chain, and because of its capacity for self-transcendence and creative choice we are now on the verge of a quantum leap into a new wholistic reality. Barbara Marx Hubbard reports in her autobiography,

> The concept of life as an evolutionary process has subtly taken hold of me. I don't live in a static eternity but in an evolving universe. I'm going somewhere. Being of the race of human, not animal, for the first time in history there's an opportunity to choose, at least a little, where and how. . . . Now, we, humanity, are in the process of forming ourselves into a synthesis, a planetary organism, one being—humankind.[52]

This vision of a new stage in evolutionary development includes the powerful individual dynamic found in the human potential movement combined with a vision of human connectedness that transcends a strictly self-centered orientation. Nature is thinking through us. Nature advances through us. Nature transforms herself through us.

This brings us to the concept of the *critical mass,* a key element in many new age understandings of transformatory evolution. According to the critical mass theory, if enough people believe strongly in something, suddenly the idea will become true for everyone. This theory assumes that a reciprocity exists between one's individual consciousness and the collective or higher consciousness. The argument goes like this: if a number of people—enough people to form a critical mass—concentrate on something, we may pass a threshold. Passing this threshold will have a spiritual and then a social impact on the whole world.

Belief in the critical mass principle is frequently articulated in the form of an emerging myth called the hundredth monkey phenomenon. The story originated in Lyall Watson's 1979 book *Lifetide,* and has been propagated through a book by Ken Keyes plus a film, both with the title *The Hundredth Monkey,* as well as Marilyn Ferguson's *Brain/Mind Bulletin.*[53] According to the story, in 1952 on the small Japanese island of Koshima, some scientists began leaving sweet potatoes out for the monkeys (*Macaca fuscata*) so they would be less inclined to raid farmers' gardens. One macaca, a female named Imo, learned to wash the grit and dirt off the sweet potatoes before eating them. Imo passed on the skill to her family and playmates. The teaching process was slow at first, one to one. By 1958 the number of monkeys that knew how to wash their potatoes had attained critical mass—Watson suggests one hundred—and suddenly a new phenomenon is alleged to have occurred. Knowledge began passing instantaneously from monkey mind to monkey mind. Even on the neighboring island of Takasakiyama, other monkeys suddenly began washing their sweet potatoes. What this indicates, new age followers believe, is that these monkeys had attained critical mass and then crossed a threshold that advanced the whole of the collective consciousness. This gives evidence of the power of shared psychic forces.

By the mid-1980s other scholars had reexamined the data, and their criticisms were devastating. The facts could not support the critical mass theory. The close documentation by the Japanese scientists on site indicates only fifty-nine monkeys were involved, not one hundred. The scientists, who had closely observed the teaching process, found that the real reason for the advance from slow to rapid transmission of the practice of sweet potato washing had little to do with the attainment of a critical number. Rather, it was due to the fact that the females eventually reached monkey menarche and began having babies, who learned sweet potato washing immediately from their mothers. As for the transmission to the other island, one potato-washing monkey named Jugo was seen swimming to Takasakiyama. The monkeys there likely learned it from him. Even if they didn't learn it from Jugo, there is no reason to think the macacas could not have figured out how to do it just as Imo had in the first place.[54]

We do not need a doctrine such as higher consciousness to explain what happened. Even Watson, when confronted with the counterevidence, has partially backed down and now denies the factual basis for the critical mass theory. Nevertheless, he continues to believe in the hundredth monkey as "a metaphor of my own making" to support "the notion of quantum leaps in consciousness."[55] Thus, despite the facts, new age groups continue to believe in the critical mass theory and continue to articulate the doctrine in terms of the one hundredth monkey myth.[56]

Variants on the critical mass theory appeared prior to Watson's monkeys, of course. The "Maharishi effect" propagated by Transcendental Meditation (TM) and its World Planetary Transformation Council is a good example. On January 12, 1975, Maharishi Mahesh Yogi announced that the age of enlightenment would dawn when 1 percent of the world's population became meditators. By 1977 the statistics had changed so that now only the square root of 1 percent or about seven thousand people would be enough. This was a manageable number. TM spokespeople claim that already, due to their meditating, the world has witnessed decreases in crime, traffic accidents, and infant mortality. With this alleged success, the Maharishi has started the World Peace Fund, for which he is soliciting $100 million to finance seven thousand people to meditate constantly. This would permit us to cross the threshold, to leap into our evolutionary future and establish peace on earth, he believes.

Thus, we humans have a chance to give the evolutionary development of the cosmos a boost. We can guide what happens through the exercise of our spiritual power. We find ourselves, then, in the driver's seat of evolution. We are steering the direction all of nature will take. The role of human consciousness becomes awesomely significant.

This is the point made by Renée Weber when reflecting on the work of physicist David Bohm. Weber says,

> *Meaning is a form of being.* In the very act of interpreting the universe, we are creating the universe. Through our meanings we change nature's being. Man's meaning-making capacity turns him into nature's partner, a participant in shaping her evolution. The word does not merely reflect the world, it also creates the world. . . . Through us, the universe questions itself and tries out various answers on itself in an effort—parallel to our own—to decipher its own being.
>
> This, as I reflect on it, is awesome. It assigns a role to man that was once reserved for the gods.[57]

We should note here that the doctrine of evolution in new age thinking is primarily Western and distinctively modern. It is naturalistic. It is humanistic. It posits a single uniting reality in which matter and spirit are integrated.

We should also note that the concept of evolution presupposes the modern view of linear or processive time, including openness to the future and progress. Contemporary gnosticism, except in its more overtly Asian and imported aspects, is modern and Western in this respect. When speculation about God is mixed in at this point, we get a dynamic and flowing divine reality. Ferguson speculates that God might be thought of as immanent, as the evolutionary drive of consciousness in the universe. She reports that for Aquarian conspirators, God is experienced as flow, wholeness, the infinite kaleidoscope of life and death, ultimate cause, the ground of being, the organizing matrix that enlivens matter.

In this regard, then, the doctrine of evolution marks a point of difference between today's gnostics and the ancient gnostics. The ancient gnostics sought to escape the material world. Today's new age gnostics celebrate what is physical and even try to harmonize the physical with the spiritual. Astrotherapist Gregory Szanto, who wants to unite the psyche with the stars, makes this point forcefully:

The spirit must be found in this world of ours and not by trying to escape from it. . . . The real imperative for this new age is for the spiritual and material aspects of life to be united again. This is what wholeness and the healing process means.[58]

Although the ancient practitioners believed in personal advance and development in consciousness, such advance carried with it renunciation of the material and ephemeral world. The attainment of saving knowledge (gnosis) for the gnostic of antiquity meant escape from the physical world of darkness into the intellectual or spiritual world of light. This antipathy toward the physical or natural world does not preoccupy contemporary new age thinkers, however. "There is no dualism," writes Ferguson, "no separation of mind and body, self and others."[59]

So it appears to me that Carl Raschke's book misses the mark on this point, especially when he says that "the new Gnostics . . . share a variety of religious and metaphysical presuppositions with their classical kin. Most important . . . is their systematic aversion to the idea of progress."[60] It seems that the emphasis on personal and social transformation along with cosmic evolutionary advance marks a decisive acceptance of temporality and progress on the part of today's gnostics. It also means an acceptance of the material world. To the extent that integrative consciousness and wholism are pursued, the world of nature is included and even celebrated.

7. Gnosis

It should be obvious from all that has been said thus far that transformation, which is the functional equivalent of salvation, is gained through knowledge, through gnosis. For the ancient gnostics this knowledge consisted in secret or esoteric wisdom, an insight into the workings of the world, and the opening of the transcendental gate so that the soul might pass from this ephemeral world of darkness into the eternal realm of light. Gnosis is saving knowledge.

The ancient Valentinean version of saving knowledge reflects clearly the cosmic unity mentioned earlier. The Gospel of Truth includes the following passage:

> It is by means of Unity that each one shall receive himself back
> again. Through knowledge he shall purify himself of diversity with
> a view to Unity, by engulfing the Matter within himself like a flame,
> Darkness by Light and Death by Life.

For the ancients, gnosis is preeminently knowledge of the divine, and this includes knowledge of the upper worlds plus an awareness of one's own ignorance, which gives way to a mystical apprehension of unity. Gaining such knowledge itself transforms the human condition. Gnosis "is not just theoretical information," writes Hans Jonas, "but is itself, as a modification of the human condition, charged with performing a function in the bringing about of salvation. . . . The ultimate 'object' of gnosis is God: its event in the soul transforms the knower himself by making him a partaker in the divine existence."[61]

The kind of knowledge involved, then, is not the kind of objectivist or controlling knowledge characteristic of modern science and technology. It is rather an intensely personal form of knowledge, often dubbed "new awareness" or "higher consciousness." Elaine Pagels explains how the ancient Greek language could distinguish between scientific or reflective knowledge ("He knows mathematics") and knowing through observation or experience ("He knows me"), which is gnosis. Gnosis involves an intuitive process of knowing oneself, and to know oneself is to know human nature in general and to know human destiny.[62] Stated the way Pagels does it, the term *gnosis* as used by the ancients is descriptive of much of new age thinking as well. For new age adherents the fundamental human problem is understood as ignorance, and the solution must then be some form of personal knowledge.

David Bohm's suggestive theory of insight provides us with an example. He describes the enfolded or implicate order of the whole as subtle, and the explicate order encountered through ordinary human thought as gross. Thought has its place, but it cannot of its own accord go beyond itself. It cannot transcend the explicate order because it belongs to the explicate order. It is gross, and the gross cannot handle or manipulate the subtle. It may even block it. Therefore, the subtle whole will itself have to act; and it does so through insight. Insight pierces through the explicate state of affairs with an experience that has a transcendent quality to it. It comes to one, cannot handle or manipulate the subtle. It may even block it. There-fore, the subtle whole will itself have to act; and it does so through insight. Insight pierces through the explicate state of affairs with an experience that has a transcendent quality to it. It comes to one, and in the process of coming it reorients and redirects the normal thought processes. It is a message from the whole—a message from the reality that connects all things—yet the hearing of the message has a deep inner personal dimension to it.

Literary critic Ihab Hassan uses the term"New Gnosticism" to refer to this personal form of knowledge. He perceives in Western culture a growing insistence on apprehending reality immediately; that is, apprehending reality without mediation by the scientific and critical disciplines. There is a "new sense of the im-mediacy of Mind, of complete gnosis or knowledge."[63] Hassan himself is a futurist in the sense that he looks forward to a developing universal conscious-ness wherein those participating are capable of im-mediate ex-changes of knowledge.

This is illustrated among other places in science fiction litera-ture, notably Robert Heinlein's *Stranger in a Strange Land.* The Martian in the novel who tries to understand this strange land, Earth, tries to "grok" his new experiences. *Grokking* means com-plete identification, total understanding, a participatory knowledge that requires a momentary fusion of two beings into a larger shared awareness. The neognosticism we are discussing here presupposes that critical or scientific thinking is itself a form of ignorance from which we need to be liberated.

Ignorance is darkness. As dawn broke under the Bodhi tree in ancient India, Gautama awakened to the light; he became "the en-lightened one." Historically, the transformation we seek has been called an "awakening." We have been mistaking our dream world for reality. We are sleepwalking. What we need to do is awaken to new insight, to see the world in the light of truth.

Jacob Needleman, who has become an overt gnostic through his study of esoteric religions and his discipleship to G. I. Gurdjieff, uses the term "sleep" to describe the situation of the modern mind from which we need to be awakened. The modern separation of the sacred from the secular plus modern indulgence in materialism and pragmatism has made us insensitive to the sacred impulse. Modern scientism and naturalism so dominate that the insights of the tra-

What we need, says Needleman with considerable conviction, is a gnosis that is salvific. To be salvific, it needs to be not only true but also effective. He puts the challenge this way:

What, precisely, is needed in order to awaken contemporary man? Or, in other terms, what is needed in our time for gnosis to be effective, for there to exist a salvational knowledge that actually brings about spiritual change in the midst of the material world as we actually find it?[64]

En route to answering this question, Needleman notes that saving gnosis contains two elements: first, knowledge of the supernal order of liberation—that is, the fundamental truth about the cosmic order; and second, knowledge of the infernal order of bondage—that is, an understanding of the condition of our modern fallenness into darkness and suffering. Then he presses on: such knowledge must have practical power if it is to be transformatory. We need more than ideas about the truth. We need something that works.

Needleman wants to begin where science begins, yet avoid ending up where science has ended up, namely, in scientism. Where science begins is with the impulse for truth—which is at bottom an impulse for the sacred. The transformatory gnosis we seek can be pursued if we can but open ourselves to the truth that transcends our modern Western civilization. If we open ourselves to what Needleman calls "great learning," then we will gain the power that will lead us inward; and as we travel inward we will gain a greater sense of the cosmos of which we are a genuine part. In short, the transformative awakening can be pursued through true learning.

Marilyn Ferguson finds this awakening in direct knowledge and in new paradigms. By "direct knowledge" she means a mystical or quasi-mystical experience of the whole. It is not that the world of appearances that we may study objectively and scientifically is wrong. It is rather that if you can penetrate through the system of things you can communicate directly with the whole. "Direct knowledge gets us out of the system. It is the awakening. It reveals the context that generates our lesser reality. The new perspective alters our experience by changing our vision."[65]

With a new mind, a new consciousness, we can transform ourselves. We obtain this new mind by reinterpreting our world through new paradigms. "We live what we know," writes Ferguson. "If we believe the universe and ourselves to be mechanical, we will live mechanically. On the other hand, if we know that we are part of an open universe, and that our minds are a matrix of reality, we will live more creatively and powerfully."[66] If we can awaken to our true nature—as free and creative—then we can choose to become new creatures. If we draw upon the resources already lying deep within us, upon our potentialities, then we can create a new vision of how the world should work. We can live that way. The mechanism of modernity will become history, past history.

8. Jesus, Sometimes

There are three ways in which the name of Jesus Christ may come up in new age spirituality, one negative and two positive. Negatively, Jesus represents the narrow-minded loyalties of an outdated and spiritually desolate Christian religion. Christianity has become a foil, a form of external religiosity that new agers are supposed to reject in favor of a more authentic internal spirituality. But new age teachers employ Jesus Christ in positive ways as well. First, as a symbol, Christ can be used as a cipher for the experience of psychological growth. Second, as a teacher, Jesus can play the role of the gnostic guru. Let us look at these two positive uses in turn.

The dying and rising Christ can symbolize the psychological experience of dying to one's old inhibited self and rising to a new expanded consciousness. This is clear in the induced experience of being reborn. One of the Esalen exercises led by psychologist Ronald Laing is birthing. Here a group of participants weave their bodies together in a line to form a pressurized tunnel wall. One participant, stripped and crawling, squirms through the simulated birth canal. Upon emerging from the resistant darkness into the liberating light, the neonate is showered with caressing care by the other participants. The parallel between the dark womb and the death tomb, plus the affinity between emergent birth and resurrection from the dead, does not go unnoticed.

In some ways, one might speculate that the whole new age movement represents a cultural rebirthing in the Western mind. It is an attempt to return to our roots, to inquire about the basic grounding of things. The postmodern critics of modern scientized society are dissatisfied with the cramped boxes into which we have forced the human psyche. They wonder why we have to live with the dualisms of subject vs. object, science vs. art, male vs. female. Why, they ask, should we tolerate such dualisms when at a deeper level we can experience the whole of things? They are suspicious that our inherited dogmatisms regarding the nature of reality might be superficial because they disregard the deeper personal dimensions. All this leads our socially conscious new agers not simply to rebellion but to the effort to rethink—or better, re-attend to our basic underlying experience—and then seek to rebuild. We have to return to our primitive womb and then reemerge with a new vision of reality, with a new cosmology.

This is what is felt so personally by new age seekers. What applies cosmically applies microcosmically. What is true for modern society is true for modern individuals. Like business executives who leave their offices for a two-week stress management seminar, new age people feel the need to step out of their ordinary structured existence and enter into another realm in hopes of finding renewal. It is not uncommon for these individuals to report a breakdown of some sort—illness, divorce, failure to achieve professional advancement, emotional disturbance—that causes them to lose faith in the given structures of daily social life. They enter into what anthropologist Victor Turner calls a "liminal" phase, a time-out in which to explore an "anti-structure" that violates the rules and routines of normal social involvement. It is during these liminal phases that the quester reassesses the structure of the old age and seeks foundations for a new age; or, more dramatically, seeks personal healing that consists in a dying to the old and a rising to the new. Once this principle is apprehended, the image of Jesus entering the tomb on Good Friday and emerging on Easter with new life takes on archetypal meaning.

What starts out as a secular avoidance of the inherited religious tradition cannot help but return to a reappreciation of its basic symbols, especially the symbols of the cross and resurrection of Jesus Christ. David Toolan notes how frequent references to scatological images in Esalen therapy serve to drive a person to hit bottom, to empty himself or herself of all sense of innate dignity, so that he or she might rise up toward a transcendent fullness.

The scatological element arises with experiences of swallowing filth and excrement, crawling in cesspools and sewage systems, drowning in blood, phlegm, and urine. Willingly, at this stage, the god-self must descend into all the mess which it has spurned and denied in the vain quest to gain self-made immortality. . . . Such images portend what a creaturely unconscious understands: the annihilation of experience at all levels, physical, emotional, intellectual, ethical, and even transcendental. But physical death, like biological birth, is but figure; the essential transaction at this stage, though the body is implicated, is a spiritual death-rebirth.[67]

The most common symbolic framework for this experience, reports Esalen LSD practitioner Stanislav Grof, is Christ's death on the cross and his resurrection plus the mystery of Good Friday and the unveiling of the Holy Grail.[68] To be reborn is to be resurrected. In the new age dawning at Esalen, death and resurrection do not apply to what happened to Jesus twenty centuries ago. They apply to our own spiritual experience today.

Moving beyond the apron strings of mother Esalen, the more overtly religious new age groups go beyond the use of Jesus as an archetypal cipher, although not far beyond. If and when Jesus appears, his role is the one he played in ancient gnosticism—namely, he is the teacher of the gnosis. In this case, he teaches primarily by example. He represents the protohuman, the one who has developed his innate human potential to its fullest actualization. He has fanned his divine spark into a full flame.

For David Spangler, formerly a teacher at Findhorn in Scotland and now a free-lance lecturer on the new age in North America, for example, Christ is the prototype or the expression of the universal cosmic consciousness inherent in us all, and indeed in all that lives. On a planetary level, from the heart and mind of God emerges a stream of living energy that is the dynamic evolutionary impulse that propels everything toward greater intensity of life. Christ, as Buddha before him, answered the call to move beyond the limits of his isolated selfhood and realize his oneness with the universal stream of divine energy. In doing so he revealed the divine potential within us and available to all of us.

Moreover, Christ released into human history a special presence of divinity from which we can draw to facilitate the process of realizing our own divinity. In fact, the world today is much closer to entering the Aquarian age than it was two thousand years ago because of this. Spangler focuses on Jesus' words to the effect that when two or more are gathered together in his name, there is the Christ. We are moving beyond individual consciousness to group consciousness, beyond ego to communion. In the interaction of two people in relationship, Christ is either made manifest or he is not made manifest, depending on whether that relationship effects wholeness or whether it increases separation. We are moving toward the Aquarian age now because in twos, threes, fives, and millions, souls are beginning to unite in a vast communion—that is, they are realizing the Christ force leading the flow toward oneness.[69]

This is also the theme of the old but now popular book, *The Aquarian Gospel of Jesus*.[70] Here it is reported that in the missing years between Jesus' twelfth birthday and the beginning of his teaching career around age thirty, he went to India. There he studied mystical esoterica at the feet of Hindu gurus. This he brought back to Palestine. The reason we normally do not associate such teachings with Jesus is that the established churches with their orthodox theology have conspired to keep this knowledge from the general public.

The Aquarian Gospel of Jesus, published first in 1907 and recently reprinted, is part of a wider genre that probably began in 1894 with the publication of *La Vie inconnue de Jésus Christ* (*The Unknown Life of Jesus Christ*) by a Russian journalist, Nicolas Notovitch.[71] Notovitch claims he journeyed to the Tibetan Himalayas and visited the Buddhist monastery at Himis. Here he claims to have read and translated an ancient document that records the pilgrimage to India by the teenage Jesus, whom they called "Saint Issa." According to the document now published in English, Jesus studied the Vedas and then chastised the Brahman priests for caste prejudice, arguing that the sacred scriptures should be available to the lower castes as well as the upper. This appears to be an import into the Indian setting of Jesus' egalitarianism recorded in the New Testament. In fact, the whole document seems to be a contrived history based on extrapolations of the New Testament picture of Jesus. It shows little or no sensitivity to the deeper insights of the Vedic tradition. Because it includes a report of Jesus' death under

Pontius Pilate, it has to have been written after Jesus' career was over. It could not have been written at the time that Jesus was actually in India. When Notovitch was criticized on this, he responded that perhaps the document was written later by St. Thomas. The veracity of this and other similar books that followed is doubtful.

How does this relate to the new age? It is important because contemporary new age advocates want to draw the connection between Jesus and the Asian spirituality they promote. The use of Jesus' name just may give Hindu and Buddhist doctrines credibility to Western audiences.

This is certainly what Elizabeth Clare Prophet does. She relies on books such as that of Nicolas Notovitch to buttress her claim that what Jesus really teaches is what was taught in ancient India.[72] She affirms belief in Jesus Christ and labels herself a Christian; but it is clearly a gnostic version of Christianity. She contends that in the ancient battle between gnosticism and Christian orthodoxy, the wrong side won. The orthodox Christians, she says, were just seeking power for the clergy, so they repressed the *true* teachings of Jesus that require no clergy to actualize. Church leaders hid the mystical sayings of Jesus from the people by excluding them from Scripture. The canonization of the Bible, she claims, was a tool whereby the clergy could consolidate their power.

She presents her spiritual cosmology by explicating a complex and colorful visual symbol she has created for this purpose, the violet flame. Against an evening landscape with a lighthouse beacon in the background, the picture is dominated by a translucent candle within which three figures can be discerned. The upper figure at the center of the flame, as if all the light were being emitted from this point, is the divine presence. She identifies the divine presence with the "I am" of Moses' burning bush at Mt. Sinai. It is also called the Divine Monad, so that the connection between Israel and India is made.

The middle figure is obviously Jesus, here called the "Christ Self." This is our real self, also called Christ consciousness, the higher mental body, and higher consciousness. The lowest of the three figures is our soul self, the self we live with from day to day in our ordinary experiences. It can be known by such titles as the etheric body, the mental body, the emotional body, the physical body, and so on. This soul self is presently engaged in an evolutionary advance through the four planes of matter: fire, air, water, and earth. Your and my spiritual task, according to Clare Prophet, is to balance our karma and thereby ascend to the level of Christ consciousness and then, after that, to the presence of the I AM. Once this ascension has occurred, then our soul will have become incorruptible and a permanent atom in the body of God.

Streaming directly down into the candle from the flame center is a thin beam of light. It begins with the divine I AM, extends through Jesus Christ, and ends with your or my soul self. This, says Clare Prophet, is the divine light that unites us with God. It is the spark of divinity that lies within each of us just waiting to be fanned into a brilliant flame. It is that piece of God within us that wants to go home. It lays the track that will take us back to our source, to God.

I personally find Elizabeth Clare Prophet impressive. She commands attention as the leader of her growing sect known as the Church Universal and Triumphant. She recently purchased the 33,000-acre Royal Teton Ranch in the mountains north of Yellowstone National Park. Devotees are moving in, building bomb shelters, piling up dried food, and angering their neighbors. They plan to survive what their leader has described as the dark transition from the age of Pisces to the dawning of the age of Aquarius.

Prophet carries herself like a prophet. Dressed in white behind a white podium, she carefully creates her ambiance. Directly behind her hangs a giant symbol of the divine self in the violet flame. This symbol is flanked by two large pictures, one of Jesus and the other of Saint-Germain, both of whom are made to look like Hindu swamis. She refers to herself as "Guru Ma." She asks us to visualize ourselves in a tube of light, in the fire of the violet cosmic light. Then she draws her disciples up into a liturgical chant. Her voice leads. The words are repeated with increasing speed and rising pitch. Her voice is powerful, eerie, and mesmerizing. It seems to carry the group into an ecstasy of sound and emotion. The "I AM" that refers to God, amidst the rhythm, tumbles upon and connotes the "I am" that refers to ourselves. Concentration on what is said reveals these among other words in the chants:

I AM the being of violet fire!
  I am the purity God desires!

I AM light, thou Christ in me,
  Set my mind forever free;
Violet fire, forever shine
  Deep within this heart of mine.

I AM the light of God . . .
  Blazing like a sun,
I AM God's sacred power
  Freeing everyone.

In conclusion, the Jesus of the new age is not the historical Jesus who became the Christ for the purpose of saving the human race solely by God's grace. Gone is the belief that the Good Friday cross and the Easter resurrection were historical events in which God did some work, in which God actually took action to defeat the powers of sin, death, or even Karma on our behalf. Gone is the belief that because of what Jesus Christ did we are given the forgiveness of sins and the promise of our own resurrection to eternal life. In short, the Jesus of the new age is not a savior. He is instead a teacher of mystical truths. Once we learn these mystical truths, then we ourselves can follow the Pelagian path toward enlightenment from our world of darkness, step by step, plane by plane, until we work our way up to the realm of pure light. The historical Christ need not bequeath to us much in the way of gifts of God's grace, because we ourselves, down deep, are already divine. All we need do is raise this divine potential into a divine actuality.

Conclusion

Let me reiterate that what we have identified here as the eightfold path represents the core teachings of the new age in its full and coherent philosophical form. Relatively few new age philosophers try to present the full picture, so our contact with the new age world view is ordinarily a bit more haphazard, as we bump into the human potential movement here or channeling there, or whatever. Many doors open into the new age, and when one has just entered and is still standing in the vestibule, what lies at the center of the house is yet unknown. As one moves deeper and deeper into the new age house, however, it becomes more and more apparent that it is built upon gnostic foundations with a superstructure that combines Asian mysticism with some key Western ideas such as evolution and psychological wholeness.

Just how these ideas should be evaluated is the task to come. Whether they should be embraced fully or rejected outright is the way the question is frequently posed. In the next chapter we will survey some recent religious reactions to the new age. We will note that some Christian conservatives are vehement in their rejection of new age gnosticism, even saying that it belongs to the work of the Antichrist. On the other end of the spectrum, some contemporary advocates of Christian spirituality are intentionally incorporating new age doctrines and psychotechnologies into their religious programs. It will be my own assessment that neither a bald bashing nor a broad baptizing of the whole new age is the way to go.

Rather, I think we need to sort through the various dimensions of the movement. In doing this, I have come to believe that the overall gnostic thrust of the new age is a big mistake. It leads to a naive and excessively innocent view of reality. It fails to acknowledge the strength of the powers of destruction and evil that are at work in the cosmos and in our own personalities, an acknowledgment that to me means two things. First, the cosmic wholeness we seek lies in the future, not at some level of essential reality we can reach through cultivating higher consciousness. Second, to combat the destructive powers, we need a power greater than ourselves. This, Christians claim, comes from God. It comes in the form of grace. The dynamic movement of grace is at best approximated in Willis Harman's notion of inspirational breakthroughs, but in general it is underdeveloped in new age thinking. To this concern Christian leaders should have something significant to say.

On the other hand, there is much in new age spirituality to commend it. Its protest against the excessive mechanism of modernity and our Western tendency to bifurcate the human person into a physical body separate from subjective consciousness constitutes a salutary critique. We do need to pursue a greater integration of the physical and the spiritual in all dimensions of life. It seems to me that Christian faith and the striving for integrative wholeness are natural complements of each other, and that the new age has much to teach us in this regard.

Chapter Three

Religious Reactions: Demonic! Divine!

 I was meeting her at the Coffee Connection. It's a little place on Euclid Avenue just north of the Cal Berkeley campus that sells capuccino or, if you are in a mood for nutrition, fruit smoothies. Along with LaVals Pizzeria across the street, it's my office. This is where I meet students, strangers, colleagues, and others.

This woman had telephoned for an appointment and sounded very eager to talk. She called me because she wanted to check out her experience with a theologian, but she needed a listener who would be receptive to discussing awkward topics. Someone gave her my name. We met. Over our coffee cups she explained that she was a former divinity student at a small seminary in Canada. She indicated that she was a small-town girl and thought of herself as very shy. Her professional preparations committee had recommended that she defer ordination for a year or so while she "worked" on her personality. She had decided at this point to come to California to study for a year at the feet of a well-known guru in Christian spirituality. I knew the program. It was a version of Esalen blended with Christian mysticism.

This was April. Her year was almost over. Things were going badly. She had come to California with high hopes; but those hopes had been dashed.

Having read books by the guru leader, she had arrived in the fall filled with enthusiasm. She quickly became a disciple. She could mouth the group's platitudes and defend its position in the papers she was writing. She was receiving A's on all her academic work. Her relationships with the faculty were warm and supportive, and she felt she was genuinely growing. Then came the fateful day when, in a scholarly paper she was writing, she offered a criticism of one of the master guru's favorite mystics. The reaction was swift and devastating. He turned on her with unexpected anger. He said her scholarship was faulty. He was rejecting her work, and she began to feel that he was rejecting her as well. Or was the threat of rejection a manipulative device to bring her back into line? She could not tell for certain. She did note that the master teacher was no longer available to speak to her. He asked his intermediaries to communicate with her so that there would be no face-to-face conversation.

"Everyone is supposed to think just one way," she told me. "If you don't, then pow!"

She had decided not to capitulate. Evidently she had enough fiber in her own constitution that she could stand up to the situation with courage. But because this event had suddenly challenged her world view, her view of reality, she was somewhat disoriented. She felt she needed to check herself by talking with someone who might understand but who was outside the group. She wanted my feedback. Was she sane? Was she standing on solid ground? Was she right in standing up for the independence of her own judgment?

"The program is wimpy," she complained. "In one semester seminar, all we read were two books, one by Ken Wilber and the other Roberto Assagioli's *Psychosynthesis*. And they have the nerve to call this a graduate program?" I could see she was gaining considerable personal strength and that she would eventually leave the program with an independent spirit. Good. She was getting out before any damage could be done.

This leads us into the issue of whether and to what degree new age spirituality can be incorporated into a Christian way of life. Opinions vary. Some voices from the right wing of Christianity denounce everything that even hints of new age influence. At the other end of the spectrum, we find endorsement of a neognostic version of Christianity as well as actual practices that synthesize traditional

Christian mysticism with new age spirituality. The theological student from Canada had confronted the latter. No doubt she was a believer in her spiritual practices. The problem she confronted had to do with the personality of her guru professor, a person who obviously wanted to maintain control over the newly constructed orthodoxy of his students.

The spectrum of religious reactions to the new age is quite wide. On the negative side, one way is to look through the eyes of conservative theology and think of new age teaching as heterodox, perhaps even demonic. This is the view of the Blue Army of Fatima, a group of zealous Roman Catholics. In the summer of 1990 the Blue Army protested and picketed a colleague of mine, Dr. Paul Clasper, who was simply trying to sort through new age concerns while leading an Anglican retreat. Blue Army spokespersons said that the new age is "The Devil's own philosophy." According to this view, what is wrong with the new age is that it teaches the wrong things.

A quite different negative way is to look at what happens to these teachings when they appear within the framework of a cult. What the seminarian from Canada was confronting was in fact the authoritarianism endemic to a rigid organization that could develop into a cult. In an actual cult setting, only those who agree with the group's espoused orthodoxy and who remain under the thumb of the master teacher may remain in the inner circle. What makes this demonic is that in the name of an open and free spirituality, religious demagoguery is practiced. This, in my judgment, is perhaps the greatest danger.

On the positive end of the spectrum are some fascinating attempts at apparent syncretism and even a whole reassessment of the foundations of Christianity.[1] Jesus is viewed less as the fulfillment of Old Testament expectation and more in terms of his spiritual continuity with ancient India or the esoteric and mystical traditions.

These are creative times for Christian thinking, and the new age orientation of some of our leaders is, in my judgment, most stimulating. Nevertheless, we must remember that leading Christian thinkers in the time of the Roman Empire found they could not get along with gnosticism because it denied the fullness of God's incarnation. Should history repeat itself? Do we need to reject gnosticism again on the same grounds? The neognosticism of today's new age has a much higher evaluation of the physical world than did its ancient predecessor. Is this enough to make it palatable to us? Before we address these questions directly, let us take a look at a most interesting array of responses to the new age stimulus.

Hidden Dangers in the Rainbow

Look at those cheery rainbow decals on automobile windows and children's school notebooks. They are symbols of innocence, simplicity, optimism, and good will. According to Genesis 6–8, the rainbow is the symbol of God's covenantal promise that the Earth will not be destroyed by flood. Yet hidden beneath the rainbow are dangers. The new age movement is said by some critics to be using rainbows to signify their building of the rainbow bridge (*antahkarana*) between the human race and the oversoul, whom these critics name Lucifer.

This warning is being given by Detroit attorney Constance E. Cumbey, who is launching a virulent attack against the new age. She has toured much of North America, giving standing-room-only lectures to Evangelical audiences. She titles her book *The Hidden Dangers of the Rainbow: The New Age Movement and Our Coming Age of Barbarism*. She opens her book by identifying her fundamental contention that the new age will bring in the aeon of the Antichrist.

> For the first time in history there is a viable movement—the New Age Movement—that truly meets all the scriptural requirements for the Antichrist and the political movement that will bring him on the world scene. . . . The Antichrist's appearance could be a very real event in our immediate future.[2]

Hiding behind a multicolored aura of respectability, the new age movement is actively recruiting unsuspecting Jews and Christians to work for their own destruction and for the destruction of the world as we know it, according to Cumbey. So, with a great sense of personal mission and Christian fervor, Cumbey sets out to wake us up to the portent afoot: "The Christian world—myself included—has been blissfully asleep for too long. It is time that somebody sounds the alarm—awaking sleeping Christians to this Movement and warning innocent participants to come out of it."[3]

Cumbey traces the roots of the current new age movement to the establishment of the Theosophical Society in the West in 1875. As noted in a previous chapter, under the leadership of H. P. Blavatsky, the theosophists sought an integration of Indian and Western metaphysics that engaged in a frontal attack on the monotheism of Judaism, Christianity, and Islam. The God of monotheism, said the theosophists, is the creation of human imagination. It is not the ever-unknowable reality we learn of in Hinduism. What we find in religions such as Christianity is a "blasphemous and sorry caricature of the ever unknowable."[4]

Having located its roots in Mme Blavatsky, Cumbey traces its growth through the careers of Annie Besant and Krishnamurti to Alice Bailey. Theosophists claimed that the masters of "the Great White Brotherhood" were using such leaders as chosen vehicles for inculcating the esoteric knowledge that the world needs if it is to rise to the true enlightenment, the enlightenment of the one whose name means light, Lucifer. The doctrines Alice Bailey taught, such as reincarnation and the innate divinity of the human being, Cumbey calls "the standard lies of the serpent of Garden of Eden days!"[5] The Theosophical Society established the Lucifer Publishing Company in 1922, which has since changed its name to Lucis Publishing Company, perhaps to hide the otherwise obvious.

Cumbey believes that the Luciferian dedication of the theosophists lives on in the contemporary enterprises of David Spangler in the United States and his confrers in the new age community at Findhorn, Scotland, as well as the Buddhist followers of Maitreya, the Planetary Initiative for the World We Choose, and other vaguely similar groups or individuals. She is suspicious of organizations such as Amnesty International, the Sierra Club, Children of God, Zero Population Growth, Bread for the World, and others. She attacks new age thinkers such as G. I. Gurdjieff, Pierre Teilhard de Chardin, P. D. Ouspensky, H. G. Wells, Nicholas Roerich, and Marilyn Ferguson. New age conspirators, she says, have infiltrated government and industry, are confusing our people with astrological horoscopes, hiding their destructive work behind ruses such as projects to feed the hungry. What she objects to is that "they openly and boldly set forth plans for a new mandatory world religion—a religion completely breaking with the concept of Jesus as the Christ and God as the Father."[6]

Satan is the spirit behind the new age, says Cumbey. This is made possible because of Satan's uncanny ability to disguise himself as an angel of light (2 Cor. 11:14), so although we may think of ourselves as getting enlightenment, we are really getting the enemy of God. What we earlier described as the experience of cosmic wholeness, Cumbey recognizes as "an experience of overpowering beauty and glory." The problem here is that the immensity of the experience may lead us falsely into thinking we have come into contact with the Lord. Writes Cumbey, "God recognized our vulnerability in this area and for this reason wisely commanded his people not to get involved in occult practices. Deception has been Satan's game since the Garden of Eden, and our times are no exception." She believes the overpowering religious experiences belong to the "great signs and wonders" we can expect from the coming Antichrist.[7]

Cumbey pits the teachings of new age occultism against those of orthodox Christianity. Whereas the Bible teaches that each person must die once and then face judgment, the doctrine of reincarnation teaches that each of us must live and die many times and then, we hope, attain nirvana. Whereas the Bible teaches that Jesus made a perfect sacrifice to secure salvation for all, today's occultists teach that we must all make our own atonement under the inexorable law of karma. Whereas the Bible teaches that Jesus Christ is the light of the world, new age mystics tell us that the light comes from our own higher selves. Whereas the Bible speaks of only one Christ, occultists tell us there have been many Christs.[8] In short, in Cumbey's view no reconciliation whatsoever is possible between what Christians teach about Jesus Christ and new age occultism. To think that there can be rapprochement is to be a victim of deception, a deception that originates with Satan himself.

One very confusing and misleading accusation Cumbey makes is that the new agers are anti-Semitic. She even goes so far as to identify them with Nazism. She says new age talk about evolutionary advance "is chillingly reminiscent of Hitler's 'master race' theories."[9] She writes,

> Jews are no better off with the New Agers than they were under their predecessors the Nazis. The New Agers also maintain the

traditional occult doctrine of a blood taint resting on those of Jewish extraction.[10]

The Movement is profoundly antisemitic, all the way through to its
esoteric core. . . . The Movement's theoreticians, including Spangler,
also speak freely of the need to maintain Aryan purity—which was
Hitler's justification for exterminating the Jews.[11]

I see no evidence that the new age is associated with Germany's
Third Reich. Alice Bailey, who claimed to be channeling Tibetan
wisdom in the 1930s and 1940s, spoke out vehemently against Hitler and his cruel oppression. With regard to the Jewish question,
many new age advocates, such as Barbara Marx Hubbard, come
from Jewish families. Most contemporary Jewish people are acutely
aware of the history of the Holocaust and extremely careful about
identifying even the slightest tendencies toward any repeat of past
atrocities. The essential doctrines of the new age are wholistic, inclusive, and peace promoting. They do not depend for their strength
on cultivating prejudice or hatred of any group, least of all the Jews.

Among those whom Cumbey attacks is Marilyn Ferguson, author of *The Aquarian Conspiracy*. Cumbey says Ferguson is culpable
because she teaches "blatant pantheism." Cumbey goes on to denounce new age teachers who are subtle, who attempt to clothe new
age concepts in Christian language. They cheat by expanding the
definition of Christ to give pagan gods equal time with Jesus. They
use the symbol of Christ to identify their own inner essence. So what
may sound like Christianity is really "another Gospel." Ferguson is
apostate, says Cumbey, by the very fact that she denies that Jesus is
the Christ yet fosters Christ consciousness as a higher state of mind.
To Cumbey's mind, this is evidence that Ferguson is supporting the
Antichrist.

Yet Ferguson wants to defend herself and does so. Cumbey, to
her own credit, publishes in her book a letter of complaint written
by Ferguson.

It is practically ludicrous that she [Constance Cumbey] charges the
New Age (and me by association) with being anti-Christian, anti-
Judaic, and anti-Catholic. I have spoken to church groups, at Catholic universities and in a Jewish synagogue. The spirit of my writing
cannot possibly be conjectured to be antispiritual, antichrist, etc.[12]

Cumbey also attacks the organization I work for, the Graduate Theological Union in Berkeley. Established in 1962 as a courageous venture in Christian ecumenism, the GTU has brought together nine Protestant and Roman Catholic seminaries for the purpose of training clergy in a setting of interdenominational cooperation. It is in my judgment the single most successful experiment in ecumenical theological education in the world. The philosophy of the GTU is that each religious group should be true to its own roots and tradition while engaging in dialogue with others doing the same. We do not seek to blur denominational lines. We do not seek to dissolve differences into an amorphous religiosity. We like it best when Lutherans are truly Lutherans, Baptists are truly Baptists, and Roman Catholics are truly Roman Catholics. It is this combination of authentic traditions that gives the ecumenical mix its tensive and exciting flavor.

Given the nearly two millennia of competition and acrimony that have frequently existed between Christian groups, the GTU represents a precious historical moment in which genuine love and spiritual unity have been the decisive force. In recent years we have added a Center for Jewish Studies and an Institute of Buddhist Studies, which have provided an interreligious context for pursuing theology in a pluralistic world. Our world is in reality pluralistic; so I for one could not conceive of an adequate theological education that does not reflect this undeniable reality. This is one of the marvelous achievements of the GTU.

Yet Constance Cumbey does not see it this way. What I think of as a great achievement she calls "apostasy." She writes that the GTU

> has brought Catholic, Protestant, and Jewish participants together
> in a sort of commonized apostasy. In fact, they are so apostate that
> they have expanded their theological horizons to include Hinduism,
> Buddhism, Sufism, Sikhism, Feminist Spirituality, New Age groups,
> occultism, and neo-paganism and witchcraft. Their activities meet
> approval with at least one important source: *The New Conscious-
> ness Sourcebook*.[13]

Reading this passage by Cumbey puzzled me. Yes, of course, we have courses taught here by Catholics, Protestants, and Jews. We even have a Pure Land Buddhist professor. But, I had to ask myself, where did her other ideas come from? Do we really advocate Sufism, neopaganism, and witchcraft? Not to my knowledge. So I looked up her reference to *The New Consciousness Sourcebook*.[14] What Cumbey in fact is referring to is a one-inch entry citing the books we have in the GTU Library on new religious movements. Of course our library would have such books. It is a research library. But Cumbey tries to give the impression—the false impression—that the GTU indulges in apostasy.[15]

The Cult Culture:
The Dark Side of the New Age

How do we discern the spirits of new age thinking? One way is to examine what the new age teaches and then ask to what extent it complements or contradicts the Christian understanding of God and the work of salvation. However, there is a second way, a way that depends on the first but with a slightly different emphasis. Here we want to ask: what effects do these teachings have on the people who hold them? Beyond recognizing the actual ideas new age leaders have in their minds, what happens in their lives? Are these ideas helpful? Are they harmful?

On the one hand, it appears to me that the new age is for the most part harmless and, in some cases, even helpful. Even if the theology is questionable, its ebullient optimism has a way of cheering up the downcast and making a damaged ego feel good about itself.

Nevertheless, there is an identifiable dark side to the new age. It can lead to abuse, to psychological damage, even to rape and death. This is not obvious when one looks only at the pacific ideals of unity and bliss. Yet there is a danger. The danger arises when new age teachings take on a cult form. The danger of serious damage increases when an alternative religious group begins to coalesce around a single leader who becomes identified as the master teacher possessing the transcendental truth. Because the teacher becomes revered as the master, he or she is given power. Then the master takes power. Then the master exerts power. And then people get hurt.

This is a point made by Susan Rothbaum, former director of Sorting It Out (SIO), a Berkeley organization formed to aid drop-outs from religious cults. When I interviewed her, she said she her-self had interviewed more than three thousand people who have been voluntary leave-takers from nearly three hundred different cult and cultlike organizations. It is not the loose collection of new age ideas and techniques that creates the problem, she says. Rather, it is the leader-centered groups that raise people's hopes for a while only to dash them on the rocks of abuse and misused power. Susan Rothbaum, herself a practitioner of Zen Buddhism for seven years with occasional stays in a monastery, has personally experienced the cycle that has often been reported to her. The lofty teachings become centered in one individual, the guru, the perfect master. Around the perfect master revolves an inner circle of devoted disciples. Beyond is a wider circle of followers. The greatest amount of power is wield-ed in the central core, and with diminishing force the farther out one gets toward the periphery.

Groups such as est and Transcendental Meditation have hundreds of thousands of interested adherents on the periphery who have experienced only an occasional weekend seminar. Very little harm is done at this distance. Yet these groups exert considerable social pressure, drawing the neophyte deeper and deeper into the heart of darkness. As one moves from the periphery toward the center, the belief system gains more and more control. It becomes the filter through which all experience is interpreted. It becomes the criterion of truth. It becomes the matrix of reality. The social effect is to make one feel more and more alienated from former friends and previous ways of looking at things. This makes one increasingly dependent on the inner group for mutual understanding and con-solation. Concomitant with this is the progressive loss of the right to criticize. The official doctrine is presumed to be above reproach because, after all, it is the criterion of truth. At the very center is the perfect master who, by virtue of being the mediator of the per-fect wisdom, stands above criticism. Whether under the counte-nance of Werner Erhard or Maharishi or some other master, this is the master to whom one risks surrendering one's freedom. At least this is the way Rothbaum sees the process as it applies to numerous groups both large and small.

Rothbaum has identified four doctrines as danger signals. The first danger signal is the belief that all must climb a vertical ladder to attain human perfection or enlightenment. The ladder includes the seven planes of existence in gnosticism plus other such steps in various cult schemes. The very fact that salvation is alleged to be found by climbing up and out of our present existence is significant to Rothbaum. It is dangerous because it means one's present existence is unacceptable. It means one's current identity is not good enough. It implies the need to sacrifice one's physical being to rise to a higher, more spiritual plane of reality.

The second ominous teaching is the affirmation of transcendence over immanence. It is the affirmation that real truth lies in the beyond, that it cannot be found in the immediacy of our daily lives. Because the transcendent truth must be pursued by the mind or the inner spirit, the life of the body and its accompanying physical emotions becomes devalued. This results in a denial of physical embodiment.

"Now, just how is this a problem?" I pressed Rothbaum.

"It opens the door to physical abuse," she answered. The discipline of the group may include physical punishment or sexual license, yet no one objects. Why? Because they can say that the physical plane belongs to the life of the lower self, and they all are seeking fulfillment in the higher self. Any pain felt is said to belong to bad karma, and persistence in spiritual discipline is believed to eventually release us from bad karma. This leads to a loss of one's ability to recognize what is healthy and unhealthy in the situation.

According to the third ominous teaching, the path to enlightenment or salvation requires surrender of self, referring to the surrender of our ego. Now this should not be surprising. Many religions teach that our individual ego is an island of selfishness, a delusion that separates us from God or prevents us from realizing our true nature. Even Jesus taught that only one who is willing to give up life can find it; and certainly the Christian religion teaches that self-sacrificing love (*agape*) best emulates God's self-sacrificing love toward us. But what happens to this teaching in the setting of a new age cult is disturbing. The disciple is subjected to a systematic breaking down of his or her individual identity. Most cult members join because they are dissatisfied with their faults and limitations; so they are ready for a remaking process. In the cult, they believe they have found the right teaching, the right community, and the right teacher. They are willing to surrender everything to the right teacher, who, like a sculptor with skilled and loving hands, will reshape their very lives and thereby reveal the beautiful potential hidden inside them.

Following closely comes the fourth teaching, total obedience. One's guru is a perfect master to whom one submits in total obedience. The logic goes like this: You have come to the teacher because you're dissatisfied with your life. You're not sure what's wrong. You feel dimly that there must be more to life—and there is. But you're so full of your own habits and opinions that there's no room for anything new. You'd only try to squeeze whatever you heard into your old viewpoint. So we need to shake you up, help you become less attached to your rigid ideas. Then you'll be able to see reality.

The voiced assumption that sets an alternative religious group apart from the rest of the world so that it takes on the characteristics of a cult is the idea that the group in question is an island of light in a great sea of darkness. Here and only here can one find enlightenment. The society outside is lost to ignorance. And, within the alternative religious community, the light beams from a primary single source, the perfect teacher who, by virtue of his or her mediating transcendental truth, is the master. The perfect master becomes the one who, directly or indirectly, can loosen the chains that bind one's higher self to the realm of mundane ego preoccupations and false opinions.

To loosen the strong hold of debilitating opinions and a self-destructive ego, disciples in cults are taught to obey teachers even if they believe the teachers to be wrong. A Zen master told Susan to plant a tree upside down. She did it. "I wondered about the tree's welfare," she said. "Nonetheless, I found the practice useful. Combined with Zen meditation, it helped me put my thoughts in perspective. I saw that many ideas I had about the way things had to be simply weren't true."[16]

Obedience means that disciples should interpret everything that happens to them as teaching, as an opportunity to learn. If the master speaks harshly, the disciple should not think critically of the master but rather examine his or her own feelings of resentment and defense mechanisms.

"Taking everything as teaching" can be very valuable. It helps us to meet and greet life wholeheartedly. It inspires us to use every situation to learn about ourselves and to avoid wasting time resisting things that cannot be changed. This practice can become distorted, however, if it degenerates into simplistic naiveté, if it leads to mental or spiritual dependency and loses its critical edge. If a disciple is abused by a master, it is not enough to hear that "God put me on earth so that I could learn patience." This opens the door to the misuse of power, a misuse that is inevitable if one is realistic about human nature.

We all need teachers. What we do not need is coercion or abuse. How can we discern the spirits here? *The signal that a teacher has crossed the line and become an abusive master is the refusal to accept criticism.* When the community of disciples becomes emotionally fragile and intellectually dogmatic, we need to ask if dissent and disagreement can be handled without division or ostracism. Susan Rothbaum reports her suspicion when the abbot at her Zen monastery in San Francisco was discussing a chapter from the teacher's latest book. "Try to listen with your heart," he said. Susan reflected: "It sounded like he was pleading with us not to judge the book or the Teacher." Her friend and colleague at SIO, Joshua Baran, was excommunicated from the Zen monastery for maintaining his right to disagree.

Once the atmosphere of permission to criticize or disagree is removed, then the curtain is drawn and the tragic drama is ready to begin.

> When isolation is combined with the placement of absolute power in the hands of a single leader, the situation is ripe for abuse. SIO participants have reported, among other things, florid group delusions, vicious scapegoating and verbal cruelty, sexual abuse, and in once case, infant deaths due to willful neglect. . . . Having formed the habit of not criticizing the teacher "even if the whole world crumbles," members often fail to notice or respond to danger signs as their group changes over time. Deeply invested in the community

and mistrustful of the outside world, they doubt their perceptions and subscribe to the group's justifications. When they leave, they face a monumental task of reassessment.[17]

All this has monumental significance for the disciples who decide to leave the cult community. There is no peaceful way to cut the apron strings. The group and its leader utilize extreme social coercion to keep members from straying. The most salient tool is guilt. The unsure member is made to feel that his or her desire for independence is letting the entire group down. Only a selfish person who is not yet fully enlightened would think of leaving, goes the line.

Beyond guilt are the psychological threats. Leave-takers are told that once they abandon the group they will return to the darkness, that the demons of selfishness will gain the upper hand and envelop them with egoism once again. For those who have internalized the teachings of the alternative religion, such techniques work with great force. "No one is holding a loaded gun to my head," one woman told Susan Rothbaum, "but that's what it feels like."

If this threat does not work, group ostracism is the next step. The leave-taker is treated as a nonperson. The perfect teacher will no longer speak to the disciple. Other cult members look right through, avoiding eye contact. It is as if the apostate had died and dropped out of existence.

Disorientation is what leave-takers experience during the period in which they are undergoing reentry. They find themselves between two worlds, the organized world of cosmic truth they are leaving behind and the frightfully chaotic world of the open society they are entering. They find themselves caught in between. While cloistered by the alternative religious community they were taught that the outside world has no interest in, or room for, their cherished beliefs and values. "I was like in a scissors," writes a leave-taker. "I had no place to go. I was in no man's land. I was in limbo."[18]

It is difficult for the leave-taker to be certain that the choice to leave was the right one. To gain some semblance of self-confidence, he or she needs to have experiences of corroboration. If these experiences are slow in coming, then loneliness is the result. If things go well, ex-cultists suddenly discover to their amazement that people in the outside world are not as blind to deep insight as they had been led to believe. There are people in our wider society who are capable of kindness and even profundity of thought. That ordinary citizens could possess such wisdom and insight without the benefit of the alternative religious cult comes as a shock to the ex-member. This realization may even be temporarily deflating. But eventually it is refreshing and liberating.

Leave-taking itself can be an experience of growing in truth. It too can be a step toward fuller enlightenment. Susan Rothbaum makes two points regarding the lessons to be learned from this experience. First, nobody's perfect. We are all fallible, and this includes the so-called perfect master who is our teacher. What we need to learn is that no human being, no matter how enlightened, is above using power for his or her own self-aggrandizement. Once we recognize this truth, we will not subject ourselves to a destructive social arrangement in which the cult leader can abuse his or her disciples.

This discovery is both terrible and wonderful. It is terrible because if the teacher is seen as less than perfect, it means that you or I will never become perfect either. This means there is no simple path to follow, no sure road to innocence. It is also wonderful, because

> At the same time as it dashed my dreams of perfection, it released me from the burden of trying to believe the lies that dream entailed. I no longer needed to try to justify the community's actions as being "all for the best." . . . I no longer had to judge myself as a saint or a sinner—I was a learner.[19]

One problem with the pursuit of perfection is that when we measure ourselves, we always find ourselves wanting. We are not perfect. So we think of ourselves as bad. This opens us to a dependency relationship with others whom we falsely believe to have attained the perfection we so earnestly desire. What happens then is that our anxiety over our own imperfection blinds and binds; it blinds us to the truth that all people are imperfect, while it binds us to a dependent relationship that is stultifying. "It is ironic that religions perpetuate the idea that we don't see the truth because we are bad," Rothbaum says, "when in fact the fear that we are bad is one of the most binding of all beliefs."[20] It makes us susceptible to the trickery and abuse of others who can exploit our own under-nourished sense of self.

The second lasting insight offered by Susan Rothbaum is her positive appreciation for human embodiment and the feelings that are associated with it. She speaks favorably of incarnation. The problem of alternative religious cults is that this positive view of the body and the individual personality is functionally denied. Since the individual ego is seen as the source of delusion, any effort we make to find out what we feel or want is dubbed a selfish act, a detour from the path toward enlightenment. We lose the ability to discern what is naturally good for us. Cult members become numbed to their genuine feelings. Overcoming this numbness and becoming resensitized is an essential part of the task at reentry.

To be able to explore their feelings openly, leave-takers must become convinced at least partially that to do so is valid and safe. To allow themselves permission to attend to their basic perceptions and emotions, they must believe that these have something valuable and truthful to offer.

Bede

Just before the arrival of spring in 1983 a German colleague, Michael von Brück, and I were winding our way along mountain roads on a bus headed for Shantivanam in southern India. The two of us were interested in Hindu-Christian dialogue and were coming east from Ananda Ashram, where we had been conversing with Swami Satchitananda and Mother Krishnavai. A few miles west of the city of Tiruchirapalli we left the bus and walked past sari-dressed women and an ox cart drawn by a beautiful white Brahman bull with painted blue horns. Finally we passed through the gate, over which stood a sign in both English and Tamil welcoming us to the "Ashram of the Holy Trinity."

This is the ashram of Fr. Bede Griffiths, a member of the Order of St. Benedict, who has sought to foster a marriage of Asian philosophy with Christian spirituality since his arrival in India in 1955.[21] Living in a manner that reflects the surrounding economy of south India, the ashram supports itself by producing rice, coconuts, vegetables, fruit, and milk. Residents live in small circular huts with grass roofs and gather daily in a central open area near the garden for tea and conversation. Before the sunrise, they go individually to the banks of the Cauvery River, sometimes called the "Ganges of south India," where they greet the rising sun in the posture of still contemplation.

Each day during our stay we attended liturgy in the chapel, built to look like a Hindu temple. Worship includes readings from the Upanishads, the Bhagavad-Gita, St. Paul's Epistles, and the New Testament Gospels. In addition to a chapel, the ashram has a meditation center. Over the entrance the sign reads, "Om Nama Christaya." In the center of the room is an obsidian statue of Jesus—actually three figures of Jesus back to back—sitting with legs crossed, his hands on his knees, with eyes closed; that is, he is in meditation position. The words on the sign, "Om Nama Christaya," identifying the name Christ with the Sanskrit holy word *om*, have become a mantra. To meditate, one begins by reciting again and again this mantra.

At Shantivanam I met four men who told me they are Christian *sanyasin*. Traditionally the *sanyasin* have been Hindu men, usually older, who leave their family home and set out to seek *moksha* (liberation or enlightenment) by practicing yoga as hermits. Most *sanyasin* in our time travel to holy places, that is, from Hindu shrine to Hindu shrine or ashram to ashram—staying only a few nights and then moving on. They are on a religious quest, the quest to realize the oneness of Atman and Brahman and thereby to escape the wheel of rebirth. But what about *Christian sanyasin?* These individuals told me they were employing a Christian mantra in their meditation and that they were seeking a Christ-centered enlightenment. This means, among other things, that they adopt a semiascetic life-style quite similar to the Christian monastic tradition. And, of course, they are being supervised by their spiritual director, Bede Griffiths, a Benedictine monk.

We carried on some long and delightfully fascinating conversations with Father Griffiths. Born in England in 1906 and graduated from Oxford, he became disillusioned with the pace and style of life generated by an industrial economy. He entered a Benedictine monastery and dedicated his life to study and prayer. His study included, among other things, comparative religion. This brought him to India, where he has remained for three decades. He is impressive. A tall lanky man with distinguished gray hair and beard,

he sat Indian style on the portico of the small ashram library while
we discussed a broad range of topics. His philosophical platform
seems to have two planks: first, a new or postmodern age is coming
and, second, we should pursue the spiritual unity of the world's
religions.

With regard to the first, Father Griffiths says the whole world
is beginning to discover the disastrous effects of the modern system
of industrialism. It is exhausting our Earth's resources, polluting the
soil and air and water. It is threatening to destroy human life
through nuclear war. The conditions of life in the modern city are
setting us in conflict with nature and even with our own selves. The
resulting psychological tension is destined to lead us either to internal breakdown or perhaps into a destructive war. Present civilization
is set on a course leading to disaster.

The reason we teeter on the brink of disaster is that Western
science and technology are based on a false philosophy, says
Griffiths. They are based on the belief, for which René Descartes
was the spokesperson, that there is a material world, extended in
space and time, that exists independently of human consciousness;
and, further, that the human mind can examine this world objectively and thereby arrive at a knowledge of "reality." This knowledge, it is purported, will give us moderns control over the world.
But this is wrong, and scientific insight itself is showing it to be
wrong. It assumes a divorce of human consciousness from nature
that does not exist. Only a radical change in the fundamental assumptions of the modern Western mind can help us.

On this point a new hope is dawning. A revolt against the whole
modern industrial system is afoot. Many people recognize that we need
a new beginning. The new postindustrial movement extends throughout the world among people of all religions and of no religion. It
consists of a reassessment of science and technology with the aim of
learning to live in harmony with nature rather then merely exploiting
it. Human relations are seen to be more important than material progress. The quality of life is seen to be more important than large-scale
organization and efficiency. Most significant philosophically, it is a
movement toward a unified vision of life. This vision pictures us humans and nature as part of a single inclusive cosmic order—what in
ancient India was called *rita* and in ancient China *tao*—an order of life
that relates us to nature and also to the eternal realm of transcendence,

on which both we and nature depend for our existence. In short, we are rediscovering that nature is sacred.

> Living close to nature is very important. For me the great discovery in India is the discovery of the sacred. In India everything is sacred: the earth is sacred; food, water, and taking a bath are all sacred, a building is sacred. Here one is still living in the old "sacral" universe, which means everything to me.[22]

This sense of the sacred can be found in many religions, including Christianity. This desire to locate the common unity of the world's religions constitutes the second of Father Griffiths' two preoccupations. Central here is the path of truth. Griffiths believes we should acknowledge truth wherever it is found. And there is truth—at least implicit truth—in every religious tradition. "If we believe that in Christ is to be found the revelation of Truth itself," he writes, "then we must recognize that all truth wherever it is to be found is contained implicitly in Christianity."[23] Griffiths assumes that each of the great religious traditions can refer us to genuine truth as it exists in basic human experience prior to misleading overlays of dogma, and that once we ascertain this experiential truth we will see how it comes to fulfillment in Jesus Christ.

What this means at Shantivanam is that the Vedanta tradition in Hinduism plays a role akin to the Hebrew scriptures in looking forward to the coming of Christ. The Upanishads replace the Old Testament. We begin with the recognition of divine mystery and move up to the level of articulation in culturally conditioned formulations. The assumption here is that exoterically, religious traditions differ greatly; that is, they have quite different doctrines and practices due to their distinctive cultural histories. But at the esoteric level, there is only one true or absolute religious vision.

> At the deepest level I don't find anything incompatible. The deeper you go into Hinduism or Buddhism, the more you see how there's a fundamental unity with Christianity. On the surface there are many differences and contradictions, and even below the surface there are still problems. But the deeper you go, the more you converge on this One. That is my vision of the future: that in each religion, as you go deeper into it, you converge on the original Source.[24]

Griffiths is not advocating syncretism, uniting differing religious practices at the exoteric or surface level. Rather, the Benedictine swami wishes to penetrate the surface of all religious traditions to find their esoteric or absolute core. "There is only one absolute religion and that is the religion of the Holy Spirit, which is the Spirit of love," he writes; and it is present in some measure in every religion and in every human being.[25] This inner truth is drawing all of us toward a transcendent unity; and it will succeed if we only yield to this draw.

Within this framework Griffiths advocates what he calls "true gnosis." This is the gnosis that exists *within* the Church. By it he refers to the mystical understanding for which we find precedents in Clement of Alexandria, Origen, St. Gregory of Nyssa, and especially Dionysius the Pseudo-Areopagite, who incorporated the esoteric wisdom of Platonism into Christianity. We need to recapture this premodern mysticism and bring it to bear on modern secularism. What we find in India has a validity of its own; yet it also reminds us of the mystical wealth buried within our own tradition. The end toward which Griffiths is working is a synthesis of mysticism— whether that mysticism comes from the ancient West or the contemporary East—with the natural sciences. He believes the challenge today is to create a Christian theology that uses the findings of modern science as well as Eastern mysticism.[26]

When it comes to the doctrine of God, Griffiths belongs in the camp of classical theism. On this point, he can find both agreement and disagreement between East and West. St. Thomas Aquinas would agree, for example, with the Vedas and the Upanishads that the primal mystery of the cosmos—God—is beyond naming. The nearest you can come to a name for God, says Thomas, is "Being." God is the "I Am." This is reminiscent of the *Katha* Upanishad, which says, "How can we speak of him except by saying he *is?*"

In the Hindu tradition, the divine is understood as *sat-chit-ananda,* the state of being-knowledge-bliss that belongs to pure consciousness. This is fine as far as it goes. But the object of Christian faith is more than a state of consciousness. The Christian needs to add something to our understanding of God here, according to Griffiths. What he wants to add is the divine communion of *love.* This is where the doctrine of the Trinity comes in. God is being, to be sure. God is knowledge and bliss, to be sure. Yet the being of

God is constantly communicating itself through love. Within the Godhead itself there is communion, a personal relationship among the three members of the Trinity. God is essentially relational. This Christian insight goes beyond what one can find in the other religious traditions.

There is another important difference. In Asia, what we call sin is considered ignorance. One's relation to God is thought to be a problem of consciousness, and our task is to raise ourselves to higher and higher levels of consciousness. But for Jews and Christians, our relation to God is determined by the dialectic of sin and grace. Whereas ignorance and consciousness are problems of the mind, sin lies in the will. "I would agree with the Semitic view," says Father Bede, "that the fundamental difference—what separates us from God—is in the will."[27]

Indeed, much needs to be done in restructuring our human consciousness. Father Griffiths begins with meditation, with focused discipline. But this is just the beginning. He wants this to lead toward a waking consciousness of one's oneness with nature and, further, one's oneness with the sacred dimension within nature. This should become a daily or even a moment-by-moment awareness. Though it may take a religious experience of the oceanic type—a moment of grace—to break through the routine of daily life, we will not understand reality until we become aware that there is another dimension beneath what we see and hear. We can apprehend our life in its true perspective only when we see it in relation to eternity, only when we are freed from the flux of time and see the eternal order underneath. The esoteric truth will be revealed when we realize that "we are no longer isolated individuals in conflict with our surroundings; we are parts of a whole, elements in a universal harmony."[28] This is a compelling and beautiful vision, to be sure.

Had the new age consciousness not arisen, Bede would probably have still taken this road. What originally elicited his interest was the path of truth as it winds its way through the classic religious traditions of Asia. Bede has been somewhat of a pioneer, a trail blazer. After some time, many new age seekers have taken notice of this Benedictine pioneer and are considering joining him on the path. Because of its roots in both classical Asian mysticism and classical Christian theism, Father Griffiths' thought represents perhaps the most serious proposal for a new age syncretism. As we turn to the work of Jacob Needleman, we will find a less serious though quite interesting proposal, a proposal to revive Christianity in gnostic form.

Needleman's Gnostic Christianity

In 1980 Jacob Needleman published *Lost Christianity: A Journey of Rediscovery to the Center of Christian Experience.* It was widely read, and it certainly intrigued me. To think that in this book I might find the "center" of Christian experience was an invitation I could not resist. I read it immediately. So did a number of my colleagues. We invited Needleman to a meeting of the Pacific Coast Theological Society and made his book the focus of a two-day analysis and evaluation. The discussion would turn out to be a good one.

Needleman is a professor of philosophy at San Francisco State University and for a number of years directed the Center for the Study of New Religious Movements at the Graduate Theological Union in Berkeley. He became widely known in the late 1960s through the publication of his book *The New Religions.* He is of Jewish background and respected for his work on the cults and their teachings. The intriguing question was: What has Jerry discovered about Christianity?

The specialist in new religions had traced the increasing influence of Asian mysticism on American soil. Somehow, he conjectured, this was serving to slake a thirst. The modern West has been going through a spiritual dry spell since the rise of natural science and its accompanying naturalism, secularism, and the quantification of everything of value. Cut off from religious roots, the spiritual sensibilities of the modern world were drying and dying on the vine. By turning East, the younger generation of the 1960s was hoping for a rerooting, a new grounding in transcendent reality. But was it necessary to go to the Orient to do this? This was the question Needleman began to ask in his book on Christianity. His answer was no. Why? Because "everything I had seen in the Eastern teachings was also contained in Judaism and Christianity, although the language of the Bible was practically impossible to penetrate, because it had become so encrusted with familiar associations."[29]

The task he set himself was to get beneath the encrustations of familiar associations to the original and recoverable secret doctrine of the Christian faith, the hidden fountain that would slake the same thirst that was taking America's young people to the pools of Hinduism and Buddhism. This fountain he called the "esoteric tradition" within Christianity. By "esoteric" he meant something effective, something that "works, that actually produces real change in human nature, real transformation."[30] What kind of search could be more exciting!

In the book's introduction Needleman reports on a conference in the Orient where he met a Christian monk and mystic named Father Sylvan, who, fortuitously, personally embodied and taught the very esoteric brand of Christianity he was looking for. This "unforgettable man," Father Sylvan, was "overflowing" with ideas and information about "worlds upon worlds of Christianity that neither I nor anyone else I had met knew anything about." Needleman reports that he told the gentle mystic, "What I need to understand is, what is the *heart* of Christianity? There must be such a heart, an inner core."[31] The monk agreed and announced that he too had been on such a search for the heart, which he believed to be now hidden, lost. Later the priest died and left a thousand pages of mystical musings for Professor Needleman to decipher. On the basis of Father Sylvan's legacy and Needleman's analysis, the remainder of the book searches out, finds, and explains Christianity's heart, its central core.

At the central core is Christian gnosis. Gnosis, says Needleman, is salvational knowledge, knowledge that transforms the life and being of the human race. He uses the Greek *gnosis* to translate the Hebrew word *da'ath*, "an extremely intimate kind of knowledge involving the whole man, not just the mind."[32] To realize this is to solve the age-old dichotomy between faith and reason. There is no distinction between these two, he says. The important distinction rather is between consciousness of one's own state and the unconscious actions of both thought and emotion. To choose between reason and faith is to miss the point. Self-attention is the point. It is self-attention that leads us not to an explanation of things but rather to the kind of knowledge that makes things different. This means, among other things, that gnostic Christianity is not Christian gnosticism. It is the *-ism* that bothers Father Sylvan and

Jacob Needleman. Gnosti*c*ism, they say, is the perversion of gnosis into a doctrinal system. "Gnosticism," says Father Sylvan, "is not a heresy of the Church, but a heresy of gnosis."[33]

The central theological problem, says Needleman, is that traditional religion has misled us regarding knowledge of God. We have been told by religious spokespersons that God is beyond the comprehension of the human mind. But what is not made clear here is that the mind can in fact "comprehend" God; it can form a thought of God. As in the case of trying to think about a difficult-to-master scientific theory, we can think about God, even if we find it difficult to grasp completely the nature of God. The problem is not the ambiguity regarding our ability or nonability to comprehend God with the human intellect. Rather, the problem is that the very presentation of this issue directs our attention away from the real issue.

The real issue does not have to do with the development of the isolated intellect, with explanations of reality. Rather, it has to do with transformatory knowing, with gnosis. The way to get to this gnosis is to attend to the forces at work within the human self; most particularly, to the force within each of us that drives us toward the truth of being.

When we fail to yield to this inner impulse toward truth, we fall. What we fall into is trusting our ordinary mind or intellect. At the level of the ordinary mind we find the Church's beliefs, its doctrines and practices bequeathed to us through the tradition. The problem is that the ordinary mind is only part of a greater whole. "The real enemy," writes Needleman, "is man's tendency to give his trust to what is only a part of the mind or self, to take the part for the whole, to take a subsidiary element of human nature as the bringer of unity or wholeness of being."[34]

When we yield to this inner impulse toward truth, we are living in faith. When Needleman uses the word *faith* he does not mean belief, of course. He is not referring to Christian doctrines, which exist at the level of the ordinary mind or intellect. In the historical stream of the Christian tradition, we have been asked to believe with our minds and conform to the moral rules and religious rituals laid down by the Church. What has not been required is that we be innerly active. Needleman wants *faith* to refer to inner activity. Faith in the sense of trusting the inner impulse is actually "opposed" to the whole of the ordinary mind, including both reason and belief as they are conventionally defined. True faith belongs to the esoteric or gnostic Christianity, which had been lost before being rediscovered by Needleman.

Needleman has his own version of the doctrine of the higher self and the divine spark. He calls it the "higher unconscious." By this he does not refer to what Sigmund Freud meant when he spoke of the unconscious. Rather, Needleman wants to call our attention to a divine implant within the human psyche that through life grows and blossoms. It is an innate impulse toward God, stronger that Freud's pleasure principle. What causes it to grow and develop are impressions of truth—nourishing forms of energy—received by the human organism.

At this point the teachings of G. I. Gurdjieff come into play. What Gurdjieff calls "the third state of consciousness" or "consciousness of self" lies between "waking sleep" (our present or fallen condition) and "objective consciousness" (which is our human birthright).[35] In this intermediate or third state of consciousness we can formulate great ideas and uphold sacred traditions and take meaningful actions in history. This is where the best of us usually find ourselves. Nevertheless, the aim of a very serious person is to awaken from even this state of consciousness. For this, the highest awakening, the term "esoteric knowing" is used. In order to say "I am a Christian," a person first needs to be able to say, "I am."

The gnostic Christianity proffered by Needleman is nondualistic. For centuries, orthodox Christians have attacked gnosticism on the ground that it is dualistic. Yet this attack misses the mark. No serious gnostic ever held the notion of ultimate dualism— the idea of a good and an evil force fundamentally dividing the universe. Needleman's gnosticism is monistic. God is the whole, and everything in creation is a part of God. Hidden in his hidden teaching is unity or oneness. What we experience as dualism is in reality the struggle of the self to find its own true existence. The genuine gnostic position is that we need to discriminate different directions of energy, to recognize that the struggle for inner perfection involves cosmic principles that operate within and outside of human nature. The term *esotericism* refers us to the study of supraindividual energy within oneself.

Gnostic truth is not antiphysical; in fact, the body is said to be sacred because, with prayerful diligence and persistence, it can come to experience directly the hierarchy of God and the confusion of the ego's striving. A disciplined body can destroy the root of the illusions of the social self, the self we each assume to be our genuine self but that in reality is only the smoke of the ego.

In a manner akin to ancient gnostic hierarchicalism, Needleman posits two levels of God. The ancient gnostics followed Plato's *Timaeus,* according to which the God who created the world is known as the Demiurge. This deity is the craftsman or working principle of the world. Beyond the Demiurge lies the God-Beyond-God, the unnameable one who is sometimes dubbed the Fore-Beginning or the Inconceivable or the Immeasurable. Following Father Sylvan's lead, Needleman says the God-Beyond-God is the God of the developed soul, whereas the lesser God is the god of morality and ordinary religion. The Demiurge represents true and good concepts regarding creation and daily life, but, as concepts, they stand as a screen between the soul and the direct experience of the ultimate reality. We need to go beyond our thoughts, linking our soul to what lies beyond the mind. What we need is a religion that links, that mediates or connects. We need an "intermediate" religion.[36]

The lost element in the Christian tradition appears, then, to lie somewhere between mysticism and belief. It is something more subtle than the experience of God. It is the experience of oneself. It is the power of listening to oneself. What we need is what Needleman names "intermediate Christianity" to aid us in realizing the nature of self-existence. The thesis of Needleman's book is that "it is precisely this intermediate, or conscious, Christianity that is being sought by the numerous Christians turning now toward Eastern teachings or responding to the challenge of the new religions by delving into the Western contemplative forms and texts that have survived over the centuries."[37] What is really needed is not so much the big experience but rather some kind of intermediate state— something without which the big experience leads to illusion or distortion of some kind. This intermediate consciousness can be described by terms like *openness, sensitivity, consciousness, feeling, presence, attention, seeing.* This leads to the recognition and acceptance of a hierarchy within Christianity and the necessity to climb the ladder.

> The conclusion is that the teachings of Christ as we know them are meant for people of a higher level than we ourselves. And the lost element in Christianity is the specific methods and ideas that can, first, show us the subhuman level at which we actually exist and, second, lead us toward the level at which the teachings of Christ can be followed in fact, rather than in imagination.
>
> In brief, there are levels of Christianity.[38]

What then, in the final analysis, is the esoteric secret of lost Christianity? It is the search itself. It is the quest. By responding to the inner impulse to pursue truth and being, we presuppose that we have already found it. This has transformatory power because, as Father Sylvan says, "the process of inquiry itself was a normalizing influence on my outer life."[39] What has been lost in orthodox Christianity is the now-forgotten power to extract the pure energy of the soul from the experiences that crowd and smother us in daily life. Our task, then, is to pursue the inner life; and this very pursuit itself has transforming power.

Shortly after the publication of *Lost Christianity*, I offered a course on postmodern and new age teachings at the Graduate Theological Union. I assigned this book. I invited Professor Needleman to come for one class session. Among the students were a number of adepts in various aspects of new age esotericism, so the anticipation of Needleman's visit was high, and when the visitor came the discussion was lively. But one interchange altered the mood significantly. A student asked the guest professor to say a bit more about this personality on whom the book is based, Father Sylvan. Needleman responded by saying that there was no Father Sylvan. He was a fictitious concoction, a mere literary device. At the next meeting the students had droopy faces. When I asked why, they all agreed that something had happened when they discovered that Father Sylvan was a fiction. Could this mean, they speculated, that Needleman's Christianity was not something lost and then found, but rather something invented?

The Fox Phenomenon:
Creation-Centered Spirituality

A near-messianic figure to some and a maverick to others, renegade Dominican Matthew Fox, O.P., spells excitement on the current religious scene. Formerly of Mundelein College in Chicago, Fox has been heading his own graduate studies program, the Institute in Creation-Centered Spirituality, at Holy Names College in Oakland, California. Like many in the new age movement, Fox is seeking—and actually promulgating—a new postmodern paradigm that allegedly integrates science and religion. He attacks two previous paradigms, the scientific mind-set of modernity plus what he dubs the "fall/redemption" mind-set of traditional Christian theology. In their place he substitutes his own "creation-centered spirituality."

The word *creation* in "creation-centered spirituality" connotes two things. First, it refers us to the natural world in all its beauty. It understands nature as a blessing to be embraced, not a curse to be overcome. It faces up to the ecological crisis by decrying the threat of nuclear war and the poisoning of our environment through pollution. Second, it proffers the idea of creativity. It connotes an ongoing dynamic of transformation, which means we ourselves can create a different future. We can renew our own lives as well as renew the world in which we live. Toward this end, Fox contends that "religion's task is to reintroduce a cosmic vision," a wholistic vision that sees each of us individuals as participants in the ongoing creativity of God's cosmos.[40]

To affirm the creation in terms of an "original blessing," Fox believes he needs to denounce the Christian doctrine of "original sin." The problem with the idea of original sin, he says, is that those who believe in it are retarded from tapping their own powers of creativity. He ridicules St. Augustine and other traditional theologians for anthropomorphizing the cosmos. For if the universe is 20 billion years old, Fox argues, then human sin is only as old as humanity, or at most 4 million years old. This means that fall/redemption theology leaves out 19,996,000,000 years of sinless natural history! What we need to do instead is appreciate the goodness of nature, our own human nature included. Fox goes on to fault Christian theologians for even thinking up the idea of original sin, because the very idea is destructive. It is destructive because it is dualistic, distinguishing sharply between the human and the divine. "The doctrine of original sin can itself contribute to sin," says Fox.[41] The sin Fox believes in is not original sin; rather, it is the sin of creating conceptual dualisms, and theologians are the ones most guilty.

Creation-oriented spirituality seeks to overcome dualisms of every sort, Newtonian as well as Augustinian. Fox lays out four paths to follow. These paths are spiral, not ladderlike. They interweave and interconnect. The first is the *via positiva,* the positive befriending of nature. According to this path, sin consists in denying what is natural in the environment through pollution or denying what is natural in ourselves, namely, our Eros. Salvation, correspondingly, means we try to heal the environment through bringing back into balance the relationships of earth, air, fire, and water. It also means we return to Eros and accept the empowerment it stimulates.

The second path is the *via negativa,* which, as traditionally understood, connotes the apophatic and ascetic traditions of meditation. What this means for Fox is that we learn receptivity. "Everything that is to be receptive must and ought to be empty," he says, citing Meister Eckhart.[42] Sin, then, would consist in the refusal to let go of our old attitudes toward things, the refusal to admit the need for receptivity. Salvation here consists of forgiveness, and forgiveness consists in letting go. It allows us to be forgiven, and this matures into the power to forgive others. Forgiveness heals, because it allows us to let go of our crazy military projections and nuclear madness. What we need to do is let ourselves "sink" into existence. We can trust this sinking because, as Meister Eckhart says, at the bottom, "my ground and God's are the same."

The third path is the *via creativa,* wherein we realize that we are co-creators with God. We are agents of cosmogenesis. Neither the universe nor the Creator is static, says Fox; "they are unfolding, pulsating, passionate, loving, creating, breathing, spiraling."[43] And we are made in the image of God. We are the *imago dei.* Thus, sin here would consist in lack of imagination, in conservatism and reluctance to change things. Salvation would consist in turning our lives into a work of art.

We are creative whether we like it or not. Unfortunately, pines Fox, the kind of creativity produced by scientists and engineers is ego-exaggerating, which has brought us to the brink of nuclear holocaust. This is the demonic creativity of the left brain, which when allowed to go too far becomes destructive. Fox prefers the intuitive and artistic creativity of the right brain. Although he usually casts his prescription for salvation in terms of a wholistic unity of right- and left-brain functions, his bias toward the intuitive and against the scientific comes through loud and clear. When our intuitive capacities are freed for expression, we are ready to realize mystically the divinity that lies within us. Fox recognizes that he is flirting with heterodoxy here.

> The fact that I am the first theologian that I know of in the West to have named the Via Creativa as an essential ingredient to the spiritual journey does not give me comfort. . . . The fear of our own divinity so haunts us that religious leaders and thinkers rarely if ever preach this truth. . . . Meister Eckhart was not so reticent to speak of our divine powers: "Now the seed of God is in us. The seed of a pear tree grows into a pear tree; the seed of a hazel tree grows into a hazel tree. The seed of God grows into God."[44]

The fourth of the paths is the *via transformativa,* which begins with the biblical symbol of the new creation. "All people are challenged to be instruments for this new age, this new creation," says Fox.[45] Advocating a doctrine of realized eschatology, Fox says that what we need to realize is the creation of a new global civilization where peace and justice reign, where the spirit of delight and play and celebration can be made to happen. This projected transformation of our world begins with the entrance of the new creation into human consciousness, which is actually a form of getting in touch with the blessing of the original creation already within. Fox is never quite clear regarding the relation between the old and the new creation. On the one hand, if the old creation is in fact the blessing, then the new creation would be an insult. On the other hand, the old creation must not be good enough for Fox. He commands us to engage with God as co-creators to transform the present world into something new. Here is an abiding ambiguity in the Fox position.

The reason we need transformation is that sin is serious. It is not trivial. Sin leads to injustice, builds ovens of genocide, wipes out whole cultures and peoples, and threatens the survival of the universe itself. Fox makes this point despite his earlier rejection of the Christian doctrine of original sin. Evidently, what Fox does not like is the idea that sin is "original." Even though sin is the product of dualistic human thinking, it is a serious matter for Fox and provides the warrant for his doctrine of transformation.

Transformation begins in the individual but by no means ends there. The first step on the way to transformation is to love oneself. We need to be freed from self-hatred and all forms of masochism. The importance of authentic self-love must not be underestimated. Only after we have begun to have compassion for ourselves can we become compassionate toward other people. Only after we have acknowledged that we are erotic physical beings who desire to enjoy life will we be empowered to become instruments of world transformation. Salvation comes "by way of Eros." It taps a power already within us. What we need to do is unleash it,

> to unleash the spirit's work of New Creation, of new possibilities for letting go and birthing, for being transformed and for transforming. In a culture that has lost its sense of Eros and celebration, the true prophets will come celebrating. Celebrating sensuality and earthiness, passion and compassion, failures and imperfections, space, time, being, foolishness, our capacity to laugh, let go, and be young again. Play itself becomes a salvific act.[46]

What understanding of God does Fox assume? He is a panentheist. Fox rejects garden-variety pantheism, according to which everything is God and God is everything. The problem with pantheism, he feels, is that it loses sight of God's transcendence. Yet Fox is deeply influenced by feminist theology, by images of God as mother and corollary images of us humans living like fetuses within the being of the divine. So he embraces panentheism, which inserts the little Greek word *en* (in) between *pan* (all) and *theism* (God). The result is a theology that asserts that "God is in everything, and everything is in God."[47] This means that there is a continuity of being between God and the world, that we humans as well as the rest of nature are essentially divine. His is a sacramental and mystical view of the world in relation to God. Anything and everything in nature, then, can be diaphanous; that is, transparent to the divine presence. Fox rejects the classical Christian commitment to theism, which sees the world as a creation of God that is sharply distinguishable from God.

This comes to evocative symbolic expression in Fox's unabashed identification of divinity with Mother Earth and with the feminine force within all human beings. With dramatic expression he exploits the imagery of the Earth Mother giving birth to us her children, yet, because of the dualistic thinking of our perverted theology, we are killing our own mother through polluting our environment. We are commiting matricide. We are crucifying God. Mother Earth is dying.

> The Great Mother archetypes of native peoples everywhere have been practically exterminated by patriarchal holocausts and colonialism. There is Spider Woman and White Buffalo Woman in the Americas; there is Gaia and Athena in Europe; there is Oshun and Yemaya (among others) in Africa; there is Sophia in Greece and Shekinah in Israel. Aboriginal mother love is in us all. . . . The goddess in everyone has been dying, along with creation, Mother Earth, and wisdom.[48]

Mother Earth may be dying, but she is not yet completely dead. There is potential for new life, for resurrection. This resurrection will take place when we return to mysticism and let the divine life force free us from our dualism and inspire us to embrace our earth and one another in ecological love. This theme of dying and rising reminds us of Jesus, and this is just what Fox intends.

What role does Jesus Christ play in Fox's theology? He is the embodiment of the new creation and, hence, our prototype. Jesus' own life was a work of art: he was a poet, storyteller, and artist. He was not a priest or theologian or an academician or a dispenser of sacraments. Rather, he was an awakener to the sacrament of the cosmos, what Fox calls the "kingdom/queendom" of God that immerses all persons. As such, Jesus invites us to be likewise. He invites us to actualize the image of God that we are. Jesus did not tell us to meditate on him; rather, we should go out and do the same works he does, which is the work of the Creator God. "Jesus' life represents the fullest creation-centered and deepest of the spiritual journeys of humankind."[49] By his life and teachings, Jesus calls us to reconciliation with ourselves and to the task of global transformation.

Is this gnosticism? Fox certainly employs gnostic imagery. He says the fire in each of our hearts ties us to the divinity of the cosmos. I have heard him say in slogan form:

> *We need no other guide*
> *than the fire inside.*

Yet it is worth noting that Fox overtly rejects gnosticism. He does so on the grounds that creation-centered spirituality has a high regard for the created physical world, whereas gnosticism in its ancient form rejected the physical so that the soul could escape. The soul was torn away from matter and sought its salvation through an ascent into the realm of the divine. The gnostic God was an acosmic God, and the soul was an acosmic soul. To this Fox objects, because as a panentheist he sees the cosmos as constitutive of God's very being. God cannot exist without the cosmos. Neither can we. In what I judge to be a very creative move, Fox proposes that we think of the global village as the planetary soul. This removes the idea of the soul as the private property of the individual person. It recognizes that salvation is communal, that our stake in the health and welfare of the whole planet is absolutely essential.[50] This tightly ties together self-interest and community interest. It provides a dramatic foundation for an ecological ethic.

Is this new age? It sounds similar, from the divine-human identity to ecological unity and social transformation. Yet Fox himself is not happy about classifying his creation-centered spirituality as "new age." This is because Fox thinks of himself as in league with the liberation theologians of Latin America, with those theologians who are asking the Christian Church to identify with the poor and oppressed peoples of the Third World. New age practitioners, in contrast, belong to the bourgeoise of the First World. This is a class distinction. The new age belongs to the educated middle and upper classes. If Fox were to identify too closely with the new age, he might lose credibility among his liberationist friends. So to a reporter he complains, "The weakness of the New Age . . . is that it often seems to me to be a fundamentalism for the rich. . . . There's a whole money thing in the New Age which really bothers me. That really goes to the heart of the justice issue."[51]

Despite such protestations, however, the Fox theology clearly overlaps with new age themes and relies upon many of the same resources. His activities are followed closely in the new age press under the assumption that they share a common lot.[52] In 1990 Fox visited Findhorn in Scotland known for its new age garden, and he finds himself frequently welcomed into new age company. Fox and the new age? Two peas in a single pod.

Fox has been and continues to be the object of critical attention. Roman Catholics are suspicious that he may be less than fully orthodox. The Vatican Congregation for the Doctrine of the Faith, heir to the former Holy Office of the Inquisition, began questioning the orthodoxy of Father Fox's work in July 1984. A commission of three Dominican theologians examined three of Fox's writings, *Original Blessing* plus two others, and in May 1985 filed a report with Cardinal Joseph Ratzinger, who heads the Congregation, saying that "there should be no condemnation of Father Fox's work." Nevertheless, Fox has continued to raise the ire of the Catholic faithful because he has invited Starhawk, a self-proclaimed witch, to serve on his teaching faculty. In defending this move, Fox dissolves the link between witchcraft and Satanism. He ties witchcraft rather to nature spirituality—to Wicca—and the sense of wholeness in nature. This tradition "reverences the earth and the mother goddess present in everybody," he told a reporter. "It's a concept that is very close to our concept of the cosmic Christ, that there is a divine sign in everybody."[53]

In December 1985 Cardinal Ratzinger advised the Dominican Master General that the conclusions of the previous report were "questionable," and he requested public redress for the "scandal of Father Fox's seeming espousal of witchcraft and the harm which his published books and teaching activities have already brought to the faithful." Ratzinger judged Fox's *Original Blessing* to be "dangerous and deviant." He objected to such things as Fox's calling God "Mother" and "Child." He accused Fox of denying the validity of infant baptism.

In September 1987 Cardinal Ratzinger informed the Master General that his own office would undertake a theological inquiry, and in September 1988 he demanded that the Master General take action to silence this outspoken priest—that Fox's position as director of the Institute in Culture and Creation Spirituality be terminated and that he cease public speaking, preaching, teaching, and publishing his views. The Master General complied. This precipitated an immediate outpouring of support for the pursued Fox. Letters of protest flooded the Vatican.

One was written by Matthew Fox himself. It has the humorous and provocative title: "Is the Catholic Church Today a Dysfunctional Family? A Pastoral Letter to Cardinal Ratzinger and the Whole Church."[54] In it he reaffirms adherence to the doctrines of original sin (redefined in terms of dualism, of course) and infant baptism. Then Fox goes on the offensive, accusing Cardinal Ratzinger of reading with a "closed mind," attacking the Congregation for the Doctrine of the Faith for its "intellectual sloth" and "spiritual sloth" because it accuses "without feeling the oppression of others that is addressed in my and other works of liberation theology."

Fox puts Ratzinger into the camp of the oppressors. He goes so far as to compare the cardinal to an alcoholic father in a dysfunctional family, a tyrannical parent who must always be appeased and placated in hopes that he will not become violent yet another time. Those who appease through silence become the "co-dependents" and inadvertently consent to the oppression. In this letter, Fox believes he is speaking out, breaking the silence and announcing just how "increasingly scandalous" Ratzinger's behavior is becoming. As if this is not enough, Fox goes on to describe the Roman Catholic church as "fascist." Near the end he writes defiantly, "Silencing me will not destroy Creation Spirituality any more than silencing Leonardo Boff destroyed Liberation Theology. The truths of the Four Paths of Creation Spirituality resonate too deeply with persons' experience to be silenced."[55]

The letter was dated August 8, 1988. Fox accepted the ban to silence beginning December 15, 1988. I was present at his last public lecture prior to the advent of the ban. It took place at the GTU on December 12. The standing-room-only program began with prayers of invocation offered by a native American and a native African. This was followed by a dramatic dance, then a short talk by Fox on the role of the mystical prophet. It continued with a long question-and-answer period with frequent applause as Fox used quips and sarcastic attacks against the Vatican. "I may have to be silent," Fox told his friends, "but you don't. You can speak and write and get the message out." The meeting concluded with a moment of group silence in honor of its beaten hero.

Cardinal Ratzinger's criticisms of Matthew Fox seem simplistic and superficial. A more substantive criticism is offered by theologian Jane Strohl. She argues that Fox's assurance that we have the ability to make the right choices does not guarantee that we have the will to do so. Dealing with sin requires more than merely the power of positive thinking. Although Fox is justifiably outraged by those who have overemphasized sinfulness and underemphasized grace, the imbalance is not redressed by reveling in original blessing. To advocate that we can be as good as God intended us to be if we only put our imaginations to the task is an invitation to despair rather than hope. Goodness is not already in us to the degree that Fox assumes. The overlooked advantage of the fall/redemption theology is that it acknowledges the activity of God's grace. It recognizes that our turning comes as a gift from God, as the first fruit of the redeeming work of Jesus Christ. In sum, by seeking the ground for hope in human creativity, Fox risks missing it; it lies not only in the divine grace of creation but also in the redeeming grace of God bestowed on us in the Easter resurrection.[56]

What I personally like about the Fox program is his attempt to reassess the place of the modern scientific mind in human consciousness and seek the foundations for a postmodern way of thinking. He has gleaned the vocabulary of the new age and has used ideas such as wholism, the new paradigm, co-creativity, diaphaneity, right-brain and left-brain complementarity, and the overcoming of dualistic thinking. Fox is adapting these things to the Christian way. And he does so in an exciting, even inspiring, fashion. Yet, I have reasons to remain cautious.

First, what is it that makes for the excitement? One way to make one's position interesting is to define it sharply over against an alternative, even to attack the alternative and impugn it for fostering things that are evil. This is what Fox does. With considerable vituperation he attacks the alleged prevailing paradigm of orthodox Christianity, which he characterizes as fall/redemption theology or spirituality. The worse he can make orthodox Christianity look, the better will his own program appear. In the heat of the argument,

what Fox does is astounding. Not only does he say that the traditional fall/redemption spirituality is mistaken, but he proceeds to
blame nearly all the problems of the secular world on this religious
vision. He blames Christian theology for the ecological crisis, for
the existence of pain and sin, for the "sin of introspective religion,"
for fear and lack of trust, and even consumerism.[57] If we were to
take Fox seriously, we would end up blaming the theologians for all
the problems of sin and evil in the modern world.

What it boils down to for Fox is that theology itself is the
source of evil. It should follow from this premise, then, that prior
to St. Augustine, who articulated the doctrine of original sin in the
fourth century, there did not exist such things as sin, pain, fear, and
consumerism. One may wonder then why the Hebrew slaves in ancient Egypt cried out for freedom. One wonders how it was that
people of the first century—still existing in Fox's alleged created
goodness—could ever get around to crucifying the Son of God. The
absurdity of the Fox position is that theology ends up creating the
fall rather than reporting on a fall that has already happened.

Second, it is not necessary to reject the so-called fall/redemp-
tion paradigm in order to make the point that the original creation
is a blessing. Nobody in Christendom disagrees with this point; so
Fox's alleged opposition is contrived. He constructs a straw theologian, because fall/redemption theologians equally affirm the essential goodness of the original creation. We all read the same Bible
with the Genesis account in which God pronounces all that he created to be "very good." There is no dispute here.

Relevant also is to note that the "original" in the phrase "original sin" refers to the state of alienation in which the created order
currently finds itself, a state that precedes our own particular existence and into which we in our generation have been born. It is the
recognition that right now, where we find ourselves in world history,
conflicting forces are at work, forces that wreak destructive havoc
and that are bigger than any individual who participates in them.
When Fox speaks about sin in terms of ecological imbalance, global
injustice, and the threat of nuclear war, this is what he himself is
talking about. Regardless of what he calls it, he himself cannot deny
the reality to which the term "original sin" refers.

Third, I am reluctant to follow Fox into panentheism. He follows this path because he wishes to identify the Eros that drives

human life with the divine life. He wants to think of us as participating in the being of God proper. He likes panentheism because it
places the being of the world within the being of God with a little
bit of extra divinity left over. This prevents us from equating God
with the world and permits God a modicum of transcendence. The
payoff for Fox here is that he can bypass the special revelation of
the Bible and find access to the divine through the beauty of the
flowers and through creations of art. This gives one a very warm
feeling, knowing that the world is not only one's own home but
God's home as well.

The problem with this conflation of the being of God with the
being of the world is that it actually diminishes the drama of what
Fox most wants, namely, creativity. What creativity means in its
fullest sense, I think, is that God is creating something other than
the Godself. Our world and we human beings within it are not
extensions of the divine being. Rather, we are creatures. We come
from nothing. We have been created *ex nihilo*. We are the result of
a gracious and loving act whereby the divine power authored something brand new. The goodness of the creation comes from God's
declaring it good because it is an object of the divine love. It does
not have to be divine to be good. It is good simply because it is
God's creation. Why does Fox feel the necessity to conflate God
with the world in order to affirm the creation as an original blessing? It is unnecessary and misleading.

I am most sympathetic with Fox's explication of the *imago dei*,
with the divine image in us, in terms of co-creativity. But I think we
can find a much clearer presentation of this concept in the work of
Philip Hefner, who describes the human being as the "created co-
creator."[58] The wording here is important. On the one hand, we are
"created." We are first the product of God's divine creativity. And,
very importantly, we find ourselves totally dependent on God for
our very existence. We are not immortal gods. We are creatures,
subject to the limits of time and space. It would be unrealistic to
deny this. On the other hand, our human task in this world is to
continue the dynamic of creative activity in concert with the divine
creator. We bring new things into being. What we create—whether
through art or engineering—however, belongs strictly within the
realm of the created order. We do not create anything divine. We
do not create God. Yet we participate in God's ongoing creative

work. In sum, we can and should think of the human enterprise in terms of co-creatorship with God, but we do not need panentheism to make this possible.

As doctrinal theology, Matthew Fox's creation-centered spirituality simply cannot pass the test of critical scrutiny. Nevertheless, perhaps its value lies elsewhere. Fox has put his pastoral finger on an open sore in Christian spiritual practice. We have too long and too often driven our most faithful servants of Christ in the direction of unnecessary guilt and self-deprecation. In the name of humility, which is appropriate, we have delivered the message that to feel worthy is to feel like a worm. In the name of fruits of the Spirit we have asked people to deny the life-enthralling Eros, the natural inclination to be natural. The ascetic practices of monastery life have bequeathed to many a mood of spiritual and psychological repression. What Fox has been rightly looking for is a key to unlock the cells of our confinement, to liberate our inner being. By declaring who we essentially are to be good, we can no longer justify to ourselves the repression of our selves. In the name of God, we can now walk through the open door to a new lease on personal freedom. For making this possible in the case of many of his students, Matthew Fox deserves a vote of gratitude.

One of the items on the Fox agenda is a rapprochement between science and religion. He contends that the Einsteinian and post-Einsteinian models of the universe are opening up new avenues of wisdom for the whole of our culture.[59] In this regard, Fox is in tune with the many non-Christian advocates of new age spirituality. What is at stake here is a cosmic vision; a reassessment of the cosmos as viewed scientifically is inevitable. His attempt to sign a peace treaty ending what some have called the centuries-long warfare between science and religion is an ambition startling in scope. It is to this attempt at reconciliation that we turn in our next chapter.

Chapter Four

The New Physics and Wholistic Cosmology

 The new age has a new science. We might call it *scientific wholism*. It combines three things: twentieth-century discoveries in physics, an acknowledgment of the important role played by imagination in human knowing, and a recognition of the ethical exigency of preserving our planet from ecological destruction. "Modern" science is outdated, say new age philosophers. Worse, modern science has placed us on the brink of disaster. Only a move forward into a postmodern science can save us.

We all know the litany of symptoms ailing our modern culture: the spoliation of nature, the continuing suicidal buildup of nuclear weapons, toleration of apartheid, racism and economic oppression, spreading illiteracy, the breakdown of personal relations, a haunting sense of futility, cynicism, uncivility, and outright violence. If these are the symptoms, then what is the underlying disease? New age theorists and other postmodernists offer a diagnosis: the sickness of the modern West is caused by the widespread habit of dualistic and fragmented thinking endemic to modern science.

The core problem is that we think badly. We think atomistically and divisively. We perceive the world as divided up into quantifiable and isolatable parts. We reduce wholes to their component parts in an effort to control them. Most important, modern scientific epistemology separates the object of study from the inquiring subject. This rips the human person out of reality and turns persons into spectators. We look at what is real as if we were onlookers, not participants. This leaves out all the affective dimensions of life—feeling, intuiting, valuing, willing—assigning them to a realm of subjectivity that is supposed to be of no interest to scholars and scientists. Because science is concerned almost exclusively with quantitative relationships, it has nothing to contribute in enabling us to deal with qualitative issues such as the ultimate meaning of existence; yet these issues are part of reality as well. This has resulted in what C. P. Snow called "the two cultures," the split between the sciences and the humanities. In cutting itself off from the affective dimensions reflected in the humanities, science has unnecessarily fragmented human consciousness and thereby fragmented the human community as well.

The appropriate medicine, then, is a good dose of wholistic thinking that reintegrates the sciences with the humanities. We need a transformation of human consciousness to heal the painful dualisms that have torn the modern world apart.

This is what futurist Alvin Toffler sees coming. The modern world, which Toffler dubs "the second wave," has dominated Western consciousness since the Enlightenment. But that wave is now receding and leaving on the beach the debris of abstract thinking, compartmentalized knowledge, warring specialisms, fragmented facts, and a general sense of alienation between human consciousness and wider reality. A "third wave" is about to break upon us. And we are thirsting for it. We desire synthetic thinking, putting back together what we have rent asunder. Toffler writes,

> Today I believe we stand on the edge of a new age of synthesis. In all intellectual fields, from the hard sciences to sociology, psychology, and economics—especially economics—we are likely to see a return to large-scale thinking, to general theory, to the putting of the pieces back together again.[1]

In short, what we need to heal divisive thinking is wholistic thinking.

To recover wholistic thinking, Columbia University professor of education Douglas Sloan prescribes exercising the human imagination. We must begin, he says, by recognizing that scientific knowing is grounded in a fuller rationality that extends beyond the boundaries of the calculating intellect. We have access to this fuller rationality through the use of our imagination. Imagination is

> that fundamental capacity for insight that is the source of all cognition and of all new meaning and knowledge. . . . Imagination is that participation of the whole person—in logical thinking, feeling, and willing—in the act of cognition. The imagination places the human being in a context of intelligibility that spans the cleavage between subject and object, a context of meaning that includes both.[2]

To cure our divisive thinking with a heavy dose of insight and imagination is to take the first step toward a cure for all the world's ills: "The recovery of the wholeness of imagination is also a healing (a making whole) of the human being—and potentially the world."[3]

Where does Sloan get his ideas? From the new physics, he says. In particular, the theory of relativity and quantum mechanics. Even more particularly, Sloan focuses his attention on one physicist, David Bohm. The work of philosopher-scientist Bohm, Sloan believes, demonstrates that insight and imagination belong to scientific research proper. Bohm demonstrates that the sciences and the humanities can be united in a world view that incorporates both physical and mental processes. Bohm paves the way through the debris of modern divisive thinking toward a postmodern wholistic form of thinking.

Sloan is not alone in his assessments. David Bohm is the scientific mascot of new age consciousness. In this chapter, we will take a look at the alleged problem of divisive thinking endemic to the modern scientific mind and the sharp criticism of it given by those seeking a postmodern consciousness. Then we will examine the physical cosmology of David Bohm and its comprehensive vision of dynamic wholeness. We will conclude with a theological evaluation, asking if and how the wholistic vision can edify the Christian understanding of God's work in the world.

Beyond Newton and Descartes

The critics of modernism say the thinking of our last three centuries has been characterized by atomism, mechanism, and objectivism. The problem is not, of course, that the modern mind thinks objectively about atoms and mechanics. The problem is that it mistakenly assumes that reality itself is so constituted. The result is fragmentation, in the sense that reality is assumed to be composed of separate atomic objects functioning according to mechanical laws, externally related to one another as subjects and objects. Where did this mistake come from? Revisionist physicists blame scientist Isaac Newton and philosopher René Descartes, the two acknowledged fathers of the modern mind.

The world view we have inherited from Sir Isaac Newton reminds me of the cuckoo clock that hangs on our dining room wall. Its gears and levers are the atomic parts that make up a mechanism that operates predictably; that is, if I remember each morning to pull the chains to lift its weights and wind it. Newton's scientifically apprehended world is a sort of cosmic cuckoo clock. God pulled on the chains once at the beginning to get everything going, but the mechanism has been running on inertia ever since. Just as I have to adjust the time once in a while to make the clock cuckoo at just the right time, however, so does Newton's God have to intervene once in a while to prevent gravitational pull from drawing the planets into the sun. Other than that, things operate pretty smoothly.

According to this view, the world is inert. This means the world has no life-force built into it. It is dead. Its power comes from beyond, from God. The world operates from day to day on inertia. God wound up the cosmic mechanism at the beginning, and it has been running like clockwork ever since.

The world view that provides the framework for Newton's physics is based on the three-dimensional space of Euclidean geometry and the notion that time flows from past to future. This provides us with a kind of receptacle of space and time into which we dump nature's laws and the course of events. In this receptacle of absolute space and time move material elements or particles, the small, solid, and ultimately indestructible objects out of which all matter is made. These material atomic units can be located in space and time. Their velocity and size can be measured. They are basically passive and inert, their relationships to one another determined by external forces of nature such as gravity. These forces or laws of motion assume a closed causal nexus or mechanistic structure. Any definite cause gives rise to a definite effect, and the future of any part of the world system can be—in principle—predicted with certainty if one knows the details of the causes. This leads to the image of the whole world as machine, an implicit and rigorous mechanical determinism.

René Descartes, who is usually called the father of modern philosophy, paved the way for this understanding of the world as machine by distinguishing sharply between the world of extended objects out there and the world of subjectivity in our own mind. Despite the fact that feelings are endemic to human consciousness, Descartes warned us that we could not truly know the world if we let our feelings get in the way. We must be objective. We must observe the mechanistic workings of objects in the external world without affectively influencing them. We can gain true knowledge as long as we think objectively, as long as we do not personally participate in those workings, as long as we picture accurately in our mind how objects relate to one another. The net effect of Descartes's philosophy over the last three centuries has been to cause us to attempt to separate human consciousness from the world processes and, in addition, by concentrating on the plurality of objects to miss seeing the world process as a single whole.

Big changes in the Newtonian and Cartesian world view came during the first quarter of the twentieth century, however. Albert Einstein's special theory of relativity dispossessed the framework of absolute space and time, at least when dealing with very high velocity movements that approach the speed of light. Because temporal sequence is dependent on and relative to one's inertial frame of reference, observations from two different frames of reference result in different sequences of events. There can be no simultaneity over great distances. Thus, the idea of a uniform receptacle of space and time had to be surrendered, at least in certain domains of physical research.

Quantum theory also disrupted the Newtonian world view, perhaps even more so, for three reasons. The first feature of quantum theory is that it sees atomic particles such as electrons as things that cannot be described simply by using concepts such as location,

velocity, or size. Thought of as particles, they travel from one location to another without traversing the distance in between. They
move discontinuously. They do not appear to function at all like the
material objects we understand at the level of common sense. Thus,
understanding them as particles of matter can be misleading. It is
helpful, say the new breed of physicists, to understand them also as
waves or wavicles.

Second, the theory recognizes that no apparent structure of
efficient causation belongs to individual subatomic events. We must
study them in groups, in quanta. Individual subatomic events are
not predictable. They do not even seem to be individually causally
determined. This is what is meant by "indeterminacy" in physics.
What we can do is predict what will happen on the basis of a
statistical analysis of a given quantum of atomic activity. In the case
of radioactive decay, for example, the point in time at which a particular radioactive atom will suddenly disintegrate is totally unpre-
dictable; but the overall half-life or rate of decay of radioactive
substances is knowable. We might use actuarial predictions of in-
surance companies as an analogy. Statistical laws can predict with
a high degree of approximation the mean number of people in a
given class of age, height, weight, and such who will die of a certain
disease in a specified period of time, even though no one can predict
the precise time of death of any individual policyholder. Furthermore, the notion of statistical laws makes sense only if there is
indeterminacy at the level of individual events.

Third, subatomic experiments can demonstrate nonlocal relationships between electrons. Einstein, Podolsky, and Rosen have
shown that when two electrons from a single atom have interacted
and then flown off in opposite directions, interference with one will
instantly affect the other, regardless of the distance between them.
This seems to indicate a sort of telepathy between the particles, an
intimate interconnection not dependent on spatial contact. This is
action at a distance, action with no connection. What we have here,
astonishingly, is a noncausal, nonmaterial, yet influential relationship.

In short, quantum theory takes us away from a material notion
of matter and a closed nexus of efficient causation, away from a
strictly mechanistic picture of the world, away from the world of
Descartes and Newton. University of California physicist and pop-

ular new age author Fritjof Capra describes the significance of these new perspectives.

> The first three decades of our century changed the situation in physics radically. Two separate developments—that of relativity theory and atomic physics—shattered all the principal concepts of the Newtonian worldview: the notion of absolute space and time, the elementary solid particles, the strictly causal nature of physical phenomena, and the ideal of an objective description of nature.[4]

For Capra, this is a signal that we should move on. We are at the turning point. As Capra makes the turn from the modern to the postmodern vision, he tries to tie together modern physics with ancient mysticism.

> The new concepts in physics have brought about a profound change in our world view; from the mechanistic conception of Descartes and Newton to a holistic and ecological view, a view which I have found to be similar to the views of mystics of all ages and traditions.[5]

Arthur Koestler sums it up similarly.

> The strictly deterministic, mechanistic worldview can no longer be upheld; it has become a Victorian anachronism. The nineteenth-century model of the universe as a mechanical clockwork is a shambles and since the concept of matter itself has been dematerialized, materialism can no longer claim to be a scientific philosophy.[6]

The new physics has brought us to the brink of a new postmaterialist and relationalist era. Where do we go from here? David Bohm recommends that we plunge wholeheartedly and whole-mindedly into wholism.

The Wholism of David Bohm

In April 1983 the Center for Theology and the Natural Sciences at the Graduate Theological Union invited David Bohm to Berkeley.

One of the world's foremost theoretical physicists, he was the last student to work with J. Robert Oppenheimer before the Los Alamos experiments during World War II. Later Bohm became known for his work on instrument design for the cyclotron and synchro-cyclotron. His research on plasma in magnetic fields led to his theory in fusion studies now called the "Bohm-diffusion." For showing that an isolated line of magnetic force is able to affect electrons that pass around it without contacting it—a prediction drawn from quantum physics and not derivable from classical physics—his name is attached to what is known as the "Bohm-Aharonov effect." Though presently a professor of theoretical physics at Birkbeck College in London, Bohm received his Ph.D. in 1943 from the University of California in Berkeley. So in a sense we were inviting him home.

We put on a conference with the title, "David Bohm's Implicate Order: Physics and Theology."[7] The physicists, including "bootstrap" theorist Geoffrey Chew, sat on one side of the room. The theologians, including David Griffin, who heads the Center for Postmodernism in Santa Barbara, California, sat on the other side of the room. During the sessions proper, physicists did not talk to theologians, nor did theologians talk to physicists. Bohm addressed the groups separately. He alternated, dealing first with a problem in physics and then with a theological issue. We did not design it this way. It just happened. After the formal sessions were over, physicists and theologians shook hands and slapped each other's backs over what a great conference it had been. We felt the discussion had been important, but we were not sure just why.

Perhaps this shows how extremely compartmentalized we have become. It shows how hard it is to find a common set of categories for carrying on interdisciplinary discourse. Bohm could do it. But then, this may be the reason that many see Bohm as on the frontier of a new paradigm for pursuing knowledge that integrates science and religion.

The reason we permit this compartmentalization of the specialized disciplines is that we are in the habit of divisive thinking, believes Bohm. More precisely, the problem is that we assume that the divided character of our thinking corresponds with an actual dividedness in reality itself. "Since our thought is pervaded with differences and distinctions," says Bohm, "it follows that such a habit leads us to look on these as real divisions, so that the world is then seen and experienced as actually broken up into fragments."[8] Hence, the cure for the ills of the modern world must begin with healthier thinking. And, noting that our word *health* in English is based on the Anglo-Saxon word *hale,* meaning "whole," healthy thinking will be (w)holistic thinking. This sets the agenda for the entire Bohm project, namely, to understand the nature of reality in general and conscious thought in particular as a coherent whole.[9] It is Bohm's thesis that the explicate order of things that we accept as part of our everyday world and that is studied by modern scientists is itself not the fundamental reality; there is under and behind it an implicate order, a realm of undivided wholeness. And this wholeness is present in each of the explicate parts.[10]

Following in Einstein's Footsteps

Although he himself had performed some of the most astonishing experiments, Einstein remained quite committed to the classical view of physics. He believed that quantum theory was still incomplete, that something was missing. There must be some as-yet-undiscovered "hidden variables" that will explain such unusual phenomena as action at a distance. It is through this gate that David Bohm enters the path previously trod by Einstein.

Bohm does not want to return to the mechanistic determinism of Newtonian physics, yet he does want to take us beyond the present state of quantum theory with his own notion of "hidden variables." The problem as he sees it is that there is at present no consistent notion at all of what the reality might be that underlies the universal constitution and structure of matter. Quantum physicists tend to avoid the issue by concentrating on mathematical equations that permit us to predict and control the behavior of large statistical aggregates of particles, while adopting an attitude that any overall view of the nature of reality is of little or no importance. On this count the practicing quantum physicists are still modern, still calculating the position and momentum of fragments, even though the fragments are of a different scale.[11]

By focusing on the quantum as an indivisible unit amidst a plurality of such quanta, and assuming only indeterminacy within the unit itself, we may miss other hidden factors that might open us to seeing the fundamental unity behind all things. Bohm wants to open us up to those hidden factors, by contending that the electron has more properties than can be described in terms of the so-called observables characteristic of quantum theory. There are underneath these, he says, hidden variables that influence the directly observable behavior of the quantum unit or system. His thesis is that "in a deeper sub-quantum level, there are further variables which determine in more detail the fluctuations of the results of individual quantum-mechanical measurements."[12]

What are these variables? The answer partially proposed by Bohm is to be found as much in philosophy as in physics. While accepting quantum theory as satisfactory for its domain, we must pursue the search for hidden variables in a different domain. They are to be found in reconceiving our world view, in speculating about the underlying unity of the whole of reality. It is to Bohm's specific cosmological speculations that we now turn.

Flow, Flux, and Holomovement

Heraclitus wins! Reality, according to Bohm, is fundamentally "undivided wholeness in flowing movement."[13] This harkens back to the ancient Greek philosophers and the contest as to which is prior, being or becoming. For Parmenides of Elea, there was one fundamental reality—being, which is through and through one in kind, homogeneous with itself, uncreated, complete, and unchangeable. Heraclitus, in contrast, gave priority to becoming. All flows. The universe as a whole and everything in it is engaged in perpetual motion, ceaseless process. You cannot step into the same stream twice, as he is quoted by Plato.[14] Bohm has taken sides with Heraclitus in this classic debate.

And in so doing, Bohm has sided with the modern and postmodern minds as well. Interpreters of Western culture attest to the triumph of Heraclitus in the age of science. Yale historian of ideas Franklin L. Baumer says the "sense of becoming is at the heart of what we mean by modernity, or 'the modern mind.'"[15] University of Chicago theologian Langdon Gilkey says that for moderns, time is the most fundamental structure of all experienced being. . . . Almost every significant aspect of the modern spirit—its sense of contingency, of relativity, of temporality, and of transience—moves in exactly the opposite direction from the concept of a necessary, self-sufficient, changeless, unrelated, and eternal being.[16]

Although we recognize that the modern mind assumes the priority of temporal becoming, we should be a bit more precise. Becoming is more important to us now than when the modern mind first squirmed out of the womb of the medieval mind. We should note that within the modern period, the triumph of time-consciousness occurs in the later phase, more in the nineteenth century. The idea of becoming does not in quite the same way dominate the mindset of Descartes and Newton in the formative period of the seventeenth and eighteenth centuries. Nevertheless, the notion of flowing movement belongs to the modern era proper. It will become a cardinal principle in the postmodern era as well.

What does Bohm mean by it? Flow means that everything is changing. But it is not a single homogeneous or undifferentiated flow, which would be undiscernible from static being. It is rather a flux, a movement of forms and shapes and units. Despite the undivided wholeness in the overall flowing movement, we can by the tools of thought abstract from it patterns, objects, entities, conditions, structures, and so on, and these have a certain autonomy and stability. What Bohm wants to stress here is that the flow as an unknown and undefinable totality is prior, whereas the flux of describable events and objects is considered an abstraction. This means that our knowledge of the laws of physics deals with abstractions; it deals with events and objects having only relative independence and existence from their ultimate ground in the unknown totality of the universal movement.

It follows that human knowing is both an abstraction from and a participation in the total flux. It is an abstraction because when we focus on either subjective knowing or objective knowledge, we temporarily forget the wider unity that binds them. We mentally extricate them from the single flow of which they are a part. And although the distinction between mind and matter is described by Bohm as an abstraction from a prior unity in the universal flux, such things as mind and matter do exist. But they do not exist by themselves, independently, in isolation. They are each modes of the one common underlying reality. "Mind and matter are not separate substances. Rather, they are different aspects of one whole and un-broken movement."[17]

This is not the bifurcated world of Descartes in which thought in the mind views the reality of objects out there, as if thinking consisted in viewing reality as an audience views a drama. Here thought is part of the reality that is the ongoing flow. Because reality is inclusive of thought, reality itself must be thoughtful. It thinks through us. It has consciousness. It belongs to us and we to it. The flow consists in a single holomovement.

Holomovement and the Implicate Order

There is more than just flow, flux, and consciousness in the holo-movement. There is also a microcosm-macrocosm correlation, a sort of presence of the whole within and implied by the part. Bohm's notion of cosmic order as flow is not to be understood solely in terms of a regular arrangement of objects (for example, in rows) or as a regular arrangement of events (for example, in a series). Rather, the total order of the holomovement is contained in some implicit sense in each region of space and time. He refers to this as the "implicate order."

Bohm observes that the verb *to implicate* means "to fold in-ward" or "to enfold," as the term *multiplication* means "folding many times." The implicate ordering of the cosmos means that the total structure is enfolded within each region of space and time. So whatever part, element, or aspect we may abstract in thought, this still enfolds the whole and therefore is intrinsically related to the totality from which it has been abstracted.

> In terms of the implicate order one may say that everything is en-folded into everything. This contrasts with the *explicate order* now dominant in physics in which things are *unfolded* in the sense that each thing lies only in its own particular region of space (and time) and outside the regions belonging to other things.[18]

Another term for these regions is *subtotalities*. The relationship between subtotalities and the whole is governed by holonomy—that is, the law of the whole. The law of the whole has a looseness about it, permitting a certain autonomy on the part of the regions within it. The exact nature of the law of the whole is not known and may even be unknowable, but what we do know is that it includes an overall sense of necessity while avoiding any mechanical determinism.

> In the holomovement, there is still an overall necessity . . . but its laws are no longer mechanical. Rather . . . its laws will be in a first approximation those of the quantum theory, while more accurately they will go beyond even these, in ways that are at present only vaguely discernable.[19]

The net effect of holonomy is to establish the implicate order, to foster subtotalities that provide access to the whole.

Manifestation and the Explicate Order

Although the nonmanifest implicate order is primary, the explicate order of manifestations perceptible through the human senses is authentic for Bohm. What is manifest is literally what can be held with the hand—something solid, tangible, and visibly stable. The manifest world consists in the external unfolding or explication of the implicate order. The holomovement admits of *verration,* the act of perceiving truth as well as attending to what truth means.[20] In other words, the forms of flux themselves do not leave us abandoned in a world of illusion. Illusion occurs only when we mistake the forms of flux for the fundamental reality, when we assume that what is explicate is all there is.

> *What is* is the holomovement and . . . everything is to be explained in terms of forms derived from this holomovement. Though the full set of laws governing its totality is unknown (and, indeed, probably unknowable) nevertheless these laws are assumed to be such that from them may be abstracted relatively autonomous or independent sub-totalities of movement (e.g., fields, particles, etc.) having a

certain recurrence and stability of their basic patterns of order and measure.[21]

Bohm believes that the notion of an implicate order becoming explicate gives a more coherent account of quantum properties of matter than does the traditional mechanistic idea of order. For example, it solves the problem of discontinuities in the track of an electron particle. Where the electron seems to pass from one state to another without traversing the states between, Bohm can say this is possible because the electron itself is only an abstraction from a much greater total structure. If we assume that the electron as a particle is the primary reality, then it appears to drop out of existence and then come back into existence. But this is something impossible. However, if we assume a hidden implicate order to be the primary reality, and that this implicate order provides the continuity, then we can accept that what is manifest to our senses (or to laboratory instruments) does not itself have continuous movement or continuous existence. The disappearance and reappearance of the particle represent multiple projections of a single higher-dimensional movement, the unfolding and enfolding of the single more comprehensive holomovement.

Scientists may very well study the manifest explicate order of electron particles and even employ mechanistic concepts as far as they are helpful, according to Bohm. But they should avoid the mistake of assuming that the explicate order is the fundamental reality. One cannot explain the harbor by referring simply to the boats and their lights. Science here, understood as the human process of pursuing knowledge, ought not to begin from an examination of the parts and then attempt to derive all wholes through abstraction, explaining wholes as simply the results of the interactions of the parts.

> On the contrary, when one works in terms of the implicate order, one begins with the undivided wholeness of the universe, and the task of science is to derive the parts through abstraction from the whole, explaining them as approximately separable, stable, and recurrent, but externally related elements making up relatively autonomous sub-totalities, which are to be described in terms of an explicate order.[22]

We have a move here from one point of departure to another that parallels the medieval move from nominalism to realism: from beginning with the part to beginning with the whole. Some might say that this represents a move from physics to philosophy. It may also represent a move from the modern age to the postmodern or new age.

Part, Whole, and Holarchy

A question we might pose at this point is: What is the relationship between the parts and the whole? In one sense Bohm resists any sort of hierarchy of relationships; there is no great chain of being from lower to higher. For him, animate matter is not a higher form of being than is inanimate matter. To say that inanimate matter is dead or that it exhibits no intelligence may lead to the mistake of placing it lower on the ladder of being. What is misleading here is to think abstractly, to abstract the explicate parts from the implicate whole.[23] Bohm begins with the whole of matter, and he holds that this whole unfolds itself—becomes explicate—in a variety of media, some intelligent and some not, some conscious and some not. To focus our attention on either the animate or the inanimate is to abstract; and to divide and separate by means of thought is simply illusion. There really is an implicate order making itself explicate. Bohm is not a simple monist, believing that the parts are swallowed up in a mystical blur; rather, he believes that the whole is immanent in the parts.

Consequently, we might press the question of the relation of whole and parts in the explicate order. Does a strictly inanimate part contain the whole that has animate qualities? Bohm seems to answer this indirectly with his notion of region or subtotality. It should follow from the previous paragraph that a subtotality necessarily contains both animate and inanimate dimensions if it authentically re-presents the whole. However, Bohm describes inanimate matter as a relatively autonomous subtotality in which life is not manifest. This raises questions. If life is characteristic of the whole but not the inanimate subtotality, then how can the whole be wholly present in the subtotality? Is life left out? Or is it just not manifest? Does he mean to say that life is present implicately even when only inanimate matter is explicate? If so, then how do we know? By faith? That is, do we believe in the nonmanifest whole even when it is not manifest to us?

In addition, we wish to ask about the relationships among various subtotalities. Do they relate directly and solely to the whole, or do they share an intermediate relation with one another that qualifies their relation to the whole?

We might refer briefly here to the work of Arthur Koestler, whose cosmology at this point seems to run somewhat parallel to Bohm's. What Bohm refers to as a subtotality corresponds roughly to Koestler's notion of the holon. Like Bohm, Koestler is seeking a wholistic world view. He defines *holism* as did J. C. Smuts, as the belief that the whole is more than the sum of the parts. In modern physics, wholism consists in the insight that the whole is as necessary for understanding the parts as the parts are necessary for understanding the whole.[24] A whole is considered something complete in itself that needs no further explanation. The whole-part relationship, contrary to widely held thought, however, is not just that. There are no completely distinguishable parts and wholes in any absolute sense. They mutually define and depend on one another. Furthermore, all things are held together by an intermediate reality, the subwhole or holon. The holon is a stable, integrated structure, equipped with self-regulatory devices and enjoying a considerable degree of autonomy, of self-government.

Holons are part of an inclusive hierarchy, which Koestler calls a "holarchy." Koestler offers the example of cells of tissue and the heart. Each cell is capable of functioning in vitro as a quasi-independent whole. The heart is made up of such cells, but it too is a quasi-independent whole, functioning according to its own somewhat autonomous principles. Each of these are subwholes that function as subordinated parts of a more inclusive whole yet, namely, the human organism. "The term 'holon' may be applied to any stable sub-whole in an organismic, cognitive, or social hierarchy which displays rule-governed behaviour and/or structural Gestalt constancy."[25] Koestler's concept of the holon serves to supply the missing link between atomism or fundamental pluralism, on the one hand, and a holism that swallows up everything individual into mystical absorption, on the other.

Koestler's holons recall the mythical god Janus, the god with the two faces. The holons face two directions within the holarchy, toward the inside and downward as well as toward the outside and upward. Internally, the holon integrates its parts into itself as a whole. Externally, it is self-assertive, preserving its individual identity, while it itself becomes integrated into a more inclusive hierarchy. Holons "are Janus-faced. The face turned upward, toward higher levels, is that of a dependent part; the face turned downward, towards its own constituents, is that of a whole of remarkable self-sufficiency."[26]

It seems to me that Bohm could agree with much that Koestler says. The concept of subtotalities denies that the whole of reality is simply an aggregate of elementary parts. The whole determines the parts as much as the parts determine the whole, perhaps even more so for Bohm. And at times Bohm speaks of an infinite regress of implicate orders, wherein a given order is implicate to the explicate order dependent on it, and at the same time is itself explicate to a higher order that is its implicate. This roughly parallels Koestler's holarchy.

However, there are some contrasts. Bohm is more egalitarian and less hierarchical than Koestler. Bohm does not develop the equivalent of the holarchy for the explicate world. In addition, Bohm may be asking for more from his subtotalities than Koestler does from his holons. To get from the part to the whole in Koestler's holarchy, one must climb the ladder of being one holon at a time until one reaches the comprehensive top, the all-inclusive reality. Bohm, in contrast, goes directly from part to whole and back again without a mediating ladder. Bohm holds that access to one subtotality or integrated region provides us with a material door that opens directly out onto the whole, that the very nature or character of the largest whole can be revealed in the smallest part.

It is on this point that Ken Wilber and David Toolan are critical of Bohm. They do not like what they identify as the "shotgun wedding" of physics and mysticism in Bohm's work. These two critics have a high regard for mysticism in the classical sense, and Bohm's egalitarianism contravenes the hierarchicalism implicit in the mystical vision. Along with the tradition of the perennial philosophy, Wilber and Toolan picture reality in terms of levels of being, each one of which includes the levels beneath it. At the lowest level is inanimate matter, for example, which is included and surpassed at the animate or biological level. Similarly, the mental level includes both the inanimate and animate below it. This continues through the spiritual levels right on up the chain of being to the ultimate unity of all things. The various levels are mutually interpenetrating and interconnecting, but not in an equivalent fashion. The higher transcends the lower, not vice versa. All of the lower exists in the higher, but not all of the higher in the lower. The mystical view is that of a hierarchy of wholes, a multidimensional interpenetration with nonequivalence.[27]

In Bohm's defense it could be said that in place of a mystical hierarchy he has substituted the image of the universe as an organism breathing in and out. Thus, Bohm is willing to accept something less than a full confluence of mystical philosophy and physical theory.

> Mysticism's positive meaning could be that the ground of our existence is a mystery—a statement which Einstein himself accepted. It was he who said that what is most beautiful is the mysterious. To my mind, the word mystic should be applied to a person who has actually had some direct experience of the mystery which transcends the possibility of description. The problem for the rest of us is to know what that may mean.[28]

The Immense Multidimensional Ground

Now we ask of Bohm: What is the nature of the whole itself? For starters, it is not limited to the four dimensions of space-time common to our everyday experience. Electromagnetic fields that obey the laws of quantum theory have already provided us with one example of reality that transcends the four-dimensional frame of reference. And, Bohm argues, quantum theory in turn is limited to a certain domain so that hidden variables must be sought elsewhere. In short,

> the implicate order has to be extended into a multidimensional reality. In principle this reality is one unbroken whole, including the entire universe with all its fields and particles. Thus we have to say that the holomovement enfolds and unfolds in a multidimensional order, the dimensionality of which is effectively infinite.[29]

Occasionally Bohm refers to this as a background reality of "higher-dimensional" space. What does he mean here? Could it be a form of space that transcends yet is inclusive of our three-dimensional space? What are the alternatives? One alternative is to conceive of the inclusive background reality as an empty receptacle, as a void. Premodern precedents exist for this conception, which became dominant during the Newtonian period. Leucippus and Democrates divided material being into a plurality of imperceptibly small atoms (*atomoi*), each one eternal and indivisible. According to these philosophers, these atoms can be separated from one another and relate to one another because they are set within a wider background of empty space, the unlimited (*apeiron*). But because true being is associated with the atoms and not with the empty receptacle, the spatial background itself cannot function as a cause or influence in the material world. It is only present due to its absence.

The other alternative is to fill the background with being. For this alternative we can thank both Parmenides and Heraclitus. Bohm, curiously enough, identifies himself with the school of Parmenides in holding that space is a filled plenum.[30] Space is filled for Parmenides because outside of it there can be only nothing. "What is, is," he wrote, which implies that there is no such thing as empty space either within or outside the being of the world. All things are finally reduced to one thing, and that great One is described as never having come into being from a previous state of nonbeing. It is eternal, imperishable, unitary, and complete. Parmenides goes on to argue that if there is a single substance behind all things, then the concept of change is logically absurd and the phenomenon of change is an illusion. To get beyond opinion to truth is to get beyond illusory change to eternal and unchangeable being.

One could think Bohm would be more interested in Heraclitus than Parmenides on this score. With Heraclitus, Bohm could have both fundamental unity and ongoing change. According to Heraclitus, there is only one basic reality in the world, which is the source for all things, and the process by which this reality becomes a plurality of things is the process of change. The never-ending flux consists in differing forms of a containing single reality variously described as fire, logos, or God. Materially conceived, all things are a different form of the ever-living fire. Rationally conceived, all things are expressions of the divine logos. Because God is reason (*logos*) and since God is the One that permeates all things, pantheist Heraclitus holds that all things move and change in accordance with the logos as the universal law immanent in the process. What we perceive to be disorder and strife between opposites will ultimately find a higher harmony in the ongoing life of the divine unity.[31] In addition to comprehensive unity and flux, Heraclitus should also have appeal for Bohm because his unifying reality, God, has the ability to influence individual events.

How does Bohm describe his own notion of the filled plenum? He describes it as a sea of energy. The forms of the flux appear as ripples or wave patterns on the surface of this sea.

> What is implied by this proposal is that what we call empty space contains an immense background of energy, and that matter as we know it is a small quantized wavelike excitation on top of this background, rather like a tiny ripple on a vast sea. . . . This vast sea of energy may play a key part in the understanding of the cosmos as a whole. . . . What we perceive through the senses as empty space is actually the plenum, which is the ground for the existence of everything, including ourselves.[32]

The sea of energy is immense. So immense is it that when Bohm discusses the big bang theory of cosmogenesis, he says, "This big bang is to be regarded as actually just a little ripple."[33] The whole twenty-billion-year history of the multigalactic cosmos is just a little ripple! When Bohm says his sea of energy is immense, he means it.

Bohm's plenum is not to be conceived as a material medium such as Heraclitus's fire or the nineteenth-century concept of a pervasive ether, both of which were regarded as moving only in three-dimensional space. Bohm wants more. This energy sea is to be understood in terms of a multidimensional implicate order, while the universe of matter manifest to our sense experience is to be treated as a comparatively small pattern of excitation. This excitation pattern is relatively autonomous and gives rise to our experience of subtotalities and the notions of three-dimensional and quantum space.

From this point on, Bohm's multidimensional sea of energy begins to pick up character and personality. As we mentioned be-

fore, because this grand reality is inclusive of human consciousness—which Bohm takes to include thought, feeling, desire, will,
and so on—in itself it cannot be less than conscious. The holomovement must be the source of life and itself be living. Furthermore, the
absence of life is dubbed by Bohm as an abstraction.

> In its totality the holomovement includes the principle of life as
> well. Inanimate matter is then to be regarded as a relatively autono-
> mous sub-totality in which, at least as far as we know, life does not
> significantly manifest. That is to say, inanimate matter is a second-
> ary, derivative, and particular abstraction from the holomovement.[34]

Like other postmodernists, Bohm is striving to get beyond the
dualism bequeathed us by Descartes, for whom consciousness or
"thinking substance" is sharply distinguished from matter or "extended substance." The problem this dualism creates is that we then
have to look for a bridge to connect matter with consciousness.
Descartes clearly understands this difficulty and proposes its solution with his doctrine of God: God, transcending both matter and
consciousness, is able to provide clear and distinct ideas to consciousness that correspond to the extended objects. During the in-
tervening centuries since Descartes, the notion of God has dropped
out of modern cosmology and physics, leaving the now divorced
mind and matter to go their separate ways. Bohm wants to reunite
them with a common higher-dimensional ground, and so his notion
of holomovement performs the job done by God in Descartes's
system.

In uniting mind and matter, the holomovement is not simply
passive, waiting for conscious thought to manipulate it. Bohm says
it projects. It presses itself into human consciousness through memory, wherein a single moment consists in the co-presence of a series
of interpenetrating and intermingling elements in different degrees
of enfoldment. Bohm is making the startling claim that human
memory is not the projection of subjectivity out toward the world
but rather the projection of the world itself into our subjectivity.
The holomovement actively prompts human consciousness.

Thus each moment of consciousness has an explicit content,
which is a foreground, along with an implicit content, which is a
corresponding background. But the holomovement here is not re-

stricted to the implicit background; it also manifests itself in the explicit foreground. It projects its own implicate order in the process of becoming the explicate manifestation.

> The more comprehensive, deeper, and more inward actuality is neither mind nor body but rather a yet higher-dimensional actuality, which is their common ground and which is of a nature beyond both. . . . In this higher-dimensional ground the implicate order prevails. Thus, within this ground, *what is* is movement which is represented in thought as the co-presence of many phases of the implicate order. . . . So we do not say that mind and body causally affect each other, but rather that the movements of both are the outcome of related projections of a common higher-dimensional ground.[35]

And Bohm goes still farther in his concept of projection. He says the inclusive ground is creative.

> Such a projection can be described as creative, rather than mechanical, for by creativity one means just the inception of new content, which unfolds into a sequence of moments that is not completely derivable from what came earlier in this sequence or set of such sequences. What we are saying is, then, that movement is basically such a creative inception of new content as projected from the multidimensional ground. . . . This we may call the ground of all that is.[36]

In sum, the all-inclusive holomovement can be understood as the sea of energy or the multidimensional ground from which all things derive. It is living. It actively projects its own implicate order in and through human consciousness, thereby becoming manifest and explicit. In doing so it is creative, because what it unfolds in a sequence of moments is not simply derivable from what came earlier.

Holomovement and Holes in the Argument

One might ask at this point if Bohm has fallen into the fallacy of composition. This fallacy is committed when one reasons without warrant from the properties of the parts to the properties of the whole. The whole, if understood as more than simply the sum of its constituent parts, will have a character or integrity of its own that is not simply the transfer of the character of the parts. It will be a composition, not merely an aggregate. For example, I would commit the fallacy of composition if I were to argue that because every part that went into making my cuckoo clock is light, the cuckoo clock as a whole is light. The error is that the clock may contain a very large number of light parts, making the whole quite heavy.

Here, in the case of the holomovement, Bohm argues that because individual human beings are conscious, the universe as a whole is conscious. But does this follow? Does it follow necessarily that if the individual parts are conscious—which implies intelligence, self-awareness, identity contrasted with other identities, and so on—that the whole *qua* whole has a parallel consciousness? It is in principle possible that the whole is the way Leucippis and Democrates thought it is, namely, an empty receptacle containing individual atomic units. Instead of a whole, the cosmos might in fact be simply an aggregate. It might just be a large collection of animate and inanimate entities, some of which are conscious.

Bohm, of course, means what he says. He understands the holomovement on the model of the hologram. The term *hologram* is derived from the Greek *holo* meaning "whole" and *gram* meaning "to write." Holography is the construction of a kind of three-dimensional picture produced by lensless photography. By letting light fall on a photographic plate from two sources (from the object itself plus a reference beam, which is light deflected by a mirror from the object onto the plate), one can reconstruct a three-dimensional likeness. What is important for the present argument is that every part of the resultant hologram contains the entire image. If the hologram is broken, any piece of it will reconstruct the whole. This is the model for the universe employed by Bohm in his notion of the holomovement.[37] The whole is fully present in the part.

But again we might ask whether some fallacious reasoning might be involved. In this case it would be the reverse of the composition fallacy, the fallacy of division. This fallacy is committed when the properties of the whole are attributed without warrant to the parts. According to the holographic model, the qualities of the whole seem to be present without remainder in each of the parts.

Yet wholistic thinking ordinarily requires as one of its premises that the whole is greater than the sum of the parts—or, to phrase it more accurately, that the whole has an integrity (integrating power) of its own. This premise would permit the influence of the whole to be present in each of the parts, but the whole itself would not be exhausted in each of the parts. The problem of the parts for Bohm is just that they are parts—that is, that they are perceived and thought of as separate and distinct from one another. What Bohm wants to affirm is unity, wholeness. Whatever unity or wholeness exists, then, belongs by definition not to the parts but to the whole. The parts even just formally cannot contain all the qualities of the whole. It seems that the holographic model then might be leading Bohm away from his target, because this model implies that all of the qualities of the whole are exhaustively present in the part.

Is the Holomovement Divine?

Can we consider the holomovement divine? Bohm refers to it as the "higher-dimensional ground" of all things, the implicate order underlying the explicate order, or even the nonmanifest that moves what is manifest. Corresponding notions in the philosophies of Descartes and Spinoza are labeled God. What functions as God and the divine subjective aim in Alfred North Whitehead's metaphysical system has an ordering responsibility akin to Bohm's implicate ordering. Theologian John Cobb can refer to Whitehead's God as an "energy-event" that gives rise to both matter and human consciousness.[38] Thus, if Bohm wished to attribute divine qualities to the holomovement, there would be some precedent.

But Bohm hesitates to follow this precedent. He is willing to speculate on the nature of the implicate order, but then he adds a caution: "We have to be careful not to linger on that too long."[39] He wishes to keep theological speculation to a minimum.

Bohm is willing to describe the implicate order as holy. He is a bit less willing to describe it as sacred. The term *sacred* has an etymological history going back to ancient religious sacrifice, and this makes Bohm nervous because it is too closely associated with organized religion. Bohm wants to avoid organized religion. The term *holy,* in contrast, comes from the same root as *whole;* therefore, he is quite happy thinking of the whole as holy.[40]

But in dubbing the whole holy, Bohm is still a long way from formulating what looks like a doctrine of God. The implicate order for Bohm is matter, not spirit. The term *spirit* in languages such as Hebrew and Greek means "breath" or "wind." It became associated with the divine because, though in itself it was not manifest, it appeared to move what is manifest when blowing things around. Modern science upset the phenomenological basis for such a theology, however, by discovering that breath and wind are themselves matter. All this brings Bohm to the frontier of theology without crossing over. "All we can say is that this view is consistent with the notion that there's a truth, an actuality, a being beyond what can be grasped in thought, and that is intelligence, the sacred, the holy."[41]

In thinking this way, Bohm follows other philosophers who similarly hesitated at this point. Parmenides, whom Bohm mentions, refrained from referring to the plenum as divine. He may even have refrained from referring to it as being. Parmenides' famous phrase *estin a ouk estin* is grammatically ambiguous, so that it can be translated either "it is or it is not" or "what is, is." The rendering "it is" makes one ask what "it" is referred to here. Some translators answer: being. The term for being, *eon,* appears in other Parmenidean texts, but not here. Why? And why does he avoid the term *god,* which was so commonly used by other pre-Socratic thinkers? Philosopher Eric Voegelin speculates that it is because of a mystical tendency in Parmenides and that the term *god* is typically used to refer to an object of thought.[42] Gods, as objects of thought, are only parts of the cosmos. The whole of reality transcends the parts and can be apprehended only through mystical insight.

Although it is worthy of note that Parmenides did not call his unifying reality divine, it may have been for reasons that do not apply to David Bohm. If Voegelin is correct that Parmenides was a mystic and that mystic reality transcends divinity, we should note that Bohm does not seem to develop his notion of the multidimensional ground in an overtly mystical direction. He restricts himself to scientific and speculative procedures, avoiding any appeal to direct mystical experience or to mystical philosophy. Bohm's theory of the implicate order is a theory about matter, not spirit. Should a realm of supramatter exist beyond the holomovement—which the Bohm theory does not forbid—then the discussion would be open for religious speculation. In the meantime, as we suggested earlier, there is no actual mixture of physics and theology in Bohm's work.

Another reason that might be given for avoiding the attribution of divinity to the holomovement is that in doing so we might fall into the "god-of-the-gaps" trap. Theologians fall into this trap when they look for the gaps in scientific knowledge and then try to plug those gaps with assertions about God. This is a trap, because what is a gap for one generation of scientists is frequently filled with empirical knowledge by the subsequent generation. The result is that the gaps become smaller and smaller, making the theologians' God proportionately smaller. Arthur Koestler, whose position is quite similar to the one under discussion, cautions us here while criticizing Bohm's hidden variables theory.

> Einstein, de Broglie, Schrödinger, Vigler, and David Bohm, who were unwilling to accept the indeterminacy and acausality of sub-atomic events . . . were inclined to believe in the existence of a substratum below the sub-atomic level, which ruled and determined those seemingly indeterminate processes. This was called the theory of "hidden variables"—which, however, has been abandoned even by its staunchest supporters because it seemed to lead simply nowhere.

> But although unacceptable to the physicists, the hidden variables provided a fertile field for metaphysical and parapsychological theorizings. Theologians proposed that Divine Providence might work from within the fuzzy gaps in the matrix of physical causality ("the god of the gaps").[43]

Although Bohm does not advocate a god-of-the-gaps position, he does advocate something parallel. It is a ground-of-the-gaps or holomovement-of-the-gaps position. The Newtonian physics of the modern era and the quantum physics of the approaching postmodern era have left gaps that Bohm wants to fill. The fragmentation of modern thinking and its corresponding breakdown of social and natural relationships has sent Bohm on a search for a wholistic actuality that can unite the fragments. He has not sought it through divine revelation or even mystical experience. He has sought rather to observe what is manifest in the explicate order, to observe the spatial gaps among what is explicate, and then to render a synthetic judgment positing an all-inclusive and implicate order belonging to the whole of reality.

Regardless of whether Bohm himself engages in theological inquiry, we must recognize that talk about the whole suggests talk about God. To raise the question of the whole of reality is indirectly to ask about the divine. In Jewish and Christian tradition all that is real is the product of God's creative work. The cosmological speculations of theorists such as David Bohm raise the kind of issues that prompt questions about monotheism.

Monotheism is the belief in one God as the ultimate reality that normally includes a distinction between God and the created order. The created order is not sufficient unto itself. Even if we conceive of it as a whole, as a totality of *finite* reality, we must recognize that we can then in principle conceive of something outside or beyond it. In fact, wholes that we have experienced (Bohm's subtotalities or Koestler's holons) are constituted as specific wholes by being separated from something else, by drawing the line between what is integrated and what is left outside the integration. We can distinguish one whole from another whole, and this is what gives each whole its identity. Unless the cosmos is an exception to the rule, then, a transcendent God is required for it to attain its own wholeness. Or else the wholeness of the cosmos, by being conceived of as ultimate and infinite, is inadvertently equated with God by transcending in itself all the subwholes within it.

Christians have historically made certain commitments regarding such a doctrine of God that usually put them in the camp of monotheists. The primary religious sentiment is to affirm that God is the ultimate reality. Regardless of how it is rationally depicted, this affirmation of God's ultimacy is expressed by St. Paul, for whom God is all in all (1 Cor. 15:28), by St. Augustine's doctrine of creation out of nothing, and by St. Anselm's notion of God as "that than which nothing greater can be conceived."[44] Note how H. Richard Niebuhr, for example, communicates this sense of divine ultimacy when depicting "radical monotheism."

> For radical monotheism the value-center is neither closed society nor the principle of such a society but the principle of being itself;

its reference is to no one reality among the many but to One beyond all the many, whence all the many derive their being, and by
participation in which they exist. As faith, it is reliance on the
source of all being for the significance of the self and of all that
exists. It is the assurance that because I am, I am valued, and
because you are, you are beloved, and because whatever is has being, therefore it is worthy of love. It is the confidence that whatever
is, is good, because it exists as one thing among the many which all
have their origin and their being, in the One—the principle of being
which is also the principle of value.[45]

For Niebuhr, radical monotheism has to do with the ultimate being
and value of all things. It is also more. There is something beyond
the being and value of all things. That "One beyond all the many,"
Christians call God.

It is in principle possible to solve the problem of the relationship between the one and the many without recourse to the
Christian God. A monism would do, and it is monism that is attracting new age devotees. Monism is the view that the plurality of
things in the phenomenal world is ultimately part of a single reality.
Parmenides and Heraclitus provide us with examples. In more recent
times monism has become attractive as a tool for overcoming the
dualism of mind and body, because one can simply posit a more
primary reality of which both mind and body are modes. This seems
to be what is attracting Bohm and attracting as well his new age
followers.

The problem with monism in all its forms is that it denies the
Christian belief in a radical distinction between God and the creation.[46] This distinction functions to affirm divine ultimacy. Although
God is present in the world, the being of God transcends the world,
the whole world. This means among other things that the creature
can never become totally divine. Although God as Trinity does participate in creation through the incarnation in Jesus Christ and
through the work of the Holy Spirit, that which has been created
will remain the created.

The distinction between God and the creation has two corollaries in Christian monotheism. First, God is not thought of as simply a craftsperson who molds and shapes and directs an already
existent world stuff. Rather, God creates *ex nihilo*, out of nothing.

He summons the universe into existence, and should he not so summon it, there would be only God.

It entails, second, that the created realm is entirely dependent on God as the source and power of its continued existence. We have a part in the universe not by some natural right, but only by the grace of God. Life is a gift. The proper creaturely response is to be thankful.[47] The purpose of Bohm's books such as *Wholeness and the Implicate Order* is not to render thanksgiving for the cosmos, of course. But perhaps the theological reader can be thankful that Bohm tries to avoid a clash with Christian theology that would result from naming the holomovement divine. Yet the clash cannot be avoided, because the claims he makes for the holomovement *do* compete with the claims theologians make for God.

History and the Whole

There is another and related issue: Can Bohm's holographic microcosm-macrocosm correlation be made compatible with the Christian emphasis on historical reality? The idea that reality is historical and that such things as creativity and irreversible change occur within history is an idea that modernity shares with ancient Israel and the New Testament. Because of the movement in holomovement, it would seem that Bohm accepts the modern understanding of reality as processive, temporal, and historical. But just how far is he in fact willing to go with this? Speculations on the microcosm-macrocosm correlation have a tendency to deny genuine historicity to events, to dissolve everything into a timeless unity. When Bohm speaks directly to the issue, he speaks of time in the holomovement in terms of "recurrence" on the analogy of the changing seasons.[48]

Bohm's notion of implicate causation carries his theory in the direction of a timeless or suprahistorical whole that minimizes the importance of the course of individual events. In Bohm's explicate order, current events do not cause or influence future events directly. Each event is enfolded into the implicate order, into the whole. The next or the subsequent event emerges from the implicate order. It is not the direct product of its predecessor. All of history is presumed here to be analogous to a movie film. Each frame is a still picture, but due to its speed through the camera we perceive the movement as continuous. So also in history each event is a unit unto itself produced by the implicate order becoming explicate. It only appears to be a sequence of causally related events. To exaggerate a bit: in order to kick the dog one must first kick the implicate order and then the implicate order kicks the dog; then, in a subsequent event, the implicate order prompts the dog to yelp. Kicking, feeling the kick, and yelping all belong already to the immense multidimensional whole and simply become explicate at arbitrary times. It just appears to us that they are causally related.

The advantage of such a theory is that we are no longer the victims of a strict nexus of efficient causation. Individual events are related to the whole. Should one want to describe divine activity in the ordinary course of events, the concept of the implicate order might be a vehicle for doing so. However, there may be a disadvantage as well. By eliminating entirely the direct continuity between the sequence of events, temporality and historicity risk being swallowed up in the achronic abyss of the implicate order.

There are grounds for taking history seriously in both natural science and Christian theology. It has been traditionally assumed that history belongs peculiarly to the human condition and that nature functions in some timeless or achronic realm, subject to unchanging laws. What is beginning to dawn on modern consciousness is the comprehensiveness of the category of history. Nature too is historical. It is not timeless. Its temporal events run in only one direction, from past to future. Space physicist C. F. von Weizsacker argues the point forcefully.

> Man is indeed a historic being, but this is possible because man comes out of nature and because nature is historic herself. . . . History in the broadest sense is the essence of what happens in time. In this sense, nature undoubtedly has a history since nature herself is in time. History of nature, then, would be the totality of what happens in nature.[49]

If von Weizsacker is correct that the natural realm is historical and hence subject to newness and to irreversible changes, then the whole of nature is not directly accessible through mental holography or microcosm-macrocosm correlation. Nor is temporal passage a totally discontinuous product of a supratemporal whole.

If one were to take the historical view seriously, so that what is engaged in temporal passage is understood as what is real, and if one were similarly open to the future and to the possibility of a genuinely new reality resulting from the processes, then one would have to deny that the whole of reality presently exists anywhere. Even if the whole of space were present, certainly the whole of time would not be. In any given moment in which one focuses on one of the parts, the whole could not become present in any complete sense. It could not do so because it is not yet the whole that it someday will be. There cannot be a microcosm that fully represents the macrocosm, because the macrocosm is itself still in process, still becoming, still incomplete. To assert that the whole is fully present holographically implies a denial of temporality. It implies that reality as a whole is achronic and unchanging. The only authentic way in which the whole can become present in the part is for the final future to become present ahead of time.

Bohm believes he handles this problem by distinguishing between flowing "wholeness" and static "totality." Totality includes the notion of completeness. What is whole, in contrast, is incomplete.[50] By the whole he is referring to what is at the present moment, in its incompleteness and without regard to its future. But, we might ask, what kind of a whole is it that is an incomplete whole? Can the whole understood this way be equated with what is real? Is not the future of the holomovement constitutive of its reality? Is not Bohm himself doing what he has warned us against, namely, abstracting and isolating the present whole from the more inclusive reality?

The concept of totality is not necessarily as static as Bohm believes. If it includes the aspect of temporal passage, then totality is located in the future and stands in contrast to the present in creative tension. It constantly draws the present beyond itself toward ever-new reality, toward fulfillment. Without the notion of future totality, the notion of wholeness is abstracted from time and becomes vacuous.

At the present moment, the totality of reality does not exist anywhere in its completeness. We can only anticipate it. In fact, that is what we do. In isolated moments of meaningfulness, we implicitly anticipate the completed whole, the total reality that will finally put all things into their respective places. To see meaning in the present moment of our lives is an act of unconscious faith. It is an act of trust that the future will confirm and extend the meaning we presently perceive and experience. Oh, yes, you or I just might have a mystical experience that will give us a sense of cosmic unity. We might also read with sympathy a theory such as Bohm's that posits cosmic unity. But these are not holograms in the sense that they reveal a presently existing wholeness to things. Rather, such experiences and theories are proleptic—that is, they anticipate *future wholeness.*

Ordinary events—as well as mystical experiences and metaphysical theories—are both causative and yet open to the future, making them reciprocally related to the future whole. Present events, or parts and subtotalities, gain their own present identity from the final future of all things. And the final future will be determined in part by present events. Meaningful events may be revelatory—that is, they may manifest wholeness—but they do so not because they are microcosms of the whole. They do so rather because by faith we recognize their dependence upon the yet-to-be-actualized whole to make them what they are. They point to the whole while not in themselves embodying all that the whole will ultimately include. Instead of holograms we should speak of *proleptograms.* Munich theologian Wolfhart Pannenberg contends that the essence of all things is yet to be determined. It will not be determined until the eschatological future. The meaning we find in the present moment is dependent upon an implicit faith that includes a foreconception of what is to come.

> Only from a fore-conception of a final future, and thus of the still unfinished wholeness of reality, is it possible to assign to an individual event or being—be it present or past—its definitive meaning by saying what it is. Thus, when someone names a thing and says, "This is a rose," or "This is a dog," he always does so from the standpoint of an implicit foreconception of the final future, and of the totality of reality that will first be constituted by the final future. For every individual has its definitive meaning only within this whole.[51]

It is at the point of this defining whole in the final future that we will find God. All events are moving ahead to meet a common future, a common future that is the reality of God. No whole exists at present. Separate subjects and separate objects and the consequent uncertainty in human knowing really do exist. Fragmentation and brokenness really do exist in our world, and no amount of thinking wholistically will make them completely go away. In fact, if we convert our minds to engage only in wholistic thinking, and if the fragmentation and brokenness persist, then our thoughts will be illusory. We will be naive. What we need to do rather is place our wholistic thinking into the category of hope and expectation. We need to be realistic about the divisions and destructive forces in our world while at the same time looking forward to a wholeness that will have uniting power. We need to look forward to a future healing. Once this vision is clear, then we can seek to make that future healing have an impact on present brokenness. This is how proleptic wholeness works.

The Yet-to-Be-Whole World

The real world is the yet-to-be-whole world.[52] This, I think, is the best way to capture the wholistic insight of new age thinking that remains realistic and that also coheres with the Christian doctrine of creation. Christians believe that God is the creator of the world. But just how God goes about the activity of creating is debatable. We can be helped here somewhat by paying attention to what scientists and philosophers are saying. Given what I have said in this chapter, let me suggest the following theological hypothesis: *God creates continually and will not finish the divine creative work until the creation is made whole in the eschaton.* The destiny of the whole will determine what the parts are. This leads to a couple of corollaries.

Our first corollary is this: *God creates from the future, not the past.* Now this may seem to contradict the commonly accepted Christian view as well as our commonsense view of causality. We in the West have commonly accepted the idea of temporality, that time consists of a linear one-way passage from the past through the present toward the future. We assume that the power of being comes from the past—that is, that everything is due to a past cause and a present effect. The power of being is assumed to come in the form of a push from the past. God is frequently said to have created all things once and for all at the onset of time. What is widely believed is that out of abject nothingness God built a lovely machine complete with parts and principles of operation, then wound it up, and it has been running ever since.

Yet I think the reverse is the case. To be is to have a future. To lose one's future and to have only a past is to die. Deep down we know this. Thinking theologically, then, we could say that the first thing God did for the world was to give it a future. Without a future it would be nothing. God bestowed the future by opening up the possibility of its becoming something it never has been before and by supplying it with the power to change. And this is something we experience constantly. Moment by moment, God is giving us a future. This means that creation is not merely an event that happened once a long time ago. Creation is continuing. It is going on right now.

Instead of as a push from the past or a kick from Bohm's achronic multidimensional ground, then, I suggest we think of God's creative activity as a pull from the future. This brings us to the second corollary: *God's creative activity within nature and history derives from his redemptive work of drawing free and contingent beings into a harmonious whole.* In other words, God heals by integrating parts into the whole. This is how God creates. This is how God saves. Creation and salvation, then, belong together as the work of the one God.

Thus, we may think of the whole of cosmic history as a single divine act of creation, a whole of which our own personal histories are minute but indispensable parts. And just as the operations of the human heart are drawn up into the decisions and purposes of the human personality as a whole, our personal lives will be drawn up into and find their proper definition through their relationship to the whole of God's creative work. But because God's creative history has not yet come to its completion, it is not yet whole. The future is for us still open. Reality is on the way to being determined and defined in mutual reciprocity between the actual course of finite events and the overall divine design. What permits us to think wholistically is the promise of the future completion of God's creative and redemptive act. In the meantime, we find ourselves within the creative work of God, a work yet to be completed, and hence appropriately called from our point of view "continuing creation."

In conclusion, I believe Christian thinkers should give ear to what David Bohm is saying because he is raising a scientific voice in behalf of the widespread yearnings for wholeness that characterize the new age and the emerging postmodern consciousness. Unfortunately, however, our contemporary theologians are paying precious little attention to this important cultural phenomenon. So preoccupied have the Church's intellectuals been with making the gospel relevant to the *modern* mind, they have scarcely noticed that the modern mind itself is now breaking down and giving way to something new. When new age consciousness finally does begin to draw the belated attention of the Church, we can expect that one of the first things systematic theologians will do is search for a philosophical system that is both authentically postmodern and potentially compatible with Christian faith. At that time David Bohm's scientific theory might be considered as an aid to theology in a manner parallel to the roles previously played by the systems of Aristotle and Whitehead.

It is with this possibility in mind that I have raised a few theological questions and suggested some cautions. Although Bohm's cosmology might very well become allied to a religious ideology in the mind of some theorists, it is fortuitous at this point that Bohm has refrained from simply labeling his holomovement God. Whether by accident or design, he shows wisdom in following Parmenides in this regard. To call it God would be to produce another god of the philosophers, a divine principle posited to save the other principles of the system from collapse. It would invite a god-of-the-gaps philosophy. Nothing in principle is wrong with a god-of-the-gaps philosophy, especially if it is done with coherence and elegance, but the problem from the Christian point of view is that once one is secure in a sound system with a built-in divinity, then one's ears are less likely to be open to the revelatory Word coming from the yet-more-transcendent God himself, the Word that takes us beyond every system into the open future.

Chapter Five

Testing the Spirits

 The task of this book is to "test the spirits" (1 John 4:1), to determine what is healthy or unhealthy about the new age movement. Testing, or as St. Paul says, discerning (1 Cor. 12:10), is the process of making subtle evaluations or judgments. I believe this is called for at the present moment, because the current tendency seems to be either to make blanket condemnations or to greet the new age as the arrival of utopia. Our human temptation is to make total or uncompromising judgments. This is a mistake, I think, on a number of counts. First, the new age movement is not merely one thing. It is a collection of a wide variety of groups and individuals, some sophisticated and some naive, some sincere and some charlatans, some who give us helpful new ideas and some who merely revive outdated superstitions. Should the same judgment apply uniformly to all of these? I think not.

Second, although we have been able to identify a central core of new age teachings that are basically gnostic, many people only dabble at the periphery of the new age without accepting the whole of the gnostic teaching. As eclectics, they borrow what they need and then go about their daily business. The degree of involvement in the new age on the part of concerned Christians needs to be reviewed carefully.

Third, some people are genuinely helped by the support networks and the increase of self-esteem the new age offers. We should recall Jesus' words, "You will know them by their fruits" (Matt. 7:16). If new age involvement bears healthy fruit, then we should have the courage to acknowledge it and be grateful for it.

Nevertheless, we do not want to get caught up in the euphoria of the new age to such a degree that we lose our critical capacity. In previous chapters I have referred to the gnostic world view and theory of salvation. Despite claims of openness and truth, new age gnosticism is in fact closed off from the truth regarding the essential nature of our relationship to ultimate reality, namely, the dialectic of sin and grace. Its doctrine of the cosmic self fails to recognize the sharp distinction between ourselves and God, between us as creatures and God as creator. It fails to accept a plain fact: although we humans were created for union with God and with one another, we are estranged from God and neighbor because of sin. It rejects the message of the gospel, that God is the one who takes action to overcome this estrangement by granting us forgiveness of sin and the gift of eternal life. The divine ground of new age gnosticism is a passive enlightenment sitting atop a spiritual ladder, waiting for us to climb through vigorous self-discipline. The God of the Christian gospel is active. He comes down the ladder into the midst of the physical world. He enters our world at all its levels and depths. The creator becomes the creature. Salvation enters the world of estrangement. Our sin is met with God's act of grace.

At stake here is the spiritual health of individuals and groups. To get at this spiritual health we need healthy theology. We want what we say doctrinally to reflect as closely as possible the truth about God and God's relationship to our world and to us personally. Indeed, the cost of bad doctrine is often measurable in the unhealth and unfreedom of the practices it reflects and reinforces. Good theology is vital and practical. It is not merely an armchair academic concern.

As a Christian I want to reflect on what has been revealed in the event of Jesus Christ: the fact that the divine entered our world, and suffered as one of us when our world saw fit to crucify what was godly. Despite our rejection of God's presence, God acted in

grace by raising Jesus Christ from the dead and promising us resurrection as well. These are the basic historical events on which we
build a healthy theology. Now, if the truth of the cosmos is genuinely reflected in these facts, we must then confront some weakness-
es in the metaphysics of the new age. For one thing, it is clear that
we as human beings are not essentially divine. We are not God
implicit. Rather, we are creatures who are estranged from our creator. For another thing, the work of salvation is not something we
can accomplish by simply turning inward toward our higher selves.
If we are to attain the blessing of an eternal life in harmony with
the cosmos and with God, our attainment of this blessing comes
from an initiating act of God. We cannot initiate our own salvation.
It will have to come from God's grace, the same grace by which
God raised the dead Jesus on the first Easter. The good news is that
this grace is already given. Its fulfillment is already promised. We
can rely on God for salvation and healing.

St. Augustine provides us with a good example here. The pas-
sion of his life was to obtain the profound gnosis, to know "God
and the soul, only God and the soul." The version of new age metaphysics he confronted in fourth-century north Africa was Neopla-
tonism. The Neoplatonists taught him that our soul within us has a
built-in propensity to make its way through mystical contemplation
back to its source, back to its origin in the divine. It was this that
led to Augustine's oft-repeated prayer to God: "You have made us
for yourself, and our heart is restless until it rests in you."[1] When
Augustine converted to Christianity, he did so because of an important discovery. He had discovered the reverse movement of grace.
Rather than the soul ascending to God, God comes down into the
soul. Because of his loving grace, God takes action, becomes incarnate in Jesus Christ, and through the Holy Spirit enters each of our
lives with transformatory power.

Sin and Grace

On one occasion I invited Barbara Marx Hubbard to lecture to my
theology class in Berkeley. She gave a marvelously optimistic de-
scription of the imminent spiritual transformation that would carry
us to Teilhard de Chardin's point omega. It was a beautiful lecture.

During the question-and-answer period, one student asked what she thought about sin. "Oh, don't talk about sin!" she exclaimed. "That's negative thinking, and negative thinking is what is blocking our way to spiritual transformation."

There is a problem here. It is the problem of honestly acknowledging the reality in which we live. Barbara Marx Hubbard may be right in saying that we need positive thinking if we are to make positive change, but this is insufficient reason for denying the reality of our situation. In point of plain fact, we live in a sinful world and, what's more, we ourselves are sinful. Whatever spiritual health we are able to achieve in the future will have to include an honest appropriation of our own sinful nature, or else it will collapse under the weight of its own naiveté.[2]

This truth has consequences for wholism. We may be parts of a greater whole, but it is a broken whole, and we contribute to its brokenness. This brokenness is part of our everyday experience. If this were not the case, then there would be no reason for us even to want evolutionary transformation into something better. Let me offer a personal example of the sense of brokenness created by sin.

I must have been about seven or eight years old, growing up in Dearborn, Michigan. It was springtime. The older boys in the neighborhood, Bobby and Louis and David, had made themselves slingshots out of very powerful rubber bands. They were bragging about how many birds they had shot down, crows and blue jays and such. I wished I could be big like them. I wished I could be a hunter, a marksman, one who could by stealth and accuracy bring down wild game.

I examined the design of their slingshots carefully. I went home and into my father's workshop and duplicated the design. Now I had my own powerful weapon. What remained was the hunt and the kill.

Into the fields I went with a pocketful of marbles and small stones to use as pellets. I shot at everything that moved. But I hit nothing. Flying birds did not even have to dodge, so poor was my aim. When I aimed at those sitting in trees, they simply watched me nonchalantly, often flying away only after the "danger" had passed. As a hunter, I was a failure.

But I did not give up. I never give up. But because my aim was not improving, I decided to look for easier targets. I knew that in

Mr. and Mrs. Starkweather's side yard was a nest of recently born robins. My mother, seeing me shooting wildly with my slingshot, had warned me: "Frankie [she called me by my middle name in those days], whatever you do, don't go near that robin's nest!" But the primitive thirst for the kill was strong.

The fledglings were a number of weeks old. They had full feathers and full color, but they were identifiable as young because of the spots on their orange breasts. They were flying from tree to tree in the Starkweather yard under their mother's supervision. They could not move as fast as an adult robin, and they as yet had not learned who might be a mortal enemy.

I spotted one in the crabapple tree. Quietly I approached with a marble in my slingshot. It did not move. It simply watched me. I came closer so as to get a better shot. It still did not move, so I came still closer. With careful aim I sent that projectile toward the stationary robin and hit it square in the chest. It fell through the branches and landed on the ground. It was dead.

The mother robin had witnessed the whole dastardly deed. She was enraged. She screamed the screams of grief and anger. She swooped between the branches and circled above me as I ran into my house.

I sat in the living room and pondered the matter for a while. When the bird's screaming had died down, I went back out to the crabapple tree to examine the evidence. It was indeed true, I had hit my target. It was also true that this defenseless fledgling had met its untimely death at my hand, and I had created immense grief in its surviving mother. I could not even have the satisfaction of bragging to Bobby and Louis and David, because there was little merit in my downing a helpless robin compared with their shooting of wild crows. They would only laugh at me. Furthermore, the punishment my mother would mete out if I were caught was terrible to contemplate. So I found myself in a dilemma.

The only way out of the dilemma, I schemed, would be to lie. I picked up the bird's warm body and showed it to my mother. "I found this dead robin, Mom," I told her. "Should I bury it?"

"Where did you find it?" she quizzed. So I took her to the spot. In the maple tree high above, the mother robin sat and occasionally screamed, as if telling my mother what I had done to make her life so sad.

"Yes, Frankie, you should bury it," she said. So I did.

After the funeral in our backyard, I returned to my chair in the living room and sat. I sat for an hour or two, just thinking about what had happened. There was more at stake here than simply the death of an innocent robin. Somehow the world was out of joint. The screams of the mother robin were in fact the voice of the whole cosmos crying in pain. I began to cry, too. My mother drifted into the living room and sat. She waited a few moments. Then, "Did you kill that bird, Frankie?" she asked.

"No," I insisted. "I just found it there, like I told you."

"Are you telling me the truth?" she pressed.

"Yes, it's just as I told you."

She left the room. She obviously knew I was guilty. I wondered why she was not going to punish me, not only for disobeying but also for fibbing. Over the years, as I've reflected on this incident, I have concluded that she must have thought I was already punishing myself and decided to leave me to my own sad fate.

Now, perhaps a hunter or a soldier reading this account might find my example trivial. Perhaps one could say it is only a law of nature that some hunt and others are hunted, and that this is not worth becoming sentimental about. Yet, what I am after here is more than mere sentiment. What I want to do is listen to the voice of the whole of nature, a voice that is emitting a cry of pain over the brokenness of our reality. The fact that we human beings by nature are fated to eat other living things to live is much more than a mere fact of life. It is an indication that suffering and grief are built right into the nexus of nature, that terror and agony are unavoidable. Plants and animals are going to die, innocently and prematurely, if not at one another's hands then at the hands of the human devourers. And, what's worse, we humans may even create situations of terror and agony that go well beyond what nature requires. I certainly did not need to slay the baby robin to put food on my family's table. My mother could buy a prepared chicken from the grocery store. No, out of my own desire for prowess in front of my friends I became bloodthirsty and was willing to sacrifice another life. Furthermore, I was willing to lie to cover up the deed. I was willing to add one more chapter to the long human history of untruths.

What this means is that we live amidst brokenness. Things simply do not fit together in complete harmony. We are slaying robins all the time. We do so through racial and ethnic prejudice that denies life chances to children growing up in the underclass. We do so by filling the world with thermonuclear terror, and then by supporting a weapons industry that robs our national budget of monies needed for education and social services. We glean our income and even our wealth from an economic system that exploits the natural and human resources of one part of the world in order to deliver profits to another. And we take those profits now, being unwilling to pay to reclothe the landscape of Mother Earth once we have stripped her of her coal and other ores. Or worse, we fill the caverns we have created with the toxic wastes we blow out of the exhaust pipe of our industrial machine. We are destructive, sometimes inadvertently, sometimes purposely. We do violence to one another, to nature, to God, and to ourselves.

In the face of all of this it does not help simply to affirm a unity of the whole without taking this brokenness into account. It does not help to advocate that we merely alter our consciousness so that we think of a higher self wherein all beings find their unity. It does not help simply to visualize myself at harmony with the cosmos. The fact is that in our everyday life we are separate beings, each with a separate consciousness, and we in fact do violence to one another. This is reality. We cannot escape it by ducking into another more spiritual level of existence where peace reigns and then say this alternative level is what is really real. I cannot escape to another metaphysical plane where I and the robin share a blissful unity, where my sin against nature ceases to have divisive repercussions. Sinful deeds have irrevocable consequences, and these consequences constitute the indelible march of historical events that make up the only reality we have.

The baby robin is dead. The mother is grieving. The pain is actual. Nothing can change that. This is the way history is written. This is what is real. To pretend otherwise is to live in untruth.

Unless we are able to face up to the pain wrought by sin, we are not ready to hear the gospel of grace. The gospel begins by acknowledging that it is God, first and foremost, who feels the pain of sin. What God has created is now broken. What God has brought into existence out of nothing is now engaged in mortal conflict with itself, sinking back into nonexistence. We, God's creatures, flip from self-pride to self-pity in narcissistic revelry, provoking distress in those close to us and then ignoring the resulting struggle. We, the apple of the divine eye, are willing to strangle each other for no good reason. Like children who have run away from home and denied that they ever even had parents, we wallow in self-destructive indulgence while our ignored God watches in deep remorse.

Because God loves the world, God feels the suffering of the world. Because God loves each of us, our inner struggles are simultaneously divine struggles. No pain is felt on earth that is not also felt in heaven. What's worse, God experiences our suffering in compound form—that is, all of it all the time. Like the mother robin who witnessed the slaying of her chick, somewhere in infinity can be heard the constant screaming of the divine heart broken with all the pain of our brokenness.

There is no corner of the creation that is too humble for God's sympathetic attention. On one occasion Jesus remarked about how cheap sparrows are. "Are not five sparrows sold for two pennies?" he asked rhetorically. Yet in falling from the sky "not one of them is forgotten in God's sight" (Luke 12:6; Matt. 10:29).

We come to learn this truth about the kind of God we have through the revelation associated with the life story of Jesus. In Jesus, God enters the world and is rejected by the world. The eternal one enters time. The infinite one takes on finite form. The deathless one dies. When light enters the darkness, the darkness rises up to blot it out. When wholesomeness imbues a part, the other parts rise up to destroy it. When the creator becomes part of the creation, the creation crucifies him.

The fact that the innocent Son of God was hung on a cross to die tells us something about the nature of the world in which we live, that it is not a safe home for God. God is not welcome here. We are rude to our divine guests when they come to visit. We slay them, just as we slay one another. God and the world are estranged, alienated.

The gospel message is that God does not want it to stay this way. God wants the estrangement to be bridged, the alienation to be overcome. And God has taken action. He has entered our plane of existence as one of us and suffered the same things we suffer. He has died innocently, just as did the robin fledgling in Starkweather's side yard. Yet in the throes of death while struggling on Calvary's cross, Jesus reveals the disposition of divine grace by saying, "Father, forgive them; for they do not know what they are doing" (Luke 23:34). God's plan is to break the cycle of violence through the forgiveness of sins.

Once I had broken the harmony of God's creation by bringing death to one of God's creatures, there was no way I could put things aright again. Even had my mother enacted the principles of distributive justice through some sort of punishment, the mother robin would still have had to endure her grief. No amount of present or future punishment can heal the brokenness of a past deed. Only forgiveness can. Only forgiveness is capable of transforming estrangement into reunion, alienation into harmony.

God showed us he means business by raising Jesus from the dead on the first Easter Sunday. The creator of life in the first place has the power to create it again. The source of the original creation has the will to bring us a *new* creation. Sin has not ultimately undone God. Death has not undone God. The gospel includes the message that our sin will be met by God's forgiveness, and our death will be met by God's raising us just as he raised Jesus. Jesus Christ is but "the first fruits of those who have died," writes St. Paul (1 Cor. 15:20). What has been true of Jesus will become true for us. This is God's promise. This is the ground for our hope.

The only hope I can have for seeing my sinful deed rectified is found in the grace of God, which is capable of healing brokenness. That healing will have to take the form of a transformation of time and space—that is, the establishment of a new creation that fulfills all the purposes of the present creation. My own tiny though not insignificant contribution to world history needs to undergo divine transmogrification if it is ever to contribute to the harmony rather than the disharmony of the whole. This is what the promised resurrection of the dead will accomplish. In this, and only in this, can I take comfort. The hopeful message of God's graciousness constitutes the gospel.

Transformation: Christian Style

One of the things that the new age movement seems to offer is its own form of hope, the hope that tomorrow can be better than today. It is no accident that *transformation* is a key term. It is curious that this term would be primary, given the basically static world view that underlies the traditional gnostic vision. We modern Westerners want to keep things on the move, because we work with the assumption that the future can be better than the past. What we want for ourselves is to realize that better future sooner. We want to get our hands on the steering wheel and put our foot on the accelerator and drive ourselves in the direction of a better life. This is what the new age claims it can provide. It poses an immensely attractive invitation to members of Christian churches who may feel that their congregational life is stagnant, that their religion merely inflicts a long list of "dos" and "don'ts" that inhibit creative living.

Unfortunately, many Christians give up on their faith communities before they tap the transformatory power in the Christian gospel. The Christian understanding of transformation is a strong one.[3] It may be that much of contemporary Christendom has forgotten about it. It may be that too many pastors are just going through the motions of "playing church" and failing to help people plug in to the power source. There may be many reasons why the Christian understanding of transformation is ignored. Nevertheless, this by no means diminishes the dynamism of God. Nor does it change the historical fact that the reason the Christian faith swept the Roman Empire like wildfire was that it actually delivered the spiritual strength and personal power that groups like the gnostics only promised.

The vocabulary we use to describe this transformation usually includes words such as *justification, faith, sanctification,* and *love.* Let us look at some of these in turn.

Justification and Faith

The word *justification* refers to the act of creating wholeness by invoking the justice of God. It is the act whereby God turns something unjust into something just. What makes justification into the gospel is the announcement that God creates just people by forgiving them. It is an act of grace. Because of Jesus Christ, God forgives us of our sin; and this is what accomplishes reconciliation.

Martin Luther among others referred to this as the "happy exchange." The imagery is that of a courtroom. You or I sit in the defendant's chair while the prosecuting attorney reads off the list of our sins. There is no doubt that we are guilty. Then comes time for the verdict. The judge raises the gavel and then looks in the defendant's box. But instead of seeing the sinner seated there, the judge sees Christ. He sees the innocent one. When the gavel is finally lowered and the verdict rendered, we are declared innocent. Or, to put it another way, the penalty for sin falls upon Jesus. He serves our sentence for us, placing us in the state of forgiveness. What has happened is that an exchange has taken place. Christ has taken on our guilt himself. We in turn have been treated according to his innocence. Though unjust, we are treated as just. We are justified for Christ's sake.

In my own case, Jesus first takes the place of the robin in the crabapple tree. The penalty of my sin falls on him. He suffers and dies. He is the innocent one. I am the guilty. But then an exchange takes place. Jesus takes up the slingshot. He bestows on me his innocence while taking on my guilt. By Jesus' taking my place in the court of judgment, I am rendered just.

Now I can sense the drama of this exchange in my present life, because the resurrected and living Christ is present. He is actually present in our faith, right now. This is what gives faith the power to transform our lives and make us whole.

When we speak of faith here we are not referring simply to belief in doctrines or stories about a carpenter who lived twenty centuries ago in ancient Israel. Faith involves belief, to be sure. But it is not belief itself that justifies. It is Christ who justifies. The important point is that for the person who has faith, Christ is actually—perhaps we could say mystically—present every moment. We are speaking here of the Easter Christ, the risen Christ, who is not bound by time or space. We are speaking here of the living Christ who is made present to us through the work of the Holy Spirit. St. Paul says we "put on Christ" (Gal. 3:27) so that our justifier is as close to us as is our clothing. Martin Luther struggles for words to express it mystically, saying that our "faith justifies because it takes hold of and possesses this treasure, the present Christ. But how he is present—this is beyond our thought."[4] It is Christ's oneness with us that effects our forgiveness and, hence, our justification.

The justified life has a double character. It is that as people of faith we are simultaneously just and unjust. We are both saved and sinful. We are both Christ-filled and self-directing. This is the paradox of forgiveness. Forgiveness applies only to those of us who sin. Forgiveness applies only to those of us who disturb the order of nature by slaying its innocents, by sacrificing its harmony for our own self-aggrandizement, by robbing it of its life-giving potential, by filling its days and nights with avarice and violence, by polluting its beauty. Forgiveness applies to us as a race as well as to each of us as individuals. Justification means justness for the unjust.

What this means for our daily life is that we can be realistic and truthful. We do not need to hide the shadow side of our lives. We do not need to pretend that we are better than we are. We can celebrate our humanity. We can accept ourselves, even our lower selves, because God accepts us through grace. The first and most important step toward radical transformation is to realize the truth of the gospel, namely, that *God has loved us in our untransformed state* (Rom. 5:8). And, furthermore, our eternal salvation comes to us as a gift from God prior to our entering into the transformation process. This is the good news. Grace is for sinners. And we know this by faith.

Sanctification and Love

Nevertheless, we do not pursue sin just to see grace abound (Rom. 6:1). The entrance of God's grace into our lives has an effect. It turns us around, points us in a new direction, and sets us on a path toward holiness as well as wholeness. We call this path sanctification, and it usually includes five elements or steps: indwelling, illumination, regeneration, conversion, and works of love.

First and foremost is the *indwelling* of the Holy Spirit. As we mentioned above, the risen and living Christ is actually present in our faith. This is the work of the divine Spirit. We are never alone. So by the indwelling Spirit we are not referring to a divine spark. We are not identifying our true self or our higher self with the presence of the divine *pneuma,* as the gnostics have done. Rather, the Holy Spirit is present as an alien though comforting visitor. We continue to distinguish our own self—a created self and hence part of the creation—from the uncreated Spirit of God that enters into our psychic life. The divine Spirit comes bearing gifts. These gifts include the presence of Christ, the forgiveness of sins, strength and courage, special powers known as *charismata,* and also inspiration to follow the road of sanctification.

As we mentioned earlier, Jesus Christ is actually present in our faith. This presence, sponsored by the Holy Spirit, can only be described as mystical; that is, he is mysteriously present. Even when we do not experience Christ, he is nevertheless present. We know he is present because he has promised to be present. This promise is given us by Scripture. Hence, Scripture is important because it is the location of the promise.

The significance of this point—that the Holy Spirit dwells in us even when we do not experience it—cannot be overstated. Our lives have ups and downs. We have our joys and our griefs. We have our bright moments and our dark nights of the soul. We simply cannot live every moment in spiritual ecstasy. And there may even be times when we feel abandoned by God, when meaning and purpose seem to have evaporated and all we are left with is an inner emptiness. Even Jesus confronted these moments. He had deep anxiety when praying in the Garden of Gethsemane. From the cross he called out, asking why God had forsaken him. No matter how close to God we are, as long as we exist in the alienation of the old creation we will from time to time experience the terror of this alienation.

But this does not mean that God is absent from our lives. He never abandoned the suffering Jesus. Rather, he took the suffering of Jesus up into himself. So also is God present amidst our anxiety and suffering, taking our anxiety and suffering up into the divine life. God feels what we feel, even if we feel abandoned. If we assume that the word *God* refers exclusively to the joyous and upbeat and ecstatic dimensions of reality, then we will miss the point of the incarnation, namely, that God experiences our reality the way we experience it.

It is a two-way street. God experiences us. We experience God. The presence of the Holy Spirit in us does not replace us. It does not dissolve our personality into the divine being. Rather, God participates in our life, and it is truly *our* life. This sense of unity with God that the presence of the Holy Spirit communicates is exhilarating and confidence-building, to be sure; but this experience of the divine does not rid us of everything human. That is the way it was with God incarnate in Jesus. That is the way it is with the Spirit indwelling in us as well. It produces a wholeness that includes both the divine and the human.

The second and significant step on the path of sanctification is *illumination*. The Holy Spirit is the spirit of truth. The Spirit's task is to open our eyes, to grant us not just sight but also insight. The Spirit's task is to open our ears so that we can hear the gospel, so that we can "hear the Word of God and keep it." John Calvin called this the "inner witness" of the Holy Spirit, the witness within our own soul that responds to the hearing of God's Word and grants us what is necessary to believe it and to live by it. The ability to apprehend the truth of God is not a common endowment of our nature; rather it is a gift, a "special illumination" of the Holy Spirit.[5] As a light bulb makes everything in a room visible, the Holy Spirit illuminates our soul so that our relationship with God can be discerned and the message of grace be received.

This means, among other things, that the knowledge produced by illumination is not just external knowledge. It is not simply objective or historical knowledge. It is rather internal. It is knowledge *for me*. It is, in effect, gnostic illumination. Its task is to turn the darkness of our heart as well as our mind into enlightened perception (2 Cor. 4:6). The primary way it works is that the Holy Spirit guides our attention so that we can interpret the ordinary things in our daily life in such a way as to see God's gracious hand at work.

Although there is a gnostic component here in that illumination involves a highly personalized knowing, I am not advocating gnosticism in the full sense. The key reason for denying gnosticism is this: we are not saved by our knowledge. We are saved by Christ's work. What the Holy Spirit does in illumination is make it known to us (Eph. 1:15–23).

This may be analogous to having your car repaired at the local garage. You drop it off about eight in the morning. Shortly after noon the mechanic calls to say that the work is finished. Your car is ready to be picked up. The phone call in itself is not what effects the repairs; rather it reports what has already happened. Similarly, illumination helps us to see that God, out of divine grace and love, has already taken action in our behalf and granted us salvation as a free gift.

Can we actively pursue illumination? Yes. Paul encourages us to grow in the knowledge of God (Col. 1:10). This leads to an important set of activities in Christian spirituality. We begin by giving attention to the Word of God, whether by reading the Bible or listening to preaching. In doing so, we pray (Luke 11:13; Eph. 1:16–18). In this prayer we invite the Spirit to enter our minds and bring enlightenment. Then we meditate. Like Mary, the mother of Jesus, we ponder these things in our hearts (Luke 2:19). Finally, we voluntarily face trials and difficulties (Ps. 119:71). Christian faith is by no means escapist. Taking courage to try to surmount the challenges of life serves to teach us, to help us realize that the power of God is actually at work in us from moment to moment.

This brings us to the third dimension of sanctification, *regeneration*. Whereas illumination is identified with the effect the Holy Spirit has on our intellect and to some degree on our heart, regeneration refers to the transformation of our human will. Literally, of course, the word *regeneration* means rebirth or new creation. It refers to the presence of new life amidst our old life. It refers to the glories of the coming new age as we enjoy them now amidst the old age. It is the act of the Spirit whereby forgiveness is applied to you or me personally, and this releases new power to our wills so that we are motivated to live creatively in tune with God's intention. It is the Spirit-given desire to live a godly life.

What we are reborn to is eternal life, and the symbol of this rebirth is baptism. In Romans 6:1–4 St. Paul likens Jesus' dying and descending into the tomb with our descending into the water and drowning. He then likens Jesus' resurrection with our rising up out of the water into a state of renewal. We live now, this side of physical death, in the power of Jesus' resurrection. We walk "in newness of life." God's life-giving Spirit now resides in our spirit. In answering Nicodemus, Jesus says, "Very truly, I tell you, no one can enter the kingdom of God without being born of water and Spirit. What is born of the flesh is flesh, and what is born of the Spirit is Spirit" (John 3:5–6). This point is reiterated by 1 Peter 1:23, that to be "born anew" is to be born of what is imperishable, namely, the abiding word of God, which lives forever.

The sign of regeneration is that the eternal will of God becomes our will. It is an unutterably good feeling to find oneself delighting in the will of God (Ps. 1:2). There is no greater sign of the power of reconciliation than this, that we want what God wants. St. Augustine described our bondage to sin in terms of a will that, on the basis of its own strength, could not voluntarily choose the ways of God. With the indwelling of the Holy Spirit and the regenerative work within us, however, our wills become transformed.[6] God's ways become our ways. Our choice to live lives of cleanliness and righteousness is made joyfully, because the divine will is now operative within our own wills.

We now move from reception to action, from the realm of God's gracious presence to the dimension of human faith and to the fourth in our list of elements of sanctification: *conversion*. It might seem that the word *conversion* applies to some people but not others. Many of us grow up in Christian environments, having received baptism as infants, and gradually experiencing illumination. Conversion in a fully conscious sense may come only later in life—so gradually it goes virtually unnoticed—because faith has been already long operative. Yet there is a logic, so to speak, built into the idea of conversion that helps us identify it as a transformational process that some pursue with enthusiasm and others neglect. It is a transformational process well worth pursuing! Conversion has three identifiable steps: contrition, repentance, and commitment.

Contrition is the sense of sorrow we feel when we examine our lives and find ourselves guilty of hurting others, yielding to unworthy motives, participating in destructive activities, or failing to live up to our own expectations. It is marked by regret. It is usually painful. It hurts. This was what I was feeling as I sat in the living room chair. I was on the verge of gaining a contrite heart. Contrition normally leads to confession—although this was much delayed in the case of my robin murder. Confession may take place in private with the person wronged or with a close friend. It usually takes place in the presence of one's priest or pastor, and of course liturgically during Sunday worship. The feeling of contrition with the act of confession motivates the next steps: repentance and commitment.

Repentance is a willing decision to put sins into the past and to turn our life around. It is a negative decision in the sense that it seeks to negate the power of the past to affect the present and the future. It says no to previous habits. It chooses a different future, a God-led future.

Commitment follows. I am now committed: I will not be shooting any more robins. This is a positive decision of the will that gives form to the future. It is the decision primarily to love others as God has loved us (1 John 4:19). The actions we take on the basis of this commitment become the fundamental signs or marks of our transformation.

Yet, curiously enough, the transformation that occurs is indirect, not direct. This has to do with the nature of love. This brings us to the fifth step on the sanctifying path: *works of love.*

Genuine love, in the Christian sense of *agape,* is love directed toward one's neighbor. It is not self-love. Its intention is not to make the lover holy. Its aim is not our own sanctification. Rather, its aim pure and simple is to meet the needs of the neighbor. What eventually may happen, of course, is that the lover's life gradually takes on the habits of loving and then unintentionally begins to glow with the divine light.

The sanctified life is the loving life. Yet, the paradox is that we cannot finally pursue our own sanctification directly, because our commitment to love is aimed at someone else's benefit, not our own. This means that sanctification, like justification, is, in the last analysis, a gift of God's grace. But whereas justification belongs to a specific point in time, sanctification is a process. Sanctification is a gift that grows gradually in us, as the indirect yet in some way natural consequence of our commitment to imbibe the love of God expressed in Jesus Christ. Love, more than anything else, is the sign that transformation is under way and wholeness is being embraced.

Faith, according to St. Paul, works through love (Gal. 5:6). It is through love that the Holy Spirit makes our lives bear fruit. The kind of love we are talking about here is the kind that takes as its first agenda the needs of the neighbor, not of oneself. It is *agape,* the kind of love that, if the situation warrants it, is even willing to engage in self-sacrifice.

Here we confront a further paradox. Although love is commanded, it is also free. Jesus sums up the law of God: we should love God and love our neighbors. Yet at the same time, there is an intrinsic and indelible quality of freedom in genuine love that transcends what can be commanded or codified in a law. It is in the context of talking about Christian freedom that St. Paul tells us that "faith is active in love."

This is a point that Martin Luther makes with dramatic force.

> *A Christian is a perfectly free lord of all, subject to none.*
> *A Christian is a perfectly dutiful servant of all, subject to all.*[7]

Freedom and servitude go together here. On the one hand, the gospel has made us free. Because of what Christ has done, the life of love we lead can add nothing to our own eternal status before heaven. Because of the indwelling of Christ through the Holy Spirit, eternal life has entered our present life. Jesus' commandment has already been fulfilled. Jesus himself loved God and loved his neighbor, and his righteousness is now our righteousness. So, we are freed from the obligations of this law. Our salvation is already assured. Our works of love add nothing as far as we are concerned. We are free.

Yet, because of regeneration, God's loving disposition becomes our loving disposition. The same love that led Jesus to "give his life as a ransom for many" works within the soul of the Christian to behave in like fashion. This is a fruit of the Holy Spirit. We look to the needs of others just as God looks to our needs. We give of ourselves as the needs of others dictate.

Because of this, Christians employ the metaphor of the dutiful servant, making us subject to the beck and call of other people. The sanctified life is one characterized by answering to this command without grumbling. It is a joyous service. It becomes natural and unpretentious. The person of faith performs "acts of mercy, with cheerfulness" (Rom. 12:8).

At this juncture freedom enters again, but in a slightly different fashion. No rigid rules tell us exactly how to love. We have to make them up as we go. That is, love is creative. We have to devise ways to love on the spot in response to whatever the situation dictates.

The necessity for love to be creative is illustrated in one of Jesus' parables on love, the parable of the good Samaritan (Luke 10:25–37). It is important to note the context here. A lawyer has just asked Jesus about the law of God. Jesus restates the law succinctly: love God and love your neighbor. But the man presses on with the question, "Who is my neighbor?" Why does he ask this question? So he can run out and find some new neighbors whom he can love? No, of course not, reports Luke. The lawyer asks this question in order "to justify himself."

Jesus is not fooled. He sees through the lawyer's motives. So he tells the story of the man beaten by robbers and left to die on the side of the road to Jericho. A priest and a Levite, both of whom were dedicated to keeping God's law, passed by the beaten man on the other side. Evidently, no previously prescribed law obligated them to meet the needs of a mugging victim under these precise circumstances. They could justify themselves because they had not broken any laws they could think of.

The good Samaritan, however, was of a different disposition. He went out of his way to help. Not only did he give a bit of first aid, but he also gave his time and some money to the innkeeper so that the injured one could be nursed back to health. The Samaritan did not act in accordance with some already prescribed moral law that told him exactly what to do. Rather, seizing upon the opportunity to respond to human need, he used his creativity to devise a plan to meet that need. This was an act of love. It is in light of this example that Jesus tells the lawyer, "Go and do likewise."

The dynamic movement of faith active in love has a free and creative character, because it seeks constantly to create wholeness where previously there was only brokenness. It cannot help but be wholistic. A life based upon liberated love establishes a new relationship with law. Instead of determining what is right by measuring its degree of conformity or nonconformity to an already established moral law or archonic precept, a Christian ethic leads us to create new laws for the purpose of fostering new levels of wholeness in community.

The life undergoing sanctification is very practical. It consists in making judgments and taking actions in the present situation that we believe to serve the long-range good of the whole. We confront concrete problems, and the most loving thing we can do in most cases is pursue the solution that works best, that is most effective in light of the long-range view. In the social and political sphere this most often means the creation of positive laws that aim at bringing people together peacefully so that they can best enhance one another's well-being. Love produces positive law for the purpose of "creating new forms of human community and uniting those who have been separated," writes Wolfhart Pannenberg. "The law that is produced by love is not some ideal order with a claim to timeless validity (and thus, in this case, it is not natural law) but the specific, concrete solution of concrete problems until something new arises; that is, until a new situation demands new solutions."[8] Thus, love, whether we express it in personal relationships or in political programs, has as its end the creation of a wholesome community. In this sense, love is wholistic as well as immediate and concrete.

The Universal and the Particular

In our own time many people do not seem ready or willing to listen to this message of God's grace as expressed in the Christian gospel and in the Christian life. Why? In part, it is because churches in our generation have failed to live graciously. They have failed to embody the truth that they have been commissioned to proclaim. It is also because of the attack against Christianity that new age philosophers make, either implicitly or explicitly. The new age claims a moral advantage over Christendom. It appears to be more liberal, more open to a variety of ideas, more inclusive, more concerned with unity despite differences in ideas. The new age vision is a universal vision, so it is said; whereas the Christian churches are considered parochial and blind because they are concerned solely with their own survival and hierarchical power structures.

Although some new age criticisms of the churches do hit their targets, some of the criticisms are mistaken. They are subtle. The new age movement must be complimented on its universal vision and its sense of human unity, but its universal unity is more apparent than real. It has a built-in hierarchy according to which we can clearly discriminate between those who have attained higher consciousness and those who operate strictly at the level of the lower self. Historically, we can see how this might enforce social stratification when we look at India. In India, society has been strictly regulated by the caste system, which has placed the spiritually minded Brahmans on the top and the strictly this-worldly Vaisyas and Shudras on the bottom, just above the outcastes, who are allegedly devoid of spiritual openness. It was the Christianized West that introduced into India such concepts as human dignity and equality. The universal vision of Hinduism had virtually no impact socially.

In addition, the Christian vision is much more universal than its critics give it credit for being. It incorporates a strong prophecy regarding the transformation of the entire cosmos, the establishment of a new creation. It has a built-in promise of a "new age," the age of fulfillment and harmony. We will turn to this in a moment. But for now, we need to focus on the problem of the relationship between the universal and the particular.

The Christian claim frequently creates scandal, because it makes a universal claim on the basis of a particular experience. New age adherents routinely act scandalized, challenging with rhetorical questions like, "How can you Christians think your Church has the only path to God?"[9] Christians are painted to look narrow-minded and exclusive. The new age, in contrast, appears to be broad-minded and inclusive because it posits that universal knowledge is universally available. We may need a guide or a guru, says the new age, but we certainly do not need a priest to mediate. Hinduism has long made this claim in a profound way, its gurus telling us to open the door of our own Atman, which leads directly to the cosmic Brahman. On this count, philosophical metaphysics and Western science have also worked with the same formal assumption; that is, all we need do is exploit our own native capacity to reason, perhaps with the help of a teacher or university fellowship, and then we will have access to the same truths as everybody else does. New age universalism, in short, sees each individual self as the center; it sees the entire cosmos as centering in the self, and self-knowledge as the knowledge of God.

Against the backdrop of these claims of universal access to universal knowledge, the particularity of the Christian claim appears to be narrow. The Christian understanding of the incarnation is that the universal truth became particular in the person of Jesus of Nazareth. It is that the infinite became finite, taking on the flesh and bones of a personality at a specific time and place. There is an inescapable offense here.

On this point I have gained considerable insight from my friend and colleague, Surjit Singh. Surjit was born in the Punjab in India and raised a Sikh. At the age of twenty he came to faith in Jesus Christ and announced his conversion. His fellow Sikhs then arranged a kidnapping and employed interrogation and deprogramming techniques to persuade him to return to Sikhism. When they found he was standing fast, they let him go. He later went on to study Christian theology and eventually joined the faculty at the GTU. He has studied extensively the philosophical traditions of both East and West, both Hinduism and Christianity, both ancient and modern. Along with the late Kevin Wall, a Dominican scholar, Surjit and I have repeatedly offered a seminar on the modern and postmodern mind.

"The real offense of Christianity," Surjit told me once in a conversation at his home in Marin County, "is that in Jesus Christ the universal has become particular. But this in itself is not a problem only for Christians. Any religious tradition that makes a similar claim is going to have a similar offense. This is true of both Islam with its Muhammed and Buddhism with its Buddha. Whenever you claim that the infinite has taken on the form of the finite, those who think they have the infinite within them are going to take offense. As for me, I put my faith in Christ and take my chances."

Being an Indian himself, Surjit is very sensitive to Indian spirituality. He affirms the notion that each finite human being should be open to infinite truth, that though we exist in time we should measure our reality against eternity. An individual is not an individual individually, he argues. We are individual persons only in relation to other persons and in relation to the whole. We are inescapably social; we are who we are only by virtue of our relation to what lies beyond us. This applies to our relation to God as well. "The temporal human person must be open to God to find definitive human meaning and destiny," he writes, "and human society must be open to the Kingdom of God to find its ultimate meaning and destiny."[10]

He goes on. There is a paradoxical relationship between our unique individuality and our universality. Each one of us is unique, yet the more unique we become the more universally human we become. The superlatively unique and universal human being is the one who is most open to God and who, reciprocally, is also open to others. God is reflected in such a being. All human persons have the potential to enter with God into such a reciprocal relationship, but history shows that only one individual actually embodied it.

Surjit cites the Gospel of John, where the creator Word takes on flesh with a specific name, Jesus Christ (John 1:14). Then he adds:

> This statement was made against the background of the existing ethos of the Graeco-Roman world. The Greeks philosophically considered it foolishness. And the Jews looked upon it as a religious scandal. Hindus, like the Greeks, will also take exception to it, and Muslims, like the Jews, will also scandalize it. He is, they will say, at best a rabbi or a prophet. There could not be an exclusive presence of God in any one man, the others will say. God is equally in all human beings and in all things. However, the New Testament affirms that he is more than a prophet and the unique and nonrepeatable manifestation of the Divine-Human relationship.[11]

Note what is being assumed here: we and God are not alike. We are different. We belong to the finite and temporal, whereas God belongs to the infinite and eternal. The dynamics of our relationship with God actually serve to help define us, to reveal to us just what we are. We are finite, not infinite. We are temporal, not eternal. This is a truth about ourselves that is either not known or else not accepted by such spiritual traditions as Hinduism and, similarly, new age gnosticism. By equating Atman with Brahman or propounding the doctrine of the divine spark, these traditions are confusing us with God. This difference—what Søren Kierkegaard called the "infinite qualitative difference"—between the human and the divine is a significant truth that we must learn, even if we can learn it only when it is revealed in the paradox of the human-divine one, Jesus Christ. The truth is this: we are not God; yet God, in his grace, has entered the human sphere and taken what is human up into the divine life.

How, then, are we related to this incarnate truth? By faith, not by consciousness raising, knowledge, or even gnosis. Faith is not a form of knowing. It may seek and depend on knowledge, but in itself faith is a relationship to the truth characterized by trust. There are two kinds of knowledge: (1) knowledge of things historical and this-worldly, and (2) knowledge of the gnostic or mystical type regarding things eternal or universal. Neither one of these in itself can comprehend the paradox present in the incarnation of Jesus Christ. Kierkegaard lays down the challenge:

> Faith is not a form of knowledge; for all knowledge is either a knowledge of the Eternal, excluding the temporal and historical as indifferent, or it is pure historical knowledge. No knowledge can have for its object the absurdity that the Eternal is the historical.[12]

The point is that one cannot come to the cosmic truth regarding God's gracious entrance into the temporal and historical sphere of human life simply by turning inward and cultivating self-awareness.

This means further that faith focuses on the person of Jesus Christ, not just on his teachings. Jesus is not simply a rabbi or a prophet. He is not merely a professor who tells us how the world works or a philosopher who shares with us his wisdom. Jesus plays these roles, to be sure; but who he is as a person is what is decisive. In his person, heaven and earth come together. Time and eternity meet. The infinite takes up residence in the finite. The whole becomes the part. The self that opens out onto the truth of the cosmos is not our own self. Rather, it is the divine self that has been manifested in this person, Jesus Christ. This leads Kierkegaard to say that the "object of faith is not the *teaching* but the *Teacher*."[13]

This means still further that the human predicament is not characterized fundamentally by ignorance, by ignosis. Our fundamental problem is not lack of self-awareness or living without consciousness of our higher self. Our fundamental problem is sin. It is sin that alienates us from God, and we can sin at the level of both consciousness and unconsciousness.

Socrates is known for having raised the question of whether one could know what is right and then willfully choose to do what is wrong. His answer was: no. Socrates assumed that the human propensity is naturally to do what is right. Therefore, if we witness ourselves as willing to do what is wrong, it follows that we must be ignorant of what is truly the right thing to do. Once we know what is right, Socrates concludes, we will do it.

Not so! argues Kierkegaard. We know that human beings can look right and wrong square in the face and choose to do the wrong.[14] We know this because the world looked straight into the face of God when it looked into the face of Jesus, and then it put him to death. Those who look only within themselves for answers to life's mysteries may find a way to avoid looking at the ugliness of sin. They may avoid sin by assuming that the human predicament is due only to lack of knowledge. What we need in order to learn the truth about sin, says Kierkegaard, is revelation. This is what we learn from the crucifixion of Jesus, a lesson we can easily miss if we do not give our attention to what has been revealed in this instance.

What we need to do is develop a wholistic concept of knowledge, whereby knowledge is understood as growth in consciousness inclusive of consciousness of the human tendency to sin, a vision of wholeness that comprehends the existence of evil. I believe the concept of integrative consciousness in Carl Jung's work can be helpful here. Recall that Jung distinguished between completion and perfection, contending that psychological wholeness includes the conscious integration of one's shadow. This integration requires acknowledgment of one's own personal propensity for evil and destruction. Jung's idea of individuation makes each of us personally responsible for knowledge of reality; and part of reality is one's own proclivity for sin. We need to know that sin is part of us, and if we deny this reality, it will only drive sin into our unconscious. Then it will become potentially more destructive. One of the temptations inherent in new age cosmic consciousness is the equation of the self with God and of psychological completion with moral perfection. The net result is a practical denial of the abiding threat of human sin.

Christian spirituality has traditionally sought to deal with this temptation to see ourselves as the God of our own life. The method: confession, contrition, repentance, and renewal. The act of confession, if sincere, is a process by which one's sinful acts and inclinations are raised into full consciousness. Our true nature is acknowledged, not denied. In addition, the declaration of forgiveness spoken to us by our priest or pastor shows our acceptance by God despite our sinfulness. It shows that God's perfection takes human imperfection up into itself. In effect, it integrates the shadow into a life that is otherwise striving to be perfect.

Concluding Theses

What should we learn from all of this? What has our attempt at testing the spirits of the new age uncovered? Let me try to summarize in a few theses.

First, *modest dabbling in new age spirituality is probably harmless; it may even be helpful.* It is simply overkill to argue that the new age is so contaminated with demonic powers that it warrants total condemnation from a Christian point of view. Reading one's horoscope, wearing crystal jewelry, practicing yoga, or taking a trip to the acupuncturist is not likely to lead to demon possession or to constitute a forsaking of one's faith in Jesus Christ. In our pluralistic society we are confronted nearly every hour with a wide variety of beliefs and perspectives and practices. It is neither possible nor desirable to require pure orthodoxy or orthopraxis. Virtually no one can be insulated from new age thinking, nor from a variety of other points of view either. In fact, an honest investigation of new ideas is actually healthy. It signals a readiness to grow. Churches ought not to react immediately in a protectionist or defensive mode when new age ideas are being entertained.

We must admit, furthermore, that some aspects of the new age are to be applauded.[15] It is a movement not bullied by the modern hegemony of science and secularism. It speaks a religious language in areas of life and learning from which religion was once banished. Metaphysical and spiritual realities can be discussed openly. Dialogue on theological matters again belongs in the marketplace of ideas.

In addition, many of the psychotechnologies proffered by the new age include groups of like-minded persons who actively seek spiritual transformation in their lives. They form support networks. They help one another. They create microcommunities that are intensely personal, loving, and supportive. In some cases, new age groups have shown themselves to be more life-enhancing than corresponding Christian congregations. If by their fruits we shall know them, we should acknowledge God's hand in the growth of healthy and ripe fruits wherever we find them.

Second, *the new age vision is a noble and edifying one.* The utopian ideals belonging to the image of the Aquarian age are inspiring. The new age movement envisions a society characterized by peace, harmony, and fulfillment. It envisions unity between ego and self, between one person and another, between the human race and nature, and between the cosmos and God. This metaphysical vision functions to ground an ethic that leads us toward love and cooperation, toward staving off nuclear confrontation, toward caring for Mother Earth and all her living things. In addition, the inherent future trajectory of the "new" in "new age" gives it a visionary, prophetic direction. It gives it the driving power to seek growth, evolution, and transformation.

All of these values are noble and edifying. In large part they are values that every Christian ought to embrace. These are the very values built into the eschatological vision of the new creation, the image of the New Jerusalem descending at the climax of history (Revelation 21–22). This is what the kingdom of God preached by Jesus stands for. This is the justice after which the blessed ones hunger and thirst (Matt. 5:6). In fact, if we were to take a look at the history of ideas, we might discover that the contemporary vision of the new age derives in large part from the Christian image of the kingdom of God that has so long been an influence on the Western mind.

We should be reminded of Pope John XXIII, who in his encyclical *Pacem in terris* said that Roman Catholics (in our circumstance, read *all* Christians) should be willing to work with every person of goodwill in behalf of world peace. This is good advice! Insofar as new age disciples are earnestly and effectively working for world peace, they should find many ready partners in our Christian churches.

Third, *pastors, theologians, and church leaders should take the new age movement seriously.* On the whole, the new age is not a laughing matter. No longer can clergy ignore what is going on by mumbling glib invectives, implying that the new age is silly or superstitious. Some silliness and superstition is present, to be sure. Nevertheless, the new age should be considered important to church leaders on two counts. For one thing, it involves large numbers of people both inside and outside the churches. New age spiritual practices are being sought because they appear to offer answers to urgent spiritual and political needs. This makes new age spirituality an issue of pastoral concern. If this is what people are thinking about and what they find meaningful in their lives, then no spiritually sensitive pastor can justifiably ignore it. This means recognizing the spiritual thirst that exists. It may mean dipping into the reservoir of the Christian tradition and retrieving spiritual practices that have been set aside, practices such as meditation and contemplation. It may mean encouraging people to pray for an outpouring of the Holy Spirit so that they can experience the power of transformation toward a God-given wholeness.

Our church leaders should take the new age seriously for another reason. The theological issues are of great magnitude. The intellectual stakes may turn out to rival those in the battle that took place in the ancient Roman Empire between Christianity and gnosticism, perhaps even the struggle between the Christian faith and paganism. It is a time for apologetic theology. This brings us to the doctrinal issues and to our next thesis.

Fourth, *the gnostic monism at the heart of new age teaching is dangerous because it leads to naiveté and to a denial of God's grace.* There are two ways in which new age affiliation can be harmful. First, it can be harmful if it leads one to enter into a cultlike organization with an authoritarian center. This leads inevitably to a loss of one's independence and often to psychological or physical abuse. Second, it can be harmful if it leads one to make a full commitment to the metaphysical world view that new age theoreticians promulgate.

What the new age teaches is clearly naive, almost blind, to the reality of human sin and the existence of evil in the world. Perhaps this is a voluntary naiveté. It may result from the fact that many of us have been hurt in our lives. With this background it is very appealing to be able to think only positively, only in terms of essential goodness. How exciting it is to hear that goodness and blessing and fulfillment are very close at hand—already within me—so that all I have to do is execute the right psychotechnique and I can bring it to full flower. In this mood of high expectancy, just thinking about sin constitutes negative thinking and may block the eruption of all this goodness. So we are tempted to buy into a fast path to bliss, into a brightness that casts no shadow.

The problem, of course, is that this is unrealistic. When we least expect it, sin will sneak up on us and attack us. This is what frequently happens in the cults. The master teacher—the one whom all expect to embody perfection—most easily becomes the one to wreak abuse. The raising of our consciousness does not transform our wills. Only grace can do that. No matter how aware we have become, we may still make decisions that lead to great harm both to ourselves and others, and even others whom we love. This is simply the human predicament in which we find ourselves. To deny it is folly.

To deny it is also to fail to recognize how the Spirit of God actually works. We have divinity within us, to be sure. But it is an alien divinity. It does not belong to our nature. It has come into us from the outside. It is a gift of grace. The Holy Spirit dwells within, empowering us toward renewal, toward transformation. Yet the Holy Spirit does double duty. The divine presence in the Spirit is also God's way of participating in our humanity. It is God's way of continuing the incarnate presence he began in the person of Jesus. The paradox is that God's presence shows us that he loves us "while we still were sinners" (Rom. 5:8) while at the same time tranforming us through spiritual power. It is this double dynamic that we dare not forget. Otherwise we will lose ourselves in unreality.

What this means theologically is that I cannot equate God with my self. Nor can I equate God with the cosmos. You and I, along with the rest of everything that exists, belong to what we call "the creation." We have been created. We are in the process of being created. We are creatures. We are not the creator in the first sense of the term. Oh, yes, in the ongoing movement of the cosmos we are co-creators with God. But in the initial and definitive sense we are creatures, totally and completely dependent on the free and loving act of God by which we were brought into existence out of nothing. We are *created* co-creators.

And with all of this we get the promise of the gospel, the forgiveness of sins and the promise of eternal life with God. Among other things, this means that with the continued empowerment of God's grace, we will continue to live lives of creative love and thereby anticipate the cosmic transformation yet to come, the consummate arrival of the new creation.

Notes

Chapter 1: The New Age Is Here . . . and Everywhere

1. *Los Angeles Times* religion editor Russell Chandler says, "The New Age is hard to define; its boundaries are fuzzy. It's a shifting kaleidoscope of beliefs, fads, and rituals . . . a hybrid mix of spiritual, social, and political forces, and it encompasses sociology, theology, the physical sciences, medicine, anthropology, history, the human potentials movements, sports, and science fiction." *Understanding the New Age* (Waco, TX: Word Books, 1988), 17. Writing for the Spiritual Counterfeits Project, Robert Burrows says, "The New Age movement (NAM) is more accurately seen as a broad and diverse cultural trend united by world view, the world view of occult mysticism." "New Age Movement: Self-Deification in a Secular Culture," *SCP Newsletter* 10 (Winter 1984–85): 4.

2. Jonathan Adolph, "What Is New Age?" in *The 1988 Guide to New Age Living*, published by *New Age Journal* (Spring 1988): 6.

3. David Spangler, "Defining the New Age," in *The New Age Catalogue*, by the editors of *Body, Mind, Spirit Magazine* (New York: Doubleday, 1988), x. From 1974 to 1987 Spangler was president of his own Lorian Association. Lorian has now fissioned into four separate organizations: Pomegranate Foundation, Morningtown, Inc., Pacifica Foundation, and Con Terra Associates.

4. Spangler, "Defining the New Age," x.

5. Marilyn Ferguson, *The Aquarian Conspiracy* (Los Angeles: Tarcher, 1980), 29.

6. Abraham Maslow, *Motivation and Personality* (New York: Harper & Row, 1954), 206.

7. Maslow was a humanistic psychologist, and wanted to avoid drawing any theological conclusions: "It is quite important to dissociate this experience from any theological or supernatural reference." Maslow, 216.

8. Will Schutz in *Upstart Spring: Esalen and the American Awakening*, by Walter Truett Anderson (Reading, MA: Addison-Wesley, 1983), 158; see also David Toolan, *Facing West from California's Shores* (New York: Crossroad, 1987), 13.

9. Roberto Assagioli, *Psychosynthesis* (New York: Viking Press, 1965).

10. Cited by W. W. Bartley III, *Werner Erhard* (New York: Clarkson N. Potter, 1978), 108, 110.

11. Christopher Lasch, *The Culture of Narcissism* (New York: W. W. Norton, 1978), xv.

12. Bartley, 221.

13. Toolan, 25.

14. Note that the terms *holism* and *wholism* can be used interchangeably. Here I use the term *holistic health,* spelled as we find it in the literature. Normally, I follow the pattern set by Granger Westberg, who prefers the spelling *wholistic,* which connotes more obviously the sense of the whole as an integrating concept.

15. Arthur C. Hastings, James Fadiman, and James S. Gordon, eds., *Health for the Whole Person: The Complete Guide to Holistic Medicine* (Boulder: Westview Press, 1980).

16. Hastings, Fadiman, and Gordon, 17.

17. Fritjof Capra, *The Turning Point* (New York: Bantam, 1982), chap. 10.

18. Ferguson, 246–48. "Each person carries his own doctor inside him," writes Norman Cousins after healing himself of an illness through a combination of laughter, vitamin C, and a strong will to live. *Anatomy of an Illness* (New York: Bantam, 1979), 69.

19. Capra, 334.

20. Granger Westberg, "From Hospital Chaplaincy to Wholistic Health Center," *Journal of Pastoral Care* 33 (June 1979).

21. See, for example, Dennis Livingston, "Experience the Often Subtle Beauty of This Visionary Music," in *The 1988 Guide to New Age Living*, 85.

22. Adolph, 6.

23. Uma Silbey, *The Complete Crystal Guidebook* (New York: Bantam, 1987). In a book review Steven Okulewicz suggests that Uma Silbey is weak on her scientific facts regarding the origin of crystals; for example, she says crystals form under the pressure of sandstone and neglects to mention their appearance in igneous and metamorphic rock. *The Skeptical Inquirer* 13 (Summer 1989): 420. George M. Lawrence says that "technical terms such as *resonance, bonding, energy*, and *electromagnetic field* are used by the mystics, not as precise descriptions of the crystals, but as metaphors for human interactions and as buzz words connoting power." "Crystals," *The Skeptical Inquirer* 13 (Summer 1989): 399. Lawrence Jerome sorts out the scientific facts from the mystical myths in "Crystal Power: Welcome to the Stone Age," *The Fringes of Reason: A Whole Earth Catalog*, ed. Ted Schultz (New York: Harmony Books, 1989), 31–33.

24. Katrina Raphaell, *Crystal Enlightenment* (Sante Fe: Aurora Press, 1985).

25. There are cracks in the crystal camp. Some make pseudoscientific claims that crystals offer physical healing through sympathetic vibration. Barbara G. Walker objects to bad science, and asserts that if crystals heal, it is because they have a placebo effect. For crystal credibility, Walker argues, we need to expunge the bad science and focus on the genuine value of crystals, namely, their ability to help us focus our meditation. Walker, *The Book of Sacred Stones: Fact and Fallacy in the Crystal World* (San Francisco: Harper & Row, 1989).

26. Jon Kilmo, *Channeling: Investigations on Receiving Information from Paranormal Sources* (Los Angeles: Tarcher, 1987).

27. Carl Jung, "On the Psychology and Pathology of So-Called Occult Phenomena," in *Psychology and the Occult*, trans. R.F.C. Hull (Princeton: Princeton University Press, 1977), 37. Jung reports that the young woman was eventually caught cheating flagrantly at one of her séances, and subsequent to the embarrassment she ceased her channeling and became on the whole a quieter, steadier, and more

agreeable person. Nevertheless, Jung had been deeply impressed by the phenomenon he had witnessed and sought to explain it in part in terms of a complicated pattern of communication between the conscious and unconscious dimensions of her mind.

28. Sandra Hansen Konte, "The Man Who Talked to the Dead," in the *This World* section of the *San Francisco Chronicle,* 22 May 1988, 14.

29. Ramtha, *Voyage to the New World* (New York: Fawcett, 1985), 84; see also 21f., 77.

30. Ramtha, 80.

31. Ramtha, 55.

32. Ramtha, 62. Philip Zaleski is critical of what is taught here. He says that Ramtha deserves "a harsh response" on the grounds that it tries to give easy answers to life's difficult questions. He contends that Ramtha's esoteric philosophy is "utterly lacking the necessary buttresses of systematic thought and sustained practice to lead to genuine self-transformation." The problem is that it only *appears* to satisfy our authentic spiritual hunger: "This worthless food fills up—in just the way that drugs do—a space meant for more nutritious fare." "Easy Answers," *Parabola* 13 (August 1988): 87f. Sarah Grey Thomason, professor of linguistics at the University of Pittsburgh, is skeptical of Ramtha's British accent. She notes that the British accent we are familiar with goes back only a couple of centuries, and wonders how there could be a connection with Atlantis thirty-five thousand years ago. "Entities in the Linguistic Minefield," *The Skeptical Inquirer* 13 (Summer 1989): 394.

33. "Ramtha has just issued a book," comments Robert J. L. Burrows, "proof that even if you perish, you can still publish." "A Vision for a New Humanity," in *The New Age Rage,* ed. Karen Hoyt (Old Tappan, NJ: Fleming H. Revell, 1987), 43.

34. Don Lattin, "New Age Women Gurus Draw Flocks to Northwest," *San Francisco Chronicle,* 4 September 1989, A4.

35. Russell Chandler has dubbed J. Z. Knight "the Tammy Faye Bakker of the New Age movement." Chandler, 54.

36. James E. Alcock observes that nineteenth-century trance mediums "were almost certainly fraudulent" and suggests that contemporary channelers are as well. Why, then, does the public pay them money? Alcock's answer: what the channelers sell is "hassle-free religion," a way of gaining "meaning in life and escape from existential anxiety without the commitment and the conformity that cults and sects demand." "Channeling: Brief History and Contemporary Context," *The Skeptical Inquirer* 13 (Summer 1989): 380–84.

37. Ernest R. Hilgard, *Divided Consciousness* (Somerset, NJ: John Wiley & Sons, 1986).

38. Ted Schultz, "Voices from Beyond: The Age-Old Mystery of Channeling," *Fringes of Reason,* 62.

39. David Spangler, *Links with Space* (Marina del Rey, CA: DeVorss, 1971).

40. Whitley Strieber, *Communion* (New York: William Morrow, 1987), 100, 224.

41. Ruth Montgomery, *Aliens Among Us* (New York: Ballantine, 1986), 15.

42. Ted Peters, *UFOs—God's Chariots? Flying Saucers in Politics, Science, and Religion* (Atlanta: John Knox Press, 1977).

43. Montgomery, 129.

44. Montgomery, 137.

45. Donald T. Regan, *For the Record* (New York: Harcourt Brace Jovanovich, 1988).

46. Cited by Ellic Have, "Astrology," *Man, Myth and Magic* (New York: Marshall Cavendish, 1970), 1:150.

47. Gregory Szanto, *Astrotherapy: Astrology and the Realization of the Self* (London and New York: Arkana, 1987), 13.

48. Szanto, 2; see also 150f.

49. See, for example, "A Retest of Astrologer John McCall," by Philip A. Ianna and Charles R. Tolbert, *The Skeptical Inquirer* 9 (Winter 1984–85): 167–70.

50. Paul Kurtz, *The Transcendental Temptation: A Critique of Religion and the Paranormal* (Buffalo: Prometheus Books, 1986), 423–26.

51. Quoted in *Time* magazine, 16 May 1988, 41.

52. Kurtz, 433f.

53. In commenting on the opening verses of Genesis, sixteenth-century Rabbi David Darshan of Krakow wrote that "the ordering of the constellations is in the hands of God." He raised the interesting question of astrology regarding the power of enemies who oppress Israel, enemies who see themselves as under the control of the benevolent stars. Following in the Talmudic tradition, the Polish rabbi concluded: "For the moment fate smiles on them, and they are successful in accordance with their favorable horoscope, but when the influence of their stars wanes, their destruction comes from themselves." David Darshan, *Shir Hama'alot L'David and Ktav Hitnazzelut L'Darshanim*, trans. Hayim Goren Perelmuter (Cincinnati: Hebrew Union College Press, 1984), 163.

54. Artwork by Joan Marie, Box 2215, Sedona, AZ 86336.

55. Barbara Goodrich-Dunn, "The Conscious Feminine: An Interview with Marion Woodman," *Common Boundary* 7:2 (March-April 1989), 12.

56. Vicki Noble, *Motherpeace: A Way to the Goddess Through Myth, Art, and Tarot* (San Francisco: Harper & Row, 1983), 7; see also 44, 242.

57. "To reclaim the word 'Witch' is to reclaim our right, as women, to be powerful," says Starhawk. *The Spiral Dance* (San Francisco: Harper & Row, 1979), 7. See also Starhawk, *Truth or Dare* (San Francisco: Harper & Row, 1987), 8; and Luisah Teish, *Jambalaya: The Natural Woman's Book* (San Francisco: Harper & Row, 1985), ix, xv.

58. A magazine with the name *New Age Interpreter* was founded in 1940 by metaphysician Corinne Heline. Going back still farther, a monthly magazine first

published in 1914 by Scottish Rite Masons was called *The New Age Magazine*. Perhaps the phrase "new age" is a common one. The identification of this phrase with the particular teachings we now call "new age," however, has direct continuity with the Theosophical Society.

59. Mme H. P. Blavatsky, *The Secret Doctrine* (Madras: Theosophical Publishing House). In his *Blavatsky Unveiled*, published in London in the early 1890s, William E. Coleman revealed that Mme Blavatsky had engaged in plagiarism. At least two thousand passages in *Isis Unveiled* had been lifted from other books without credit, and *The Secret Doctrine* was derived from three other books that Coleman could identify.

60. John Symonds, "Blavatsky," *Man, Myth, and Magic* (New York: Marshall Cavendish, 1970), 2:289.

61. Catherine Lowman Wessinger, "Annie Besant and the World-Teacher: Progressive Messianism for the New Age," paper presented at the American Academy of Religion annual meeting, Chicago, 19–22 November 1988. See also by the same author, *Annie Besant and Progressive Messianism* (Lewiston, NY: Edwin Mellen Press, 1988).

62. Jay Kinney, "Déja Vu: The Hidden History of the New Age," *Fringes of Reason*, 22–30.

63. See Benjamin Creme, *The Reappearance of the Christ and the Masters of Wisdom* (London: Tara Press, 1980) and *Maitreya's Mission* (Amsterdam: Share International Foundation, 1986).

Chapter 2: The Eightfold Path

1. Ferguson, 366f.

2. Elaine Pagels, *The Gnostic Gospels* (New York: Random House, 1981), 181.

3. Aldous Huxley, *The Perennial Philosophy* (New York: Harper, 1944, 1970), vii; see also Jacob Needleman, *Lost Christianity: A Journey of Rediscovery to the Center of Christian Experience* (Garden City, NY: Doubleday, 1980); Huston Smith, *Beyond the Postmodern Mind* (New York: Crossroad, 1982), 32ff.; and Willis Harman, *An Incomplete Guide to the Future* (San Francisco: San Francisco Book Company, 1976).

4. Frequently the term *metaphysics* is used in new age vocabularies, even in bookstores to identify the occult section. René Guénon makes the point that "pure metaphysics" is transcultural, belonging to both East and West. The reason the West is now looking East, he says, is that the modern West has "forgotten, generally ignored and almost entirely lost" the metaphysical approach to reality. He goes on to say that although we ordinarily go first to Hinduism to see metaphysics at work, the same basic teachings can be discerned in Buddhism, Taoism, Islamic esotericism, and such. See René Guénon, "Oriental Metaphysics," in *The Sword of Gnosis*, ed. Jacob Needleman (London: Routledge & Kegan Paul, 1974, 1986), 40f.

5. Carl A. Raschke, *The Interruption of Eternity: Modern Gnosticism and the Origins of the New Religious Consciousness* (Chicago: Nelson Hall, 1980), xi.

6. David Bohm, *Wholeness and the Implicate Order* (London: Routledge & Kegan Paul, 1980), 3.

7. J. C. Smuts, *Holism and Evolution* (New York: Macmillan, 1926), 106.

8. Carl Jung, "Answer to Job," in *Collected Works* (Princeton: Princeton University Press, 1958, 1963), 11:469.

9. Carl Jung, *Aion,* 2nd ed., trans. R.F.C. Hull, in *Collected Works* (Princeton: Princeton University Press, 1951, 1959), 9:68f. For an analysis of completion—a completion that integrates one's shadow side—without alleged perfection and its significance for Christian theology, see Ann C. Lammers, *A Study of the Relation Between Theology and Psychology: Victor White and C. G. Jung,* unpublished Ph.D. dissertation, Yale University, 1987.

10. Carl Jung, introductory remarks in *The Tibetan Book of the Great Liberation,* ed. W. Y. Evans-Wentz (Oxford: Oxford University Press, 1954, 1980), liii.

11. Renée Weber, ed., *Dialogues with Scientists and Sages: The Search for Unity* (London: Routledge & Kegan Paul, 1986), 1.

12. Weber, 5.

13. Ferguson, 98.

14. Toolan, 75f.

15. Szanto, 97.

16. Marvin Henry Harper, *Gurus, Swamis, and Avatars* (San Francisco: Harper, 1976), 10. One might at this point protest my use of the term *perennial gnosticism* to describe new age thinking on the grounds that ancient gnosticism has a reputation for being dualistic, not monistic. In one sense this is correct, making new age thinkers a bit closer to someone such as Plotinus, for whom the phenomenal world is finally an emanation from the single source of being. However, in a sense one could say that all mystical monisms are simultaneously dualistic in that they divide sharply between the truth of the whole and the illusion of multiplicity among the parts, between reality and unreality, or between enlightenment and ignorance. The gnostics did this as well. Dualism and monism, therefore, are not systematically exclusive as long as monism is the inclusive category. In addition, the term *gnostic* is chosen here because it is a general term communicating that salvation is gained via a form of transcendental yet personal knowledge.

17. Lama Anagarika Govinda, for example, prefers a Buddhist approach over the Hindu one, because it maintains the dialectic between unity and diversity. "If oneness and diversity occur together, then I can understand that there can be diversity in oneness. But oneness by itself is meaningless. It is like one big mush—featureless, without any differentiation. Therefore I say that the Buddhist *advaya* is quite different from *advaita*. *Advaya* means 'the not twoness,' whereas *advaita* means the one against the many—the one and not the many, or the denial of the many.

Everything is then the same." "Of Matter and Maya," in Weber, *Dialogues with Scientists and Sages,* 63f.

18. Barbara Marx Hubbard, *The Hunger of Eve* (Harrisburg, PA: Stackpole Books, 1976), 15.

19. J. D. Salinger, *Nine Stories* (New York: Bantam, 1954), 189. The nonsentimental deity Teddy wants could be found in Hinduism's Bhagavad-Gita, where Krishna says, "My face is equal to all creation, loving no one nor hating any."

20. Sri Aurobindo, *The Life Divine* (Pondicherry, India: Sri Aurobindo Ashram, 1977), 1:45.

21. Goodrich-Dunn, 14.

22. Ferguson, 98f.

23. Ferguson, 366.

24. Harman, 103.

25. Willis Harman and Howard Rheingold, *Higher Creativity: Liberating the Unconscious for Breakthrough Insights* (Los Angeles: Tarcher, 1984), 9, 48.

26. Bartley, 184f.

27. A similar version of this distinction between ego and self is at work in the complex cosmoanthropology of Ken Wilber. Our evolutionary objective is to rise above the ego into the more comprehensive self. But this prospect causes anxiety. "As long as one remains identified with the ego," he writes, "as long as one operates through egoic desires and incests, then one is open to *egoic castration.* Because the ego translates with concepts and ideas, if you attack the ego's ideas, the ego experiences it as a death. . . . If the self can sustain egoic separation anxiety, then it can differentiate from the ego, transcend it, and integrate it." *The Atman Project* (Wheaton, IL: Theosophical Publishing House, 1980), 143.

28. Richard B. Miles, "What Is Holistic Health?" in *Holistic Health Review* (Fall 1977): 10; cited by Brooks Alexander in "Holistic Health from the Inside," *SCP Journal* (August 1978): 9.

29. Sri Aurobindo, *The Essential Aurobindo,* ed. Robert McDermott (New York: Schocken, 1973), 55. Aurobindo here is carrying on a pre-Hindu tradition regarding the self-world relationship that extends back to the Upanishads. "The Self, who is free from evil, free from old age, free from death, free from grief, free from hunger, free from thirst, whose desire is the Real, whose intention is the Real—he should be sought after, he should be desired to be comprehended. He obtains all worlds and all desires, who, having found out that Self, knows him. . . . That is the immortal, the fearless, that is Brahman." *Chandogya Upanishad,* 8.7f.

30. Jung in *Tibetan Book of the Great Liberation,* xxxix.

31. Aurobindo, *Essential Aurobindo,* 70.

32. Ramtha, 78.

33. Ramtha, 77.

34. Quoted by Hippolytus and cited in Pagels, xix.

35. Stephen Appelbaum, *Out in Inner Space: A Psychoanalyst Explores the New Therapies* (New York: Doubleday, 1979), 47.

36. "At the center of the consciousness movement's problematic, it seems to me, lies the scourge of C. P. Snow's 'two cultures,' the division between the exact sciences and the humanities. ... At the center of its agenda lies the project of healing this cultural schizophrenia." Toolan, 28.

37. Jacob Needleman, *A Sense of the Cosmos* (New York: E. P. Dutton, 1965, 1976), 23f., 97.

38. Sam Keen, "Self-Love and the Cosmic Connection," in *The Holographic Paradigm*, ed. Ken Wilber (Boulder: Shambala, 1982), 117.

39. See William Hulme, "Human Potential in the Lutheran Church," *Dialog* 16 (Fall 1977): 264.

40. Lowell D. Streiker, *Cults* (Nashville: Abingdon, 1983), 19.

41. See, for example, Ian Stevenson, *Twenty Cases Suggestive of Reincarnation*, 2nd rev. ed. (Charlottesville, VA: University of Virginia Press, 1974), and a theological response by Hans Schwarz, *Beyond the Gates of Death* (Minneapolis: Augsburg, 1981), chap. 4.

42. "Shirley MacLaine: An Interview That Will Amaze You," *Ladies' Home Journal*, June 1983, 26. Ms. MacLaine claims to have had an affair—"very sexual, by the way"—with the right-hand man to Tibet's Dalai Lama. "Every love affair I've had was a deep commitment while it was going on," she says. "I think sex is a pathway to spiritual growth if you engage in it with generosity, sharing, give-and-take." And about her book *Out On a Limb*, she says, "I was so overwhelmed by the profundity of what I was saying that I made myself want to throw up."

43. Bettye B. Binder, *Past Life Regression Guidebook* (1985).

44. *The Tibetan Book of the Dead*, ed. W. Y. Evans-Wentz (Oxford: Oxford University Press, 1960), x. Salinger's little Teddy reports that had he not met a beautiful woman during a previous incarnation as a man in India he would not be here today. He would be with Brahman and free from the cycle of rebirth. It is doubly unfortunate, because he has to spend the present incarnation in the West: its materialism prevents him from concentrating on spiritual things. "It's very hard to meditate and live a spiritual life in America," he complains, undoubtedly reflecting a social critique from the pen of the author. Salinger, 188.

45. Evans-Wentz, *Tibetan Book of the Great Liberation*, 19.

46. Terry Cole-Whittaker, "Love and Power in a World Without Limits: Women's Guide to the Goddess Within," workshop at the Whole Life Expo, San Francisco, 29 April 1989.

47. It may appear incoherent to put together evolution with the gnostic approach to metaphysical truth. Such truth is eternal and absolute, whereas evolution seems to presuppose fundamental change. Some advocates of the perennial philosophy have seen the contradiction and have elected to reject the doctrine of evolution as simply another form of the modern aberration. See Frithjof Schuon, "No Activity

Without Truth," and René Guénon, "Oriental Metaphysics," in *Sword of Gnosis*, 38f., 50.

48. "The Joys of Mastery," an interview with George Leonard by Phillip Whitten, *New Age Journal* (May-June 1990): 38.

49. Sri A. Ghose, *Essential Aurobindo* (Great Barrington, MA: 1987), 55.

50. "Letter from Chairman Edgar D. Mitchell," *Institute of Noetic Sciences Newsletter* 8 (Winter 1980): 3.

51. Harman, 104; see also 32f.

52. Marx Hubbard, 54f.

53. Lyall Watson, *Lifetide* (New York: Simon & Schuster, 1979). See also Ken Keyes, Jr., *The Hundredth Monkey* (Coos Bay, OR: Vision Books, 1982).

54. The devastating critique can be found in Ron Amundson, "The Hundredth Monkey Debunked," plus Maureen O'Hara, "Of Myths and Monkeys," both in *Fringes of Reason*, 174–86.

55. "Lyall Watson Responds," *Fringes of Reason*, 180–81.

56. James Edward Gulick of the Bennett Martin Library in Lincoln, Nebraska, delivered a fascinating paper documenting the history of the critical mass principle at the Annual Meeting of the American Academy of Religion, Chicago, 19 November 1988, titled: "The Coming Transformation of the World According to the Transcendental Meditation and New Age Movements."

57. Weber, 19. This is the assumption in the evolutionary-transformatory scheme of Ken Wilber. For Wilber, the whole of evolutionary history has been aiming at self-realization through transcendence. He calls it the Atman-project. By it he means "the drive of God towards God, Buddha towards Buddha, Brahman towards Brahman, but carried out initially through the intermediary of the human psyche." Wilber, *The Atman Project*, ix.

58. Szanto, 10; see also 100.

59. Ferguson, 372.

60. Raschke, 24.

61. Hans Jonas, *The Gnostic Religion*, 2nd ed. (Boston: Beacon, 1963), 35.

62. Pagels, xviiif.

63. Ihab Hassan, *Paracriticisms* (Urbana, IL: University of Illinois Press, 1975), 144.

64. Needleman, foreword to *Sword of Gnosis*, 3.

65. Ferguson, 372; see also 97f., 350.

66. Ferguson, 146; see also 45f.

67. Toolan, 79.

68. Stanislav Grof, *Realms of the Human Unconscious: Observations from LSD Research* (New York: E. P. Dutton, 1976), 142, cited by Toolan, who adds that there are two basic symbol structures, the Eastern mythos of the eternal return

with its return to union with the Great Mother, and the Western mythos of the dying-rising god. The Eastern way is a pilgrim's regress because of its return to primal beginnings, whereas the Western constitutes a pilgrim's progress into and beyond death. Toolan, 83.

69. David Spangler, *Towards a Planetary Vision* (The Park Forrest, Scotland: Findhorn Foundation, 1977), chap. 6.

70. Levi, *The Aquarian Gospel of Jesus* (Marina del Rey, CA: DeVorss, 1907, 1978).

71. Notovich's work has been republished in English by Elizabeth Clare Prophet in *The Lost Years of Jesus* (Livingston, MT: Summit University Press, 1987).

72. Elizabeth Clare Prophet, *The Lost Years of Jesus* (Livingston, MT: Summit University Press, 1987).

Chapter 3: Religious Reactions

1. Positive yet nonsyncretistic assessments of the new age on the part of Christians are rare. One example, however, is the *Christian New Age Quarterly,* edited by Catherine Groves. Groves can speak of "two frameworks of exchange," of "Christian–New Age friction" and of "dialogue." What she favors is a mood of "both/and" to replace "either/or" thinking. Copies of the quarterly can be obtained from Bethsheva's Concern, P.O. Box 276, Clifton, NJ 07011-0276.

2. Constance E. Cumbey, *The Hidden Dangers of the Rainbow* (Shreveport, LA: Huntington House, 1983), 7.

3. Cumbey, 34.

4. *Golden Book of the Theosophical Society* (1925), 64, cited by Cumbey, 46.

5. Cumbey, 49.

6. Cumbey, 57.

7. Cumbey, 174.

8. Cumbey, 175.

9. Cumbey, 64.

10. Cumbey, 58.

11. Cumbey, 69; see also 90f., 99f.

12. Cumbey, 145.

13. Cumbey, 149.

14. *The New Consciousness Sourcebook,* intro. by Daniel Ellsberg and Marilyn Ferguson (Berkeley: Spiritual Community Publications, 1982), 64.

15. I am not alone in criticizing Cumbey. Russell Chandler criticizes Cumbey and other similar authors for inadequate research, saying: "Facts are mishandled, claims are undocumented, conclusions are biased, and logic is flawed at vital connection points." Chandler, 229.

16. Susan Rothbaum, "Leave Taking: A Convert vs. Herself," *Express* 2 (13 June 1980): 2.

17. Susan Rothbaum, "Between Two Worlds: Issues of Separation and Identity After Leaving a Religious Community," in *Falling from the Faith*, ed. David Bromiley (Beverly Hills, CA: Sage Publications, 1988), 212.

18. Rothbaum, "Between Two Worlds," 208.

19. Rothbaum, "Between Two Worlds," 212.

20. Rothbaum, "Leave Taking," 7.

21. Bede Griffiths, *The Marriage of East and West* (Springfield, IL: Templegate Publishers, 1982).

22. Bede Griffiths, "Sacred Simplicity: The Style of the Sage," in *Dialogues with Scientists and Sages*, 160.

23. Bede Griffiths, *The Golden String* (Glasgow: Collins, 1954, 1979), 175.

24. Griffiths, "Sacred Simplicity," 170.

25. Griffiths, *Golden String*, 5.

26. Griffiths, "Sacred Simplicity," 163.

27. Griffiths, "Sacred Simplicity," 171.

28. Griffiths, *Golden String*, 11.

29. Needleman, *Lost Christianity*, 2.

30. Needleman, *Lost Christianity*, 4.

31. Needleman, *Lost Christianity*, 6f.

32. Needleman, *Lost Christianity*, 127.

33. Needleman, *Lost Christianity*, 195.

34. Needleman, *Lost Christianity*, 40.

35. G. I. Gurdjieff, cited by Needleman, *Lost Christianity*, 120.

36. By way of comment, the Christian patristics rejected flatly and openly the suggestion that Plato's demiurge could be identified with the God of Israel. If any identification were to be made, it would equate the Father of Jesus Christ with both the creator and the ineffable God-Beyond-God. Cf. Justin, *First Apology*, chaps. 60, 61; and *Second Apology*, chaps. 6, 7 in vol. 1 of *The Ante-Nicene Fathers*, ed. Alexander Roberts and James Donaldson (Buffalo: Christian Literature Publishing Co., 1886).

37. Needleman, *Lost Christianity*, 145.

38. Needleman, *Lost Christianity*, 155.

39. Needleman, *Lost Christianity*, 174.

40. Matthew Fox, *Original Blessing* (Santa Fe, NM: Bear & Co., 1983), 13.

41. Fox, *Original Blessing*, 51.

42. Fox, *Original Blessing*, 159.

43. Fox, *Original Blessing,* 214.

44. Fox, *Original Blessing,* 183.

45. Fox, *Original Blessing,* 251.

46. Fox, *Original Blessing,* 300.

47. Fox, *Original Blessing,* 90.

48. Matthew Fox, *The Coming of the Cosmic Christ* (San Francisco: Harper & Row, 1988), 27.

49. Fox, *Original Blessing,* 166; see also 239f., 300.

50. Matthew Fox, *A Spirituality Named Compassion and the Healing of the Global Village, Humpty Dumpty and Us* (Minneapolis: Winston Press, 1979), 257–66.

51. "The Sounds of Silence," by Laura Hagar, *Express* 11 (6 January 1989): 10.

52. See Shepherd Bliss, "Creation Spirituality Challenged by the Vatican," *Common Boundary* 7 (January-February 1989): 5–7, and Mark Matousek's interview with Matthew Fox, "Toward a Spiritual Renaissance," *Common Boundary,* 8 (July-August 1990): 14–20.

53. "Vatican Reviews Local Theologian's Work," *The Catholic Voice* (7 October 1985): 7.

54. Published in *Creation* 4 (November-December 1988): 23–38.

55. *Creation* 4:23–38.

56. Jane E. Strohl, "The Matthew Fox Phenomenon," *World and World* 8 (Winter 1988): 42–47.

57. Fox, *Original Blessing,* 13, 33, 50, 82, 112.

58. Philip Hefner, "The Creation," in *Christian Dogmatics,* ed. Carl E. Braaten and Robert W. Jenson (Philadelphia: Fortress, 1984), 1:325–28; and "The Evolution of the Created Co-Creator," in *Cosmos as Creation,* ed. Ted Peters (Nashville: Abingdon Press, 1989), chap. 6.

59. Fox, *Original Blessing,* 10.

Chapter 4: The New Physics and Wholistic Cosmology

1. Alvin Toffler, *The Third Wave* (New York: William Morrow, 1980), 146.

2. Douglas Sloan, *Insight-Imagination: The Emancipation of Thought and the Modern World* (Westport, CT: Greenwood Press, 1983), 69.

3. Sloan, 158.

4. Fritjof Capra, *The Tao of Physics* (New York: Bantam, 1977), 50.

5. Fritjof Capra, *The Turning Point* (New York: Bantam, 1982), 15. Renée Weber draws the connection between science and mysticism with some eloquence: "Science seeks the boundaries of nature, mysticism its unboundedness, science the droplet of the ocean, mysticism the wave. Science works to explain the mystery of being, mysticism to experience it." *Dialogues with Scientists and Sages,* 6. Stephen

Hawking repudiates the connection between physics and mysticism, saying that Capra and Bohm do not understand well enough the mathematics of physics. *Dialogues with Scientists and Sages,* 210.

6. Arthur Koestler, *Janus* (New York: Random House, 1978), 249f.

7. This chapter is based in part on my own presentation to this conference, which was later published as "David Bohm, Post-Modernism, and the Divine," *Zygon* 20 (June 1985): 193–217.

8. Bohm, 3; see also xi, 206f. See also "The Enfolding-Unfolding Universe: A Conversation with David Bohm," by Renée Weber, in *The Holographic Paradigm,* ed. Ken Wilber (Boulder: Shambala, 1982), 71, 76. Bohm's position here regarding the self-deception created when we mistakenly assume conceptual distinctions are fundamental to reality itself seems to be, at minimum, an attempt to avoid Alfred North Whitehead's fallacy of misplaced concreteness and, at maximum, a flirting with Asian mysticism wherein the phenomenal world of multiplicity and distinction is illusory.

9. Bohm, 172.

10. These being terms of David Bohm's, *implicate* and *explicate* will be explained more fully as we proceed.

11. Bohm, 85.

12. Bohm, 85.

13. Bohm, 11.

14. Plato, *Cratylus,* trans. B. Jowett, *The Dialogues of Plato* (New York: Random House, 1937), 402a.

15. Franklin L. Baumer, *Modern European Thought: Continuity and Change in Ideas 1600–1950* (New York: Macmillan, 1977), 21.

16. Langdon Gilkey, *Naming the Whirlwind: The Renewal of God-Language* (Indianapolis: Bobbs-Merrill, 1969), 54. Bohm introduces a subtlety when he says, "There is nothing which is wholly time-bound or wholly time-free." Wilber, *Holographic Paradigm.* 190.

17. Bohm, 11. Some critics have sought to identify the new age world view with a variant of subjective idealism, with the supposition that our consciousness actually creates so-called objective reality. See Dean C. Halverson, "Science: Quantum Physics and Quantum Leaps," in *New Age Rage,* 82f. Some new agers do take the extreme position that reality is the product of human imagination. But Bohm himself does not belong to this extreme. He is more subtle. Halverson rightly notes that Bohm recognizes that a great deal happens in nature apart from any participation by the observer. There is an objective reality beyond—even if inclusive of—human subjectivity.

18. Bohm, 177; see also 149, 185.

19. Bohm, 181; see also 156.

20. Bohm, 42.

21. Bohm, 178; see also Wilber, *Holographic Paradigm,* 204. The degree of reality attributed to concrete experience with distinction and multiplicity is not clear here. The option taken by Asian philosophy—an option at times resisted by Bohm—is to treat the explicate order as illusion. New age commentator Marilyn Ferguson employs the work of David Bohm along with that of Karl Pribram of Stanford in speculating on a microcosm-macrocosm correlation following the holographic model. "If the nature of reality is itself holographic, and if the brain operates holographically," she writes, "then the world is indeed, as the Eastern religions have said, maya: a magic show. Its concreteness is an illusion." Ferguson, 180.

22. Bohm, 179.

23. Wilber, *Holographic Paradigm,* 191.

24. Koestler, 26, 256.

25. Koestler, 293; see also 26f., 37, 304.

26. Koestler, 27; see also 301.

27. Ken Wilber, "Physics, Mysticism and the New Holographic Paradigm: A Critical Appraisal," in *Holographic Paradigm,* 160; Toolan, 215f.

28. Wilber, *Holographic Paradigm,* 188.

29. Bohm, 189.

30. Bohm, 191.

31. Heraclitus writes, "Things taken together are whole and not whole, something which is being brought together and brought apart, which is in tune and out of tune; out of all things there comes a unity, and out of a unity all things." Cited in G. S. Kirk and J. E. Raven, *The Presocratic Philosophers* (Cambridge: Cambridge University Press, 1960), 191.

32. Bohm, 191f.

33. Bohm, 192.

34. Bohm, 195.

35. Bohm, 209.

36. Bohm, 212. Because the multidimensional ground for Bohm is living and self-initiating and inclusive of personality, Christian critics who argue that Bohm promulgates a doctrine of an impersonal God partially miss the mark. For example, see Halverson, 88–90.

37. Bohm, 145, 177.

38. John Cobb, *God and the World* (Philadelphia: Westminster, 1969), 71.

39. Wilber, *Holographic Paradigm,* 71, 83.

40. Wilber, *Holographic Paradigm,* 69f., 194.

41. Wilber, *Holographic Paradigm,* 70. On one occasion Bohm describes the holomovement as an interpenetration of matter and spirit, but on no occasion does he give ontological priority to spirit. Wilber, *Holographic Paradigm,* 206f.

42. Eric Voegelin, *The World of the Polis,* vol. 2 of *Order and History* (Baton Rouge: Louisiana State University Press, 1957), 210f. The problem is raised as well by John Burnet, *Early Greek Philosophy* (New York: Meridian, 1957, 1982), 178f., and Kirk and Raven, 269ff.

43. Koestler, 250f.

44. We can see here that Anselm's understanding of God is worlds apart from that of Parmenides. Parmenides was still pagan and saw the gods as parts of a more ultimate natural world. For Anselm, God is the ultimate reality. Nothing transcends God.

45. H. Richard Niebuhr, *Radical Monotheism and Western Culture* (New York: Harper, 1943), 32.

46. This is the primary objection to the new age offered by evangelical critic Douglas R. Groothuis in *Unmasking the New Age* (Downers Grove, IL: InterVarsity Press, 1986). He affirms a distinction between God and the world, and describes God in very personal rather than impersonal terms. Similarly, the new age conflation of God with the self is problematic. "God is effectively silenced when the concept of God is incorporated into humanity itself," writes Frances S. Adeney in "Transpersonal Psychology: Psychology and Salvation Meet," in *New Age Rage,* 127.

47. See John Hick, *Philosophy of Religion,* 2nd ed. (Englewood Cliffs, NJ: Prentice-Hall, 1973), 7.

48. Wilber, *Holographic Paradigm,* 89f.

49. C. F. von Weizsacker, *The History of Nature* (Chicago: University of Chicago Press, 1949, 1966), 7.

50. Wilber, *Holographic Paradigm,* 203.

51. Wolfhart Pannenberg, *Basic Questions in Theology* (2 vols.) (Philadelphia: Fortress Press, 1970–71), 11:62; see also 1:156f., 229f.; and *Theology and the Philosophy of Science* (Philadelphia: Westminster, 1976), 310.

52. See Ted Peters, "The Real World Is the Yet-to-Be-Whole World," *Dialog* 26 (Summer 1987): 167–74; and my chapter in *Cosmos as Creation,* ed. Ted Peters (Nashville: Abingdon Press, 1989).

Chapter 5: Testing the Spirits

1. Augustine, *Confessions* (trans. John K. Ryan), 1.1.

2. This is an important point in the evaluation offered by Russell Chandler. He reports Shirley MacLaine saying that there is no such thing as evil . . . evil is only what you *think* it is. This bothers Chandler, so he writes, "New Age transcendence revels in innate human potential; Christian faith confesses the innate *inability* to please a righteous God but glories in the potential of his grace to transform human personality into the likeness of the face of Christ (II Cor. 4:6)." Chandler, 272, 305.

3. This is a point made by theologian John Newport. "The Christian religion made available a new consciousness to the Mediterranean world of the first century. Rich and poor, slave and free, and humble and mighty embraced this dynamic new religion. . . . Consequently it is difficult for Christian believers to understand the significance of a statement by Theodore Roszak that the hope of the West is in a synthesis of the non-Christian New Consciousness groups." John Newport, *Christ and the New Consciousness* (Nashville: Broadman Press, 1978), 9. See also Theodore Roszak, *Unfinished Animal* (New York: Harper & Row, 1975), 236f.

4. Martin Luther, *Commentary on Galatians—1535*, in *Luther's Works*, American ed., trans. Jaroslav Pelikan (St. Louis: Concordia, 1963), 26:130.

5. John Calvin, *Institutes of the Christian Religion* (Philadelphia: Westminster Press, 1960), 1:79; 278f.; 287.

6. Augustine, *The City of God* (trans. Marcus Dods), 22.30.

7. Martin Luther, "Treatise on Christian Liberty," in *Three Treatises*, rev. ed., trans. W. A. Lambert (Philadelphia: Fortress Press, 1970), 277.

8. Wolfhart Pannenberg, *Ethics* (Philadelphia: Westminster, 1981), 54.

9. The Christian claim is misunderstood in the very framing of the issue. The claim is not that the Church provides a path *to* God, a path we follow in order to arrive at a divine destination. If we assume that we have to work our way toward God, then Christians might appear smug at claiming their path is superior to the others. However, the distinctive claim of the Christian faith is that it is God who has traversed the path *to us*. This is the beginning of grace.

10. Surjit Singh, *A Philosophy of Integral Relation* (Madras, India: Christian Literature Society, 1981), 28.

11. Singh, 29.

12. Søren Kierkegaard, *Philosophical Fragments*, trans. David Swenson, rev. by Howard V. Hong (Princeton: Princeton University Press, 1962), 76.

13. Kierkegaard, *Philosophical Fragments*, 77.

14. Søren Kierkegaard, *The Sickness unto Death*, trans. Walter Lowrie (New York: Doubleday, 1954).

15. Karen Hoyt, executive director of the Spiritual Counterfeits Project, identifies ten areas in which Christians might find agreement with the new age. Hoyt, *New Age Rage*, 12; see also Chandler, 222.

Index